PURPOSEFUL EVALUATION

A Practical Guide to Design,
Development and Delivery

David Parsons

P

First published in Great Britain in 2026 by

Policy Press, an imprint of
Bristol University Press
University of Bristol
1-9 Old Park Hill
Bristol
BS2 8BB
UK
t: +44 (0)117 374 6645
e: bup-info@bristol.ac.uk

Details of international sales and distribution partners are available at
policy.bristoluniversitypress.co.uk

© Bristol University Press 2026

DOI: 10.51952/9781447376156

British Library Cataloguing in Publication Data
A catalogue record for this book is available from the British Library

ISBN 978-1-4473-7612-5 hardcover
ISBN 978-1-4473-7613-2 paperback
ISBN 978-1-4473-7614-9 ePub
ISBN 978-1-4473-7615-6 ePdf

The right of David Parsons to be identified as author of this work has been asserted by him in accordance with the Copyright, Designs and Patents Act 1988.

All rights reserved: no part of this publication may be reproduced, stored in a retrieval system, or transmitted in any form or by any means, electronic, mechanical, photocopying, recording, or otherwise without the prior permission of Bristol University Press.

Every reasonable effort has been made to obtain permission to reproduce copyrighted material. If, however, anyone knows of an oversight, please contact the publisher.

The statements and opinions contained within this publication are solely those of the author and not of the University of Bristol or Bristol University Press. The University of Bristol and Bristol University Press disclaim responsibility for any injury to persons or property resulting from any material published in this publication.

Bristol University Press and Policy Press work to counter discrimination on grounds of gender, race, disability, age and sexuality.

Cover design: Liam Roberts Design
Front cover image: iStock/Elena Kopusova

Contents

List of figures, tables and boxes v
List of evaluation examples viii
About the author x
Acknowledgements xi
Preface xiii

PART I Starting points

1   Why purposeful evaluation? 3

PART II Setting the foundations

2   Defining the purpose 29

3   Managing evaluation objectives and expectations 48

4   Managing the ethical dimension 65

PART III Choosing the right method

5   Understanding the choices 85

6   Process evaluation 100

7   Economic evaluation 121

8   Fully experimental impact evaluation 140

9   Quasi-experimental impact evaluation 159

10 Theory-based impact evaluation 181

11 Meta-evaluation 205

PART IV Putting it in place: preparation into delivery

12	Preparation and groundwork	221
13	Managing challenges and delivery	245

PART V Presenting and mobilising evidence

14	Delivering the evidence	265
15	Optimising evaluation influence	288

Notes	305
Bibliography	310
Index	320

List of figures, tables and boxes

Figures

1.1	Research, monitoring and evaluation: separation and complementarity	8
2.1	Positioning the scope of an evaluation	33
6.1	Component parts of an intervention	102
8.1	The 'nine-step' approach to an RCT	145
10.1	Essential content for a theory of change (ToC)	187
10.2	Key inquiry stages for contribution analysis	192
12.1	The eight-step model to setting evidence needs	239
15.1	Influencing change	289

Tables

1.1	Purpose for policy, programme or initiative review	10
1.2	Some potential evaluative contributions from generative AI	23
2.1	Stakeholder interests in evaluation purposing	38
2.2	Stakeholder engagement opportunities for evaluation scoping	41
2.3	Summative vs formative evaluation	45
3.1	Setting 'SMART' objectives for purposeful evaluation	54
4.1	Indicative information for a pre-participation consent briefing	69
4.2	Demonstrating fairness across the evaluation process	74
4.3	Contrasting gender dimensions in an evaluation	81
5.1	Purpose and focus for the four types of evaluation	89
6.1	Likely inquiry issues for a performance process evaluation	105

6.2	Principles of method choice for developmental evaluation (DE)	111
6.3	Common issues for 'granular' assessment of effectiveness	113
6.4	Some pointers to determining 'process' quality indicators	117
7.1	Scope and coverage of the main types of economic evaluation	128
7.2	Costs to be considered in a cost-description evaluation	129
7.3	Cost-effectiveness and CE-EC ratios	131
7.4	Comparative (indicative) content of economic evaluations	135
9.1	Options for matched comparator designs	166
9.2	Understanding unintended consequences	178
10.1	Other complexity 'push' factors to justify TBE preference	185
10.2	Some pros and cons of integrated theory-based methods	193
10.3	Some pros and cons of selected adaptive theory-based methods	197
10.4	Some pros and cons of selected configurational methods	202
11.1	Key stages in systematic review	208
11.2	A three-phase approach to rapid evidence review in evaluation	210
11.3	Systematic review and rapid evidence review	213
11.4	A four-step approach to realist synthesis	215
11.5	Other options for meta-evaluation	217
12.1	Evaluation timing and the consequences for planning	223
12.2	Some pros and cons of internal vs external commissioning	225
12.3	Potential stakeholders for evaluation planning and development	230
12.4	Coproduction and engagement in stakeholder participation	234
12.5	Principles for proportionate design of purposeful evaluation	235

13.1	From work packages to workplan	252
13.2	A practical framework for risk-foresighting an evaluation	256
13.3	Governance and steering roles in an evaluation	257
14.1	Indicative content for the reporting plan for an evaluation	267
14.2	Narrative progress reporting options (or combinations)	270
14.3	Indicative structure and content for a summative evaluation report	275
14.4	Appropriate language and style for purposeful summative reporting	277
14.5	Substantiation and internal and external validity for an evaluation	285
15.1	Evidence needs, circumstances and scope for evaluation influence	292
15.2	Guidelines for preparing actionable recommendations	296
15.3	Pre- and post-reporting promotion options	301

Boxes

2.1	Scoping an evaluation and 'theory of change' – the UK *Magenta Book*	36
3.1	Scrutinising the objectives to set inquiry issues	58
3.2	Setting the inquiry focus – objectives to 'research questions' (RQs)	60
7.1	A hypothetical example of opportunity costs	124
7.2	Setting purposeful metrics for a cost-effectiveness evaluation	131
8.1	Using prognostic factors to reduce risks of 'chance bias'	149

List of evaluation examples

Example 1	An early empirical evaluation	4
Example 2	Evaluation leverage – a timely caution about the impact of evaluation	16
Example 3	Widening the 'user' platform	30
Example 4	Harnessing stakeholders – stakeholder engagement in a theory of change working group	43
Example 5	From wants to needs – using a theory of change or logic chart	50
Example 6	Purposeful specification – where the evaluation objectives fall short	52
Example 7	Shifting ambitions – managing mission creep and disruptive expectations	55
Example 8	Expectations realism – a close encounter with organisational power dynamics in an evaluation	62
Example 9	Anticipating influences – using a theory of change to anticipate 'hidden' influences on programme effectiveness	114
Example 10	Small 'n' RCTs – small sample sizes mean little or no confidence in proof of effect	148
Example 11	Confounding variables – the examples of 'Hawthorne' and 'John Henry' effects	156
Example 12	QEDs and matched comparators – selecting geographical comparators using matched variables	163

Example 13	Harnessing 'difference-in-difference' – an evaluation of the impact of the enhanced minimum wage in New Jersey, 1992	167
Example 14	RDD and eligibility cut offs – evaluating education and health awareness outcomes from a multi-donor programme in Cambodia	170
Example 15	Applying synthetic controls – an impact evaluation of police officer lay-offs in Oregon, US, on fatal road traffic accidents	173
Example 16	Developmental 'theory-based' evaluation – evaluating capability-building impacts for school business managers	195
Example 17	Applying QCA – assessing austerity-related social disturbance in countries supported by IMF debt renegotiation funds	199
Example 18	Structuring an RER evaluation – applying an RER to a meta-evaluation for an early years learning programme	211
Example 19	Optimising working with clearance processes to provide fast starts for an evaluation	248
Example 20	Using synthesis reporting – a themed evidence policy brief from the impact evaluation of the UK's Teaching and Learning Research Programme	280

About the author

David Parsons is a practising evaluator with long experience of independent evaluations of public policy and programmes. A specialist in impact evaluation, he has led over 50 independent evaluations for numerous government departments, for non-departmental agencies, devolved administrations and regulators in the UK, and for leading charities. Outside the UK, he has directed and co-directed cross-national studies for international bodies including the European Commission, International Labour Office, and Organisation for Economic Co-operation and Development (OECD). His early career in academia was followed by posts in the (then) UK National Economic Development Office, and later as specialist advisor to the European Commission, before 15 years as partner in a policy research consultancy.

David is Visiting Professor and a long-standing contributor and collaborator at Leeds Beckett University and, since 2016, Lead Tutor for evaluation practitioner development at the Social Research Association. He continues to advise public bodies on evaluation practice and strategy, and in 2018 was elected to the Academy of Social Science for contributions to cross-conceptual evaluation practices. He is a member of, and active contributor to, the UK government's Evaluation Trial and Advice Panel (ETAP). Among other methodological publications, he is author of *Demystifying Evaluation* (Policy Press, 2017). He regularly contributes to professional conferences and networks on evaluation practice.

Acknowledgements

My previous foray with Policy Press, *Demystifying Evaluation*, started with an apology that the book was long overdue; in tardiness this book is only a little better. My enthusiasm to assuage some of the guilt from not covering all that I would have wanted has been conditioned and constrained by too many other enticing opportunities over the last seven and a bit years.

In at last progressing to this contribution, I owe much to the stimulus, and privilege, of running practitioner development courses for the UK's Social Research Association (SRA). In the intervening years since 2017, two courses have expanded to six. Each is run several times a year, and from these I constantly draw energy, enthusiasm and my own learning. Tutors can learn a lot from their 'students', and this book is informed by the many plenary and post-course discussions and practitioner questions which enliven those courses.

Evaluators can be rather insular in their practice, but I have had the great benefit of colleagues, old and new, at Leeds Beckett, SRA and elsewhere for keeping that at bay. They are too numerous to name individually, but I give special thanks to Rhodri Thomas, Kenneth Walsh and Sally Cupitt whose challenge and insights fuel (for me) what Einstein described (for him) as being 'passionately curious'. I also thank my good friend Stuart Matthews for stretching my thinking on matters of 'theory of change' well beyond my comfort zone of social policy. I am grateful for co-panel members from ETAP for their shared expertise; I cannot name them, but they know who they are. To this I would like to add my thanks to my editors and guides at Policy Press, and in particular Paul Stevens who has helped to shape the balance of the book, and both Izzie Green and Ellen Mitchell for their patience in its editing and composition. Thanks also to Rachael and her colleagues for their very thorough copyediting efforts.

Last, but certainly not least, my final acknowledgement is to Dorothy Smith, my wife, partner in practice and challenger on all matters of evidence-based policy influence. She has laboured long and dutifully on this manuscript as unpaid but insightful reviewer and critic of the first draft and grammar detective, providing constant encouragement and freedom from interruption in the stickier stages of putting together this content.

Preface

Standing sentinel in my kitchen is a tea mug with the legend: 'We love policy that works'. A gift from the government's Evaluation Task Force, it serves to remind me why evaluation is important in providing information that can contribute to shaping and making policy decisions, and in their actualisation. It is also a daily reminder that evaluation still has some way to go before that potential is widely realised. This is the starting point for this book.

This is not to criticise what evaluation, in its many guises, does; it is instead a reflection on what it is currently not (widely) achieving. This is, of course, an unfair generalisation. Evaluations, and evaluators, can and do make a difference, not just in the domain of public policy but also elsewhere. Overall, however, the conversion of an evaluation process (and delivery) into a distinct, valued and maximised contribution to decisions would appear to be sub-optimal.

Evidencing any evaluation impact is itself challenging, especially when the dynamics of decision-making means it is impractical to isolate an acknowledged contribution from any one influencing source – evaluative evidence or otherwise. Nonetheless, the lack of contribution and profile of systematic, objectivised evidence is a widespread concern in the evaluation community and a commonly shared frustration in evaluator networks.

Paradoxically, more political institutions, public interest bodies and others are explicitly committing to using evidence in decision-making. Some go so far as to say they are, or are aiming to be, evidence-led in their policy and practice. While not universal, this is a growing aspiration for many institutions and organisations in democratic states, as they reach out to demonstrate more openness and transparency. There is inevitable caution and even cynicism about those organisations 'walking the talk', but the aspiration is an increasingly common feature where public interest actions are guided through robustly democratic governance.

So why this paradox? Why do organisations that aspire to be evidence-based find themselves with evaluation (and research) evidence that is sought or commissioned but ineffectively mobilised? Why is systematic evidence the apparent 'Cinderella' within the influences shaping decision-making? Why is it too often sidelined or neglected?

A now extensive literature aiming to stimulate evidence use, and optimise its influence, has sought to answer those questions. It posits a melange of limited aspiration by users, fear of negative findings and a preference for confirmatory evidence, all reinforced by an often immature 'managing' culture, lack of ambition or weak skills mix, for harnessing evaluation evidence in many organisations. It is also seen as a consequence of the profile, and leverage, of other more established and powerful influences with less, or no, commitment to systematic evidence.

My experience – from working both within and as an independent advisor to policy-making bodies, and as a jobbing evaluator – suggests other constraints are at play. A shortening of decision-making cycles and more fast response, agile and embedded 'test and learn' timeframes intensify the pace needed to evidence what does or does not work, why and its implications. Even evidence-orientated decision-makers consequently have their frustrations with evaluative processes which are seen as too slow and lacking the pace and responsiveness needed to deliver many of those needs.

It would, of course, be wholly unrealistic to expect evaluation evidence to be the sole, or even main, influence on decision-making. Any aspiration for decisions to be *evidence-based* might be better framed as *evidence-influenced,* not replacing but ratcheting up the evidence contribution alongside others. Looked at this way, the transformation needed is not so ambitious; it is one of raising evidence profile and using that to moderate the influencing balance.

This book represents a small, and humble attempt to motivate and support those seeking such transformation. It starts with a recognition that, while evaluators, on their own, cannot bring about more consistent and effective evidence-informed use, there is much they can do. Indeed, any such transformation cannot be sustained without going beyond solid method choice and application, to embed use and utility throughout the evaluation journey. For some evaluators, this may involve only small changes in practice; for others, the demands may go deeper.

What is *not* needed is a new evaluation paradigm. The book does not offer this and recognises that the necessary transformations already have much on which to build. Many organisations are at least potentially more open to greater evidence influence – and there is a plethora of tried and tested, as well as emerging, evaluation methods to meet an infinite variety of evaluative circumstances and evidence needs. There are also widening and deepening capacities to respond within (some) organisations and in the evaluation community outside. Nonetheless, the necessary transformations are unlikely to come about from continuing with 'business as usual'.

What *is* needed is a change of emphasis. The book consequently works within the panoply of existing techniques by, firstly, proposing a pluralist approach recognising that evidence hierarchies can sometimes over-emphasise evidence robustness over situation, use and utility. Secondly, it sets out an intent-centred focus which, while respecting method choice, moves away from method dependency to emphasise end-to-end, utility-centred judgements across the evaluation's whole journey. Thirdly, it sets out a persisting need for user and key stakeholder engagement in delivery judgements and processes as essential to amplify trust, confidence and credibility in eventual findings. Finally, and perhaps (for some) the only controversial suggestion, it proposes that the evaluator act as an agent for the evidence, adopting a proactive stance to maximise its potential for use while continuing to respect necessary impartiality and independence.

The whole is framed simply as *Purposeful Evaluation*. It offers a practical framework for addressing the current underwhelming use of evaluative evidence in decision-making, especially in social and community-based settings. I hope the ideas and suggested practice will make their own contribution towards raising the impact that evaluation evidence can, and should, make for 'policy that works' to the benefit of wider society.

PART I

Starting points

The true voyage of discovery is not a journey to a new place; it is learning to see with new eyes.
Marcel Proust

1

Why purposeful evaluation?

Introduction

At its heart, evaluation is something simple made complex. Much of the complexity comes from the necessary choices within the (very) many ways in which it can be carried out and the diverse situations those choices need to reflect. Professor Scriven, a giant in the evaluation cosmos, suggested that balancing this simplicity–complexity dilemma with the numerous method possibilities came down to one overriding consideration: 'Practical life cannot proceed without evaluation, nor can intellectual life, nor can moral life, and they are not built on sand. The real question is how to do evaluation well' (Scriven, 1991).

Purposeful evaluations, and this book, are centred on making appropriate choices about 'how to do evaluation well'. Making those judgements, however, can be discomforting especially when surrounded by long-standing controversy about what methods and techniques work 'best' for what evidence and when. To avoid that confusion, a solid starting point is realising that making sound methodological judgements is not confined to knowledge about, and selecting appropriately from, a technical menu. To be purposeful, an evaluation needs to combine both technocratic knowledge with 'political' sensitivities about the practical context of the situation for what is being evaluated – the so called 'evaluand'.

Combining the technical and political, however, may not come easily to many evaluators, especially those coming from research or analytical backgrounds (as most do), where the technical comes most readily to the fore. Yet, bringing together these two dimensions is at the heart of doing an evaluation 'well' not just for decisions made at its start but from end to end. Superimposed on this, is the more prosaic need to tread carefully in accommodating the often-conflicting demands of time, budgetary and other resource pressures on an evaluation with the need for responsiveness, relevance and robustness.

With care and attention, a little caution and persistence, the challenges to purposefulness are readily surmountable. This book offers an introduction to making and applying many of the choices needed. It does not argue for, or against, different method and delivery choices, but offers a plural and practical perspective on how to integrate the technical and political dimensions to optimise its value and use. This is framed as 'purposeful evaluation'.

What is evaluation about; where are its roots?

A deep dive into the literature would show ideas about evaluation have developed over time, and continue to do so with changes in philosophical thought, practice and utility. Those roots might be traced as far back as Aristotle's concept of 'deliberative imagination' guided by rational action. Although the idea of a 2,000-year legacy of evaluative thinking may be appealing, scholarly discussion has rightly focused on more recent origins. Much is owed to the so-called Age of Reason (Patton, 2018) and the earlier influences of Francis Bacon's ideas of inductive reasoning, and later John Locke, René Descartes and others in the 17th century and later.

The practice of evaluation, and how we now regard it, stemmed mostly from the later 18th century and early 19th century, those early contributors did not see themselves as 'evaluators' or as evaluative pioneers. Their practice was rooted in empiricism and applying critical, evidence-based reasoning to inform societal progression or to tackle specific challenges (see Example 1).

Example 1: AN EARLY EMPIRICAL EVALUATION

An early recognised example of experimental 'evaluation' design was to develop a practical solution to the disabling problem of scurvy affecting sailors on long sea voyages. Some ships saw two thirds or more of crews dying from what is now known as the lack of fresh fruit and vegetables on long sea voyages (and consequent vitamin C deficiency).

The search for a practical solution included James Lind who had witnessed the effects of scurvy as a surgeon's mate and later surgeon in the British Royal Navy in the 1730s. In 1747, on the 300-man frigate HMS Salisbury, he carried out a controlled 'evaluation' with 12 affected crew members divided into 'matched' pairs testing six conjectured remedies. Lind monitored consumption and recorded symptomatic and physiological changes to show '... the most sudden and good effects' of oranges and lemons added to the normal shipboard diet.

Dr Lind left the navy to be a physician in Edinburgh, and later Chief Physician to the Royal Naval Hospital at Haslar, publishing his results in 1753 and 1757. His 'evaluation' may have fallen some way short of what is now expected of a randomised control trial, but it was systematic, evidence-based and controlled. Now regarded as the father of nautical medicine, his efforts provided the evidence for the British Admiralty to later mandate the necessary changes to supply and diets for its mariners (Bown, 2005).

Recognising the diverse roots of evaluative thinking is a start to answering for ourselves, and for those seeking results from an evaluation, just what is it for? This is not always an easy question to answer when, beyond the practitioner community, even the term 'evaluation' can be surrounded by ambiguity.

In its everyday use, we evaluate what is commonplace and even mundane: 'was the restaurant service up to scratch?'; 'is this red wine acceptable?'; 'is this jacket good value at this price?'. This informal, 'small-e' take on evaluation is very different to that for systematic 'big E' evaluations on which this book is focused, but it can fuel widely different ambitions (and misunderstandings) for evaluation practice and use.

For 'big E' evaluation, the professional literature contains numerous insights and extensive scholarly debate about its systematic roots and how this shapes what evaluation is, or should be, about. The debate is informed and expansive but will lack accessibility to the non-practitioner, and also risks confusing new or less experienced evaluators venturing into this domain. Users and novice practitioners alike can be left with an impression of a mystique about what evaluation is for, when it is of value, and how to go about applying it in practice.

A first step to demystifying this debate is simply to recognise that, while evaluation has deep, shared roots, its useful practice varies greatly with intent and the circumstances of the intervention it is to assess. There can be no all-embracing answer to 'what is it for'. This needs to be individually reasoned, going beyond any theoretical standpoint on how it is systematic, to set its rationale in the context of its particular intervention circumstances.

Purposeful evaluation puts a lot of effort into localising, and harmonising, what an evaluation is for within a specific intervention circumstance. The following chapter looks at some of the nuts and bolts of how to approach this robustly and reliably. This builds on the inherited legacy of evaluative thinking while also recognising its discipline and practice are quite contemporary and still evolving. Indeed, evaluators early in the 21st century find themselves in a period of rapid evolution of thought – one where different evaluator experiences and standpoints influence how to interpret both established and new thinking on practice (Mason and Hunt, 2018).

Mark and colleagues (Mark et al, 2006) have condensed these differences in evaluative thinking down to those emphasising method choices and practice through the prism of evaluation utility, with others driven more by methodological purity. For those coming from the perspective of utility, an evaluation's focus lies with the intended end-use, for example, an evaluation to evidence options for greater cost-effectiveness of an intervention or for scoping its transferability to similar situations. For others, evaluation is driven by an overriding focus on evidence quality through optimal technique and conditions.

Mark's implied dualism characterises significant differences in evaluators orientations but, in the author's experience, there are risks in evaluation practice to overemphasising either. Purposeful evaluation, as set out in the rest of this book, recognises these different perspectives as not mutually exclusive but complementary. In aiming to meet Scrivens ambition to 'do evaluation well', 'purposeful' evaluators need to seek the most effective balance between these two viewpoints, one which meets individual intervention circumstances and needs.

Evaluation, research or monitoring?

A practical point of departure in balancing utility and technique is a recognition by evaluator and user of what an evaluation is not. Evaluative thinking is old and possibly ancient, but as a label and distinct discipline it is modern. This fairly recent evolution has led to a self-consciousness (Mathison, 2008) about what is distinctive about evaluation and especially from research and monitoring. There are important differences between these three areas of evidential inquiry but at the risk of further confusion they can also be seen as complementary (Figure 1.1).

Understanding those differences and complementarity is a recurrent issue for evaluators when making sensible judgements for a purposeful evaluation.

Evaluation and research

Those new to or recently entering evaluation practice are commonly confused about how research and evaluation are different. Many will have come from research or related backgrounds. They are likely to be quick to see concurrence between research and how an evaluation goes about collecting, and analysing, evidence, but slower to appreciate important differences in aspirations and placing.

Understanding those dissimilarities goes beyond philosophical debate about epistemological boundaries and is fundamental in making judgements about methods, and this can have an impact from the earliest stages of scoping an inquiry. For example, in the UK, many other European countries and Australasia, a proposal for a health-geared research study will require health service governance approval, but a health service evaluation

Figure 1.1: Research, monitoring and evaluation: separation and complementarity

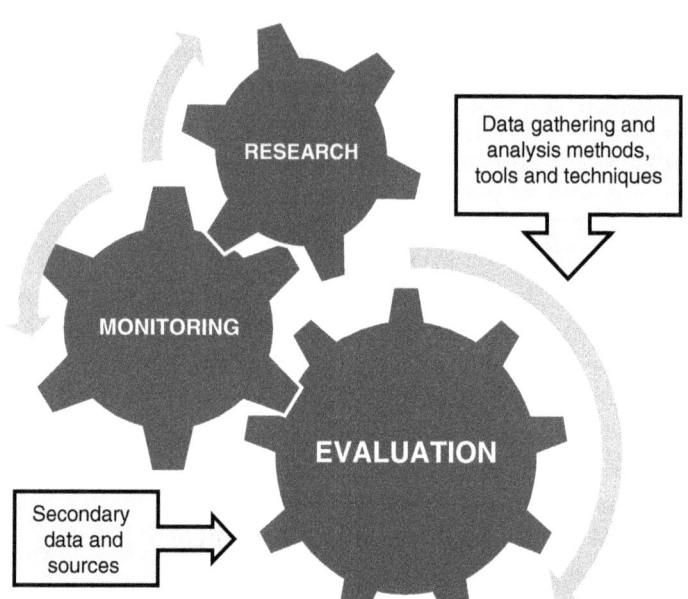

commonly does not (although it will still probably require ethical approval).

There is now an extensive literature interpreting different facets of research–evaluation differences, but here again Michael Scriven comes to our rescue. He condensed the semantics to set out a common underpinning for any evaluation: 'Evaluation is the systematic process to determine merit, worth, value, or significance' (Scriven, 1991). Perhaps the shortest of the many attempts at definition, this was later (2014) adopted by the American Evaluation Association and is generally (if sometimes notionally) supported (Picciotto, 2011). Others have taken this further to match a defining general purpose with the necessary conditions underlying any evaluation's specific context (Clark, 1999. Carol Weiss, another giant in evaluative thinking, has drawn particular attention to this: 'Evaluation is the systematic assessment of the operation and/or the outcomes of a program or policy, compared to a set of explicit or implicit standards as a means of contributing to the improvement of the policy or program' (Weiss, 1998: 4). These definitions, among many others, help provide distinctive roots for evaluation as a field of inquiry with an inclusive logic which sets it apart from aspects of research. It can also help define areas of complementarity.

Evaluation is bounded by a constituent logic (Scriven, 1999) and by underpinning theories that shape its practice and standards (explicit and implicit). Forging this inclusive 'logic' came about largely from the United States in the 1960s into the 1980s with a growing recognition in social and behavioural sciences that something distinctive was needed in applying conventional research methods to influencing policy decisions. Scholarly debate may point to other influences, but this stemmed largely from those responding to burgeoning, mainly federal, demand for assessing programme outputs and efficacy who started to question how well research methods, of themselves, were suited to this. Much of this concern was about their suitability for answering policy makers' questions about the value of complex, multi-faceted and multi-stakeholder programmes.

All this spurred a substantial growth in literature and the practice of what we now see as evaluation which went beyond traditional research applications. By the early 1980s Cronbach, and later others, emphasised the centrality of evaluation in providing evidence for decision-making for publicly funded social and education programmes (Cronbach, 1982). By the mid-1980s, others were describing the differences between research and evaluation as 'monumental' (Guba and Lincoln, 1986). A growing sense of an inclusive 'logic' for evaluation can be characterised in three areas of difference between the practice of evaluation and research:

- the underpinning purpose of inquiry;
- the constituent knowledge necessary for practice;
- the quality and focus for engagement in the inquiry process.

Purpose: Evaluations inevitably vary greatly with their circumstances and needs but all have some features driving their intent which are different from those of research (and monitoring; returned to a little later) as summarised in Table 1.1.

Table 1.1: Purpose for policy, programme or initiative review

	Overall purpose	Characterised as ...
Research	Providing groundwork for programme design and implementation (including for evaluation and monitoring scope and focus)	• Systematic, sometimes extensive and disciplined inquiry • Providing new or updated knowledge or understanding; inquiry driven • Evidence to test hypotheses, affirm or established conclusions • General or specific in scope; usually summative review • Conceptual, applied or blue sky in focus
Evaluation	Staged or summative assessment of achieved intent or delivery for operation, effectiveness, performance, value and consequence	• Systematic, usually extensive and disciplined inquiry • Providing an assessment of merit, worth or value of something • Applied focus; objective driven; formative or summative review • Evidence to support decision-making needs • Specific to a targeted inquiry
Monitoring	Information and intelligence to support ongoing implementation and necessary adjustments	• Targeted, usually constrained (targeted) and data-based • Formative and regular review • Evidence to inform operational management • Specific, applied but narrow 'key points' performance and quality focus

Source: Author's teaching materials

These differences can be subtle – for example, when contrasting evaluation with policy-related research, but they remain distinctive. Research is about systematic and disciplined inquiry which can be applied, as in policy research, or more exploratory, such as for 'horizon scanning' or 'blue-sky' research. In all cases, it is driven by the need for new, updated or extended knowledge or understanding which can be general or specific in its ambition, but is usually centred on affirming or establishing a conclusion about something.

Evaluation shares the need for a systematic approach, but its underpinning focus is on determining Scrivens 'merit, worth, or value of something' specific. That 'something' is whatever is its targeted focus – an initiative, scheme, or programme, or something larger such as a policy or strategy; throughout the book we use the term 'intervention' to cover all and any of those. Its inquiry is focused on something specific, not general, and its purpose is almost always to provide evidence to support some aspect of timely decision-making relating to it. How much or what role evaluation evidence and analysis should have in informing those decisions remains an area of controversy when decisions are influenced by many factors (returned to in Chapter 15). In this, however, evaluation may be the only contribution which is systematically evidence-based, objective and impartial.

Reduced to its essence, the difference between these two fields of inquiry is intended use. While both adopt 'research' methods for evidence-gathering and analysis, evaluation does so for different purposes. This is not to say that research has no role in decision-making. Well-founded policy-related studies often aspire to influence policies and practices, but any such influence is likely to be indirect, and may involve a long chain of influence. Results from an individual research study are rarely seen as sufficient on which to base a decision about a course of action, although that single study may contribute to an eventual body of influencing evidence.

In contrast, the connection between evaluation and decision-making is more singular and specific. An individual evaluation study should be timed and crafted to specifically and directly influence necessary or intended decisions. How much influence is subsequently achieved will, of course, be another matter. The link between 'good' evidence and 'sound decision-making' can be tenuous, and sub-optimal use of evaluation evidence in decision-making continues to be a grievance for many evaluators. Nonetheless, the utilisable potential for evaluation evidence should be at the heart of Scriven's concept of 'how to do evaluation well'. Looked at in this way, all evaluation is applied and will be judged not only on reliability but also on its utility for decision-making.

Knowledge: Most evaluators generally come to practice from other disciplines, often but not always from one of the social or behavioural sciences. They bring knowledge of social research methods, and these are valuable starting points.

Novice evaluators do not need to learn afresh about how to design a stratified sample, a self-completion questionnaire, or an interview schedule for an evaluation; their social research methods experiences are usually sufficient. However, they are often less well served by understanding the application of those 'research' tools for an evaluative purpose. There may also be gaps in knowledge of other necessary tools in the evaluator's toolkit, including, for example:

- characterising and searching for unintended consequences, or unintended and indirect effects;
- accounting for and understanding experiences and values from different points of view;
- how to deal with inconvenient or controversial issues and values;
- how to synthesise facts and values (Mathison, 2008);
- tackling the empirical challenges of separating cause and effect to assess attribution of assessable outcomes and impacts (Parsons, 2017).

Individually this range of 'know how' may not be unique to evaluation, but put together it adds up to a distinctive whole, without which an evaluator is left short-handed in necessary skills and knowledge.

Engagement: A distinguishing feature of evaluation is the attention to be paid to stakeholder engagement. This issue will be returned to later in this book (Chapter 12) but here we are concerned with how it is a distinctive feature of evaluation. Just how much attention is paid to engagement, when and how, will vary for different evaluation contexts and circumstances, but appropriate stakeholder engagement is often crucial. Social science research may draw in stakeholder perspectives, but this may not be needed at all for some such studies.

Stakeholder engagement and its integration in evaluation may be for practical reasons such as securing data and other issues for operationalising the evaluation. It is also commonly critical to scoping what is (and is not) to be done, informing proportionate judgement for collecting available evidence or experiences, accessing intervention participants or practitioners (stakeholders themselves) or others from whom evidence is to be drawn, as well as for any contributions to steering the evaluation or scrutinising subsequent findings. The other driver for engagement is the subsequent credibility of the evaluation findings and any implications for policy and practice. Stakeholders having a voice in the utility of the evaluation and engagement helps to condition their understanding of what is being done and how, and to create confidence in the validity of the findings.

Evaluation and monitoring

Both monitoring and evaluation are important to the review of an intervention; they are different but complementary. Monitoring processes are usually put in place by funders or operators to collect, periodically analyse and report information about selected inputs, actions, or outputs from the intervention. Monitoring data provides a finger on the pulse of what has (or has not) been done, against some expectations of performance (for example, performance indicators) or standard to be achieved. It is there to actively manage progress and performance, and to optimise outputs by looking not only at what's happening but also where it is likely to progress to within a funding period.

The information to be collected in monitoring varies with an intervention's circumstances and management needs. This may involve some of: performance progress, trends and trajectory; the operating environment (including possibly some aspects of the external context); the scale (and perhaps quality) of delivery; emerging results; financing; and, risk management and compliance. All this usually centres on administrative data collected systematically and routinely across the intervention and perhaps from external data sets.

Monitoring consequently shares some common ground with evaluation, but differs in important ways, in particular:

- Monitoring collects selected 'performance' information but is narrower in coverage than evaluation and will cover many fewer variables.
- Data for monitoring is operationally embedded, collected frequently and regularly across the activities whereas evaluation data may typically be collected on a staged and usually much less frequent basis.

- Monitoring data are reported more regularly than for evaluation: perhaps quarterly, monthly or more frequently, and typically at equal intervals to maintain a consistent flow of information. Evaluation may only report once in the life of an evaluation (that is, 'summative' reporting), although more commonly also with interim or interval reports. These will be much more extensive than for monitoring but produced less frequently and not necessarily at equal intervals.
- Monitoring may need to be delivered at whole and sub-intervention levels, such as for a regionally or sectorally devolved project, perhaps through separated monitoring functions. Evaluation may also be producing disaggregated or separate reports for the different constituencies, but this will usually be organised as a single activity.
- Monitoring is usually conducted internally, perhaps by funding or commissioning bodies, but more often by those undertaking the intervention itself. It is uncommonly contracted externally, except for very large-scale programmes. In contrast, evaluation may be conducted internally or commissioned from an external supplier or perhaps as a hybrid combination of both.

Monitoring and evaluation are consequently different but are also likely to be mutually supportive, as reflected in the increasing integration in evidence-based management practices of 'Monitoring Evaluation and Learning' (MEL) frameworks (Markiewicz and Patrick, 2016). Sound evaluation will always make best use of the available monitoring information. In this, MEL frameworks can steer their early cohesion, ideally with evaluation expertise engaged at an early stage of an intervention development to influence what information is to be monitored. Such integration helps to minimise demands on those supplying data, avoid duplication and set foundations for a more cost-effective and purposeful evaluation design.

Evaluation evidence, use and utility

The practical boundaries between evaluation, research and monitoring are sometimes blurred but these have in common the generation and use of evidence for a particular inquiry. The essential differences are in the purpose of that inquiry and where evaluation is led by a reasoned assumption that evidence will contribute to judgements to be made about something specific. The taproot of any evaluation is consequently the responsiveness to that use and utility to the evidence sought, how it is generated and assessed.

This importance of use and utility may seem self-evident, yet it can be easily neglected when making any of the many 'technical' choices needed for the 'good' evaluation. The reasons behind this vary as much as with the circumstances to be evaluated. This may reflect a vagueness of purpose from commissioners, misdirection or lack of clarity on the intended use or perhaps in intangible or unrealistic aspirations for the evidence. Pressures to get an evaluation underway can also leave unresolved ambiguity about what difference the evaluation is meant to make, and to what.

In any of these situations, the evaluator is well advised to recognise and unpick any lack of clarity or realism on underpinning use before starting to make method judgements. The next chapter (Chapter 2) looks at how to go about this, but a starting point is recognising that different evaluation needs can have very different ambitions for evidence and its use.

Discussion about evidence strengths and use over many years have included proposals to rank evaluations according to an evidence hierarchy (Lipsey, 2007, and others). There have also been calls for a theory of evidence to support this (Schwandt, 2008). These frameworks are touched on later in this book, but applying such hierarchies to judgements on an evaluation's necessary methods needs to be guided by intended use. In this, ambitions about 'use' have changed a lot in the last few decades with a progressive transition from use to demonstrate accountability for a funded activity, to wider ambitions to evaluate consequent impacts and often their added value. More recently, those impact ambitions have often been expected to dig deep into process-outcome mechanisms to determine what works, in what situation and how.

Accountability-based uses for an evaluation generally have their ambition limited to an end point assessment of the way resources for an intervention (the 'evaluand') were used, what they resulted in and perhaps their achieved value. These uses dominated much evaluation activity prior to the 1990s and emphasised looking at the performance for specific targeted or contracted 'outputs'. For an evaluated new training programme or course, for example, that would centre on results for participants recruited, retained and completed, certification or qualifications attained.

The 'what have we got for ...?' emphasis on accountability is now more often subsumed into wider aspirations. Around the mid and late 1990s, earlier in the US and later in Europe and Australasia, there was a gradual movement away from 'output'-centred review to outcome-based evidence, to assess what change resulted from the intervention. For that hypothetical new training course, for example, it would have gone beyond evaluating recruitment, retention and qualification attainment to look at what resulted from individuals securing the qualification, perhaps a job, a better job, promotion or progression, enhanced earnings, or better productivity. This transition took place in parallel with the rising influence in public policy of evidence-informed decisions and promoted the use of evaluation evidence to support programme or policy development (and improvement).

In practice, the actual influence of output or outcome-based evaluation evidence to support decision-making remains work in progress. In long experience, the author, along with very many others, remains cautious about the extent to which evaluation evidence helps to shape decisions in public policy or outside. Too often evaluators come to realise their well-designed and robust efforts to gear evidence to use find little or no leverage on the subsequent decision-making they were intended to inform (Example 2).

Example 2: EVALUATION LEVERAGE – A TIMELY CAUTION ABOUT THE IMPACT OF EVALUATION

The author was asked to lead an external evaluation of a government-funded staff development programme for school business managers. Contracted through a semi-autonomous, government-sponsored body, the evaluation was to draw on extensive management information across a tiered programme, supplementing this with process and impact evidence from schools, stakeholders and the participants. The evaluation goal and objectives set by the sponsor government department anticipated a multi-faceted three-year evaluation to inform a planned expansion for the programme.

The evaluation was delayed by departmental shut-down ('purdah') due to a parliamentary general election. Post-election, incoming ministers reviewed the programme, and new providers were brought in. The programme manager also changed and challenged the previously agreed evaluation objectives and framework, resulting in changes to the evaluation scope and delivery. Over the three years there were two further changes of programme manager, with each change of personnel followed by a change in emphasis to reflect their (different) interpretations of 'need'.

Change has consequence. On each occasion, the author cautioned changes would constrain comparability across the programme cohorts and impair the counterfactual. Shortly before the conclusion of the evaluation, in a wider reorganisation, the programme was subsumed by the sponsoring department (from the non-departmental public body, NDPB). Receiving the evaluation report and recommendations, the department queried changes to the evaluation scope and the consequences for comparability and attribution. The changes were subsequently endorsed as contractually compliant and the report 'signed off', but no action was taken on any of the recommendations for improvement. A year later, the programme was suspended.

Utilisation of evidence is a long-standing concern for evaluators, whether for accountability, measuring or understanding impacts and added-value, or for transferring 'what works' evidence into future focus or efficiencies. Neither are the frustrations when the evidence provided is side-lined or neglected by decision-makers in favour of other considerations or influences (Cousins and Leithwood, 1986).

Some evaluators consequently may adopt a wholly technocratic standpoint, seeing their role as starting with a brief which is taken at face value and ending with reported evidence. Evidence use would be seen as an issue for others to act on, or not. The separation of evidence generation and use is well-aligned with the evaluator's necessary impartiality and independence (Chapter 4) and with an evaluator's comfort zone of methods, choice and application. Yet technocratic solutions on their own risk compromising utility by neglecting or unbalancing the necessary combination of both the technical and political dimensions of any evaluation.

Put simply, the technical judgements needed to make an evaluation robust and responsive need to recognise a coherent purpose and apply that understanding to condition technical judgement on method and approach across the evaluation journey. This is at the heart of 'purposeful evaluation' as set out in this book. While providing no certainty or guarantees, this necessary profile of use and utility is also central to raising the wider potential for optimising the influence of evaluation on decision-making.

So, what makes an evaluation purposeful?

Earlier we established that 'purposeful' evaluators need to seek the most effective balance between evidence utility and optimal technique. But how? What is it that underpins purposefulness in evaluation choices and application?

Hopefully, evaluators (and commissioners) will always start off with a broad aspiration for their efforts to be purposeful, but as we have seen some of the practicalities and pressures faced can work against meeting that ambition. Those challenges commonly start early in the evaluator's journey for any requirement. They can work together or in isolation to confound the ability to make purposeful choices, compromising the eventual genuine utility of the reported evidence and its implications.

In focusing on the centrality of purpose and purposefulness in evaluation, this book calls for evaluator, funder and stakeholders to re-energise, sharpen and sometimes re-focus aspirations for intent. What follows in the subsequent chapters is bundled together under the clarifying label of 'purposeful evaluation'. It is not offering a new paradigm for evaluation, but an interpretation of 'purposeful' practice aimed at utility responsive choices of method. As such, it is plural in its emphasis on choosing whatever technical approach and delivery is best fitted to its situation and 'political' circumstances and most likely to optimise evidence use and utility. Making those choices purposeful is guided by four cornerstones:

- setting out a clear, well situated, timely and actionable purpose (intent) for the evaluation which is well-communicated to constituent users;
- adopting the primacy of a decision-centred focus, soundly based on realistic expectations of use, utility and users, reflected in responsive timing;
- fostering a utility value-based approach within well-aligned and reasoned method choices and deliverables;
- habituating considered and intentional actions to manage and deliver these, with appropriately communicated evidence and implications.

Understanding purposeful evaluation does not need new theory and is not complicated. These cornerstones can be seen as simple, practice-based principles to shape and steer utility responsive choices for how to make an evaluation purposeful.

Some may see these 'how to' principles as commonsense. If so, this is commonsense which can soon be overwhelmed by practical considerations and constraints which distort or confound their use. Harnessing these principles for purposeful practice needs to steer a reasoned course through the constraints likely to be imposed by an evaluation's resourcing, its contracting or commissioning arrangements, time and other pressures. The book is intended to provide a framework for addressing those pressures to make any evaluation 'purposeful'.

Evaluation in transition: what else is changing?

A lot that is fundamental to well-purposed evaluation can be traced back a long way and often beyond the recognition of evaluation as systematic inquiry to study how well an intervention has achieved its goals. The last sixty years have seen how an extensive literature on evaluative thinking and practice has contributed to widening foundations for professionalisation, notably in North America, the UK, elsewhere in Europe, and Australasia. In parallel, methodological options have multiplied to form a plethora of possibilities

Many emerging methods and techniques have had their respective exponents, but take-up has often lagged substantially behind ideas being formulated and published. In particular, evaluation theorists and practitioners have often proven more open to new ideas than those commissioning evaluation studies. This continues to be a brake, if not on new ideas, then on the conversion of innovation into mainstream practice. A legacy for many of those rigidities remains.

This is not the place to look more deeply at the historiography of evaluative thinking, but within the focus of this book two strands of evolving practice are worth particular attention:

- the position and use of theory platforms and, in particular, theory of change (ToCs) in framing evaluations and in interpreting findings;
- the emergence of generative Artificial Intelligence (AI) as an evaluative tool.

The author makes no apologies for the particular focus on these two areas which will loom large for many practitioners coming to terms with emerging practice.

Theory platforms and ToCs

Theory has always been a necessary part of method choice and application in evaluation. More recently it has taken on a different guise in its use for informed positioning of evaluations and their priorities, and especially for placing evaluation when facing complex situations for cause and effect. In this, 'theory platforms' aim to explore the circumstances, anticipated operationalisation and success pathways for an intervention, ideally as a preliminary to an evaluation.

This is certainly not new to evaluation; Funnel and Rogers suggest that theory platforms emerged from early roots in the late

1950s (Funnel and Rogers, 2011). What is 'new' is the influence of theory platforms on how evaluations are shaped. In the UK, for example, this enhanced influence can be traced to a watershed in 2020 when the updated version of central government guidance on evaluation practice – the *Magenta Book* – required that: 'Good policy-making necessitates a thorough understanding of the intervention and how it is expected to achieve the expected outcomes … [this] is typically done through synthesising existing evidence and producing a Theory of Change' (HM Treasury, 2020: 24). *Magenta*'s subsequent guidance on harnessing ToCs was built on already broad foundations for practice and especially Programme Theory (Kilpatrick, 1959; Stufflebeam, 1967; Suchman, 1967). This was referred to (Funnel and Rogers, 2011) as the first 'boom period' in articulating the potential for programme theory and its uses in evaluation.

For most evaluators, the early expression of programme theory was in the logical framework approach. Although referred to under different labels (logic charts, logic chains, log frames, intervention logic models), logic charts and their siblings were taken up early by some United Nations (UN) agencies to help shape evaluation focus. Logic charts had their own distinctive rationale. While they fell short of the causal chain exploration subsequently expected of theories of change, they provided for a readily absorbed, pipeline model of how an intervention was expected to proceed and achieve. They offered a rudimentary intervention theory which influenced aspects of evaluation design for over 30 years.

Much more could be said of these origins, but from our perspective programme theory, and its evolution in theories of change, was slow to be embraced by both sceptical evaluation commissioners and many practitioners. Its emergence into the mainstream is consequently an important part of what is currently changing in evaluation. Theory platforms have great potential for informing necessary priorities for evidence focus and analysis especially in complexity evaluation circumstances (considered later in Chapters 2, 3 and 10).

Generative AI

Various proprietary software and AI embedded tools have quite recently become available for text processing, data and code generation and advanced data processing, and more controversially for formative inquiry and text generation. Once again this is far from wholly new. Artificial Intelligence in the form of machine-based learning (ML) has been a feature of evaluation for some time (Norvig and Russel, 2010; Thornton, 2023); what is 'new' is the potential emerging from large language models and generative AI (Ferretti, 2023).

These are early days for AI and evaluation. The opportunities, and perhaps regulatory and other constraints, on its use are evolving remarkably rapidly so this assessment is brief. It also cautions that AI's potential in evaluation settings is fraught with issues of access and choice, accuracy, potential bias, regulatory and intellectual copyright issues, and also perceptions of trustworthiness. That said, generative AI will likely soon be integral to aspects of evaluators' practice.

The current uncertainty is just what aspects of viable practice? Current potential appears to emphasise evaluations facing time and cost-effectiveness pressures, especially where there is potential to reduce labour intensiveness in data-rich inquiries. Its opportunities and options are likely to go much further (Table 1.2) and merit deeper exploration than is possible here.

What is clear, is that for most evaluators it is not a case of whether AI could or should be used in their practice; for many this is already a feature of some of their work. This is especially for scoping, literature review and, where large data sets are involved, possibly for data preparation and processing. Generic search engines integrate AI-geared chatbots, deep language learning models or other embedded AI functions which will automatically guide and inform search procedures.

The paradigm shift that some have implied for AI and evaluation (Montrosse-Moorhead, 2023) remains some way off for its more embedded use in design, direct delivery and communication. Deepening use in evaluation is likely to go beyond fast-evolving AI platforms or applications, their functionality and fit. The breadth of take-up will be conditioned also by the nature of AI's commercialisation, practitioner skills and confidence as well as market pressures from rising intensity and cost-effectiveness pressures on evaluations. Future evaluation may also offer opportunities for AI in interdisciplinary collaboration, professional networking and knowledge sharing.

Table 1.2: Some potential evaluative contributions from generative AI

Evaluation contribution	Potential functional inputs for ...
Scoping and formative analyses	• Accelerating and/or extending online scoping analysis and literature review (Note: Via stand-alone protocols or search engines with embedded AI tools) • Framing, identifying, and synthesising thematic areas and past evidence to produce attributable summaries • Past evidence, trends and patterns review to identify evidence gaps to inform priorities for evaluative focus • Identifying possible comparative situations or data for counterfactual analysis
Evaluation design	• Use of AI algorithms to scope design decisions and prioritise evidence needs • Isolating important conditioning or independent variables • Framing specific research questions and inquiry terminology • Guiding priorities or focus for any causal analysis
Data processing and analysis	• Streamlining large data set processing (classification, coding frame determination/testing, encoding, and so on) (Note: AI is not faultless in syntheses, nor is human judgement in setting coding frames and populating them) • Production of preliminary analysis (trends, correlations, unanticipated consequences, and so on) for further quantitative or qualitative exploration
Communication of findings	• Support to routine aspects of reporting findings (proof-reading, editing reports, and other written deliverables) • Streamlining production to help with intensity, accuracy and digestibility of reports • Contribute directly to specific aspects of drafting (Note: With appropriate quality control arrangements in place)

Source: Modified from author's teaching materials

Hanging over these many issues affecting breadth and pace of take-up are persisting concerns over the (lack) of openness on the content and functionality of some of the constituent AI algorithms in commercialised products. These concerns may ease over time, or they may generate a mosaic of regulatory or procurement boundaries which will directly affect evaluation opportunities. All the while AI's more general potential as a disruptive technology is contested, its more specific implications for embedded use in evaluation will remain largely obscure.

How to use this book

Purposeful Evaluation aims to provide a guide to practitioners exploring or already committed to plural approaches which best fit method to circumstance and the need to optimise the potential for use and utility. It is aimed at those new to evaluation, as well as those with some experience who are looking to optimise evaluation credibility and influence. Purposeful evaluation cannot be brought about by the understanding and actions of those carrying out evaluations alone; the book will also be of value to commissioners, contract managers and those in policy or similar roles using evidence.

For all readers, this first chapter (Part I: *Starting points*) has set the scene for what this book is about and its starting points. What follows continues the practical emphasis in four further parts:

- Part II: *Setting the foundations*, looks at setting a clear, well-situated, actionable purpose for an evaluation (Chapter 2). It adds guidance on managing expectations to steer responsiveness (Chapter 3) and how purposeful evaluation can foster a value-based approach to making high-utility choices (Chapter 4).
- Part III: *Choosing the right method* provides a plural view (Chapter 5) of method choices and mixing them. This is followed by separate chapters on the main evaluation 'types' and sub-sets of method: process evaluation (Chapter 6); economic evaluation (Chapter 7); and impact evaluation divided into fully-experimental 'control' approaches (Chapter 8); quasi-experimental 'comparator' approaches (Chapter 9); and, theory-based impact evaluation (Chapter 10). It concludes with an introduction to meta-evaluation approaches (Chapter 11).
- Part IV: *Putting it in place*, sets out how to deliver a purposeful method through 'intent-led' planning (Chapter 12) and management of an evaluation (Chapter 13).
- Part V: *Presenting and mobilising evidence* entres on the practice and constraints to giving evidence the best chance to be purposeful through optimising the end-processes for evidence delivery (Chapter 14) and maximising the potential for its influence (Chapter 15).

Throughout, the book has sought to emphasise practicality. It sets out 20 mini-case studies and illustrations of 'how to' (and sometimes 'how not to') drawn from past purposeful practice, some from the author's own experience. There are also some content boxes and figures which may help to navigate some of the more specific subject matter. Much more detail could be provided, especially on individual methods (Chapters 5 to 11) but the focus has been to introduce these and not to provide a user-manual. A well-signposted and concluding bibliography will help to guide readers who want to dig deeper on specific applications. Put together, these five sections set out a loosely sequenced and complementary pathway on how to give any evaluation a better chance to make a difference and to be (more) valued.

PART II

Setting the foundations

The secret of success lies in the preparation undertaken beforehand … the dedication and effort put into laying the groundwork that ultimately leads to success.
                    Hindu text in the Atharva Veda

2

Defining the purpose

Introduction

A cornerstone for a purposeful evaluation is well-defined intent. Although few evaluations start without some statement of that intent, too many lack the forethought needed for a well-defined purpose. Getting there means taking a journey from initial 'wants' to well-specified and utility-geared 'needs' so as to provide the clarity and sharp focus needed to take the evaluation forward in the necessary direction.

Setting that intent is not as simple as it might seem. Evaluators, and especially those conducting their roles as funder agents, contractors or consultants, may have little or no direct input to purposing; they will be on the receiving end of what has been done by others and any gaps they have left. They nonetheless have potential in early preparation and planning, to act as 'critical friends' in assessing the utility of what they have received and filling in those gaps where refinement is needed. This chapter focuses on what can be done with those opportunities.

Whose purpose?

Defining purpose sets the scope and 'needs' parameters of an evaluation, but just whose purpose is it? The answer is not always straightforward. This is often taken simply to be whoever is seeking the evaluation or providing the resources for it, typically the funding agent, co-funders or commissioning body. Yet often the 'funder' is an agent acting for others who will be the intended end-users for the evaluation. In public bodies, regulators or larger commercial bodies, this might be the policy or strategy teams, perhaps themselves acting on behalf of senior managers or executives. Elsewhere, the intended users may be those who have direct accountability for the funding or direction of whatever the evaluation is going to evaluate.

Defining the intended users may raise unexpected challenges, but whoever these are they are unlikely to be the only interested players. Evaluators may be in situations where the funding body or intended user requires buy-in to the evaluation from key stakeholders. For example, evaluation commissioners or intended users may also wish to embrace the views of professional, regulatory or representative bodies with an active interest in where the evaluation evidence will lead.

Evaluation funders or commissioners will often be institutionally or operationally involved with other, perhaps numerous, partners, community or other bodies, who may be sensitive to what an evaluation is intended to do. The breadth of 'users' to be taken into account in purposing the evaluation may consequently be wider than expected (Example 3).

Example 3: WIDENING THE 'USER' PLATFORM

A university team was commissioned to evaluate the likely impacts of a city centre 'super-casino' in Leeds, only the fourth of that size to be developed in England. The development offered regeneration of a rundown part of the city centre and an enhanced night-time economy, but raised community concerns about higher problem gambling rates. The ex-ante evaluation was to assess likely enhanced problem and at-risk gambling levels (measured by the 'Problem Gambler Severity Index') and the support capacity of public and voluntary sector capacity support services.

The evaluation for the City Council was to be guided by a twelve-agency, multi-stakeholder steering group, which ahead of the casino opening was to put in place an evidence-based action plan for community adaptation. An early focus for the evaluators was a scoping stage, to comparatively map gambling prevalence and the diverse range of viable support agencies related to gambling harms ahead of refining indicative evaluation objectives. The scoping stage identified a number of 'non-official' support services which were often the first port of call for problem gamblers facing domestic, financial or mental health crises. This included various religious-run community shelters, often a first stop for crisis gamblers.

The evaluation scoping stage proposed church and mosque centre representatives were added to the evaluation steering group. Both were, and subsequently provided important insights for sharpening the evaluation focus and its utility, access to 'difficult-to-reach' problem gamblers and enhanced community credibility.

A practical way of looking with the necessary breadth at 'end-users' is to see them as 'primary' and 'other intended' users (Funnel and Rogers, 2011). Commissioners (primary users) are increasingly open to wider user engagement in purpose-setting precisely because it can strengthen credibility in the process. However, some may still be unwilling or nervous to engage with 'other intended' users in purpose-setting due to political, legacy or competitive pressures. Inter-agency rivalry may also be a constraint. Where this is the case, the evaluator may have little opportunity to change rigid views, but will need to make the primary user(s) aware of the value of accommodating at least some wider interests, and risks of not doing so.

Scoping the evaluation intent

Put simply, the judgements needed from evaluators of 'good' design and delivery need to be founded on well-placed, cogent aspirations and timely expectations of them. Yet evaluations commonly start off with aspirations which lack the necessary clarity or realistic aspiration about intent, leading to ill-defined or ambiguous goals or objectives which will be open to (mis)interpretation. Often, this also leads to either insufficient or over-ambitious objectives for what is necessary (or possible) within likely constraints of resources, data availability or access, and timeframe.

An evaluation encumbered in this way, will set off on unsound foundations. Even if time is pressed, purposeful evaluators need to ensure that purpose-setting (or refinement) is a conscious process and neither rushed nor over-simplified. Ideally, this will be an iterative process starting with initial scoping of (broad) purpose, moving to objectivising needs, and finally to setting the inquiry focus – and all of this ahead of determining a method focus. Along the way, stakeholders are engaged to help the evaluator manage (different) expectations as well as sense-checking the focus for viability and realism. This chapter is concerned with the first part of that process – scoping. The following chapter (Chapter 3) looks at how to take forward a well-defined scope, into formal evaluation goals and precise objectives to steer the inquiry focus and subsequently its method choices.

Is such an incremental approach to setting purpose overly fastidious or time-consuming? It need be neither. Scoping purpose and moving on to objectives and then to a viable inquiry focus can be, and often needs to be, intensive but it should build in opportunity to tap wider views. Conflating those stages risks insufficient reflection or scrutiny, and can result in less (or no) trust or credibility in what is subsequently done among some stakeholders. The touchstone is pace and not speed, because once an evaluation is underway it is very difficult to reset its foundations without comprising the quality of evidence.

Purpose-setting starts with understanding the bigger picture, so as to position the necessary scope for the evaluation (Figure 2.1) as outlined in the following sections.

What is the evaluation to look at?

Scoping is the departure point for determining what the evaluation is about and clarifying the nature of the intervention (evaluand) and the implications for what should and should not be considered by the evaluation of it. Scoping digs into the circumstances or backcloth to the intervention, its formulation and emphasis, to

Figure 2.1: Positioning the scope of an evaluation

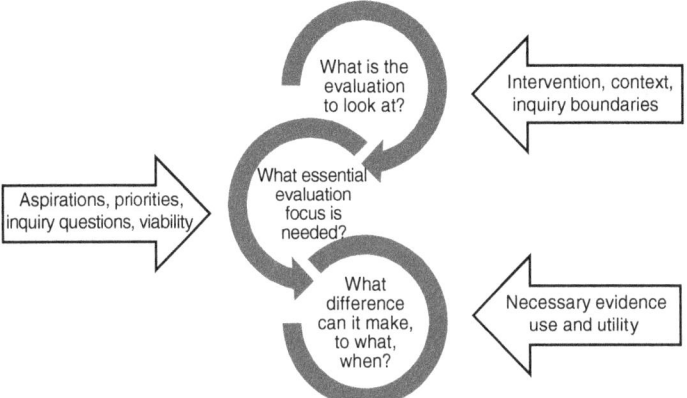

define and draw a boundary around what is to be covered, what is in and out of scope of the evaluation.

That boundary is probably going to be multi-faceted. It might set out what component parts of the intervention are to be included, and perhaps any participant or geographical limitations or focuses such as targeted priority groups or areas. The timeframe for what is to be covered will also be a boundary to be defined; this might go beyond the evaluation's start and end points, when necessary evidence is to be drawn in, to include if, and over what duration, 'legacy' data is needed for assessing changes or impacts or comparisons to past practice. These boundaries are set against the circumstances of the intervention and what it is appropriate to evaluate; when assessing a long-standing intervention, for example, it may be proportionate not to look at the whole period but only the most recent years if new aspirations or modified practices were introduced.

What essential evaluation focus is needed?

Within the set boundaries, scoping will need to explore what the evaluation needs to emphasise within what is in scope. The evaluation will not be looking at everything; scoping informs where it needs to be selective about what it is to address often within a wide range of potential evaluation issues or questions. Transparency here is crucial, with the evaluator well-advised to avoid making untested assumptions about issues of scope not clarified with funders and perhaps stakeholders.

Scoping focus builds on the exploration of the intervention's circumstances and aspiration. This helps develop a coherent map of the aspirations for the outputs or changes expected from the intervention and any wider intended consequences, as well as how these were or are anticipated to come about. This guides how to scope what is most important and feasible for the evaluation to look at.

Deciding just what is 'important' and 'feasible' will also need to take into account existing evidence of what available information can be readily harnessed, and where there are significant gaps. This may come about from an earlier evidence synthesis (for example, a pre-intervention rapid evidence review to inform its design) or existing documentation (such as a scoping study or business case rationale for the intervention). If available, it will also be informed by an intervention logic chart, or better still, a theory of change (of which more later). This picture also sets a practical baseline to later help interpret evaluation findings on, for example, consistency, quality compliance, and achieved or gaps in outputs (and for impact evaluation outcomes).

What difference can it make?

This part of scoping is easily neglected in favour of more immediate methodological concerns with boundaries, evidence availability and necessary focus. It may be reduced to little more than a (funder) statement of what's to be delivered and when. Although commonplace, especially under many commissioning and grant-funding processes, this will be a serious omission when scoping for a purposeful evaluation where it is critical to have an early understanding of how the evidence is intended to be used, what difference it will make, for whom, how and when. Here, three broad purposes for users' aspirations for evaluation have been proposed (Chelimsky and Shadish, 1997):

- evaluation for accountability (that is, for the use or value of funding and resources put into an intervention);

- evaluation for development (that is, evidencing development to better understand and improve how change is brought about by an intervention);
- evaluation for knowledge (that is, furnishing evidence-based understanding and knowledge of often complex interactions within an intervention, which may include assessing causal effects and added-value[1]).

Although proposed nearly 30 years ago, this typology is the prism through which to determine the distinctive expectations of any evaluation. Scoping helps to set out which, or which combinations, of these are important and to explicitly define what is expected of the use and utility of the evaluation namely:

- How are evaluation findings expected to be used and what are the implications for the strength of evidence needed?
- What is the necessary evidence focus? Evaluation typically focuses on evidence to support learning, measure change or achievement, and/or to better understand processes; what is the necessary priority among these (or balance of needs)?
- What difference will sufficiently robust and well-positioned evidence make, and to what?
- Who will be using the findings, and how will this integrate with decision-making processes or requirements, including, for example, consultation?
- What decisions are needed which the evaluation evidence could inform or influence?
- When are those decisions to be made and is the timing of the evaluation appropriate for this timeline?

This is not about the evaluator setting user aspirations, but a process for surfacing often ill-defined and sometimes intangible user aspirations.

Scoping boundaries, focus and utility aspirations will be aided greatly if funders have conducted a previous 'evaluability assessment'. The Organisation for Economic Co-operation and Development (OECD; Organisation de Coopération et de Développement Economiques, OCDE) has defined these as: 'The extent to which an activity or project can be evaluated in a reliable and credible fashion' (OECD-DAC, 2010: 21). These assessments can inform much of the scoping groundwork. Although a feature of scoping evaluations for some time (Davies, 2013; Trevisan and Walser, 2014), they are not yet commonplace outside big budget interventions in the public sector. Elsewhere, they are starting to be used as commissioners recognise their value in optimising the cost-effectiveness, and utility, of a subsequent evaluation.

Scoping can also be informed and intensified by drawing in a 'theory of change'[2] where it has been put together ahead of any evaluation. This has great value in stretching considerations of what it is most important to look at, and why, and is being encouraged as a scoping tool by some commissioners (Box 2.1).

Box 2.1: Scoping an evaluation and 'theory of change' – the UK *Magenta Book*

The *Magenta Book* is the long-standing, regularly updated, guidance from HM Treasury in the UK on effective evaluation practice in government. The 2020 version, the most recent at the time of writing, includes substantial guidance on scoping an evaluation as the first of several stages to framing and delivering a robust, credible, proportionate and useful evaluation. For the first time, *Magenta* in 2020 directly linked scoping and evaluability assessment with harnessing a 'theory of change' (ToC). In this, *Magenta* anticipates scoping to provide for:

- understanding the intervention and what it aims to achieve, by when and for whom;
- understanding the (existing) evidence base surrounding the intervention;
- developing the Theory of Change (ToC) (or harnessing an existing ToC);
- understanding the evaluation 'questions' which need to be answered.

ToCs are presented as a generic pathway to scoping a utility-coherent evaluation, to inform not only focus but also decision-points, learning goals and the implications for the type of evaluation needed. For *Magenta*, the key to effective scoping is combining the understanding of intervention rationale and evidence review with the additional insights offered by the ToC for:

- establishing how the intervention is expected to work, an anticipated causal chain, and the conditions needed to bring about intended changes;
- exposing the assumptions upon which the intervention actions (and causal chain) are based and the strength of the evidence supporting these;
- examining the wider context within which the intervention takes place, including other policy actions, or changes in economic, social and environmental factors.

While *Magenta* sees great value in harnessing ToCs for scoping an evaluation, it recognises many other uses including for (pre-evaluation) stress-testing an intervention design and building consensus on how the intervention is expected to work.

There is much more that can be said of the value of ToCs to purposeful evaluation and this is returned to for goal- and objective-setting (Chapter 3) and theory-based evaluation (Chapter 10).

Scoping the stakeholders: who is to help with purposing?

This chapter opened with the question: 'for whose purpose' is the evaluation? Scoping necessarily involves some wider consideration of that purpose, through the eyes of, and interaction with, 'others' with an interest in what it is to do and its later use. Many evaluations take place in multi-stakeholder situations, so a recurrent challenge is making proportionate judgements on which 'others' have the potential and motivation to play a role.

There is no template for stakeholder engagement in scoping (or other stages of) an evaluation. Determining which stakeholders to involve (how and when) will need to navigate between two opposing tensions. The first puts an emphasis on narrowing stakeholder engagement in scoping, perhaps because of demands to get an evaluation underway or resource constraints. There is also the all-too-common legacy of funders' caution about involving outside bodies early on in an evaluation. As one commissioner recently observed to the author: 'This is our [programme], our evaluation and we are funding it. We know what we want and what for … we do not need others to tell us what we need to do.' The second tension pushes in the opposite direction. It encourages breadth in stakeholder engagement, to widen the range of insights drawn on, demonstrate openness or raise credibility among diverse stakeholders through early engagement.

Resolving this 'narrow' versus 'broad' tension for stakeholder contributions may be heavily influenced by the institutional culture of funders or their views on how stakeholders can add value at this stage. Where the evaluator, or those involved in early planning, have some influence or discretion on who contributes it can be guided by mapping just which primary and other intended users might be involved (Table 2.1).

Table 2.1: Stakeholder interests in evaluation purposing

Primary users	Other intended users	Stakeholder	Stakeholder interest
√		- Decision-makers - Policy teams/ policy originators - Accountable leads	Intervention influencers/ initiators. Includes others with the most to gain from what a well-scoped evaluation shows is working (or not)
√	√	- Accountable or budgetary leads - High-level scrutiny bodies (Note: Might include government, parliamentary or regulatory scrutiny)	Individual(s) with executive or scrutiny responsibility for effective use of intervention funds/cost-effectiveness
√	√	- Aligned policy or programme influencers. (Note: Internal and/or external to initiating agency)	Those with an active interest in, or responsibility for, intervention improvement or transferable evidence or lessons for future policy formation
√		- Partner organisations (to initiators) - Co-funders - External collaborators in formation	Actors contributing to intervention resources, ideas-building or operationalisation (Note: In pilot actions, might include local government, community or sectoral bodies where piloting occurs)
	√	- Delivery agents who are directly engaged - Contracted providers	Provider bodies likely to be (or have been) directly involved in intervention delivery with insights on delivery effectiveness

Defining the purpose

Table 2.1: Stakeholder interests in evaluation purposing (continued)

Primary users	Other intended users	Stakeholder	Stakeholder interest
	√	- Practitioners and/or representatives - Professional bodies	Bringing grounded experience or knowledge of (likely) participant engagement, motivations, behaviour, and/or change leverage
	√	- Intended participants - Likely service users or direct beneficiaries (Note: Pre-intervention these are likely to be representatives or past (similar) service users)	Those with direct or proxy knowledge or lived experience of interventions intended/targeted users (Note: Participants are unlikely to be homogeneous so 'users' might include representatives of different needs groups)
	√	- 'Consequence' bodies - Professional/standard setting bodies - Regulators, and so on	Agencies not directly involved in the intervention or policy formation but with interests in delivery processes or outcomes
√	√	- Knowledgeable others (Note: Might include relevant academics or researchers with direct experience of the user/needs group)	Those responsible for evidence-gathering or appraisal with insight into articulating different data sources, additional data needs, data quality and its use, and so on

Of course, many evaluations will have the need or potential to engage with only a few of these stakeholders. Others may face a plethora of possible stakeholders where not all can be involved in purposing discussions. In both situations, early judgements will need to be made on:

- Which individual stakeholders are the most relevant to the scope and purpose of the evaluation?
- Which (of those organisations) have the capacity and capability to contribute?
- Which of those are likely to be willing to engage constructively?
- Are there others it is also important to involve for operational or credibility reasons?

Making necessary choices will need to keep an eye also to who plays a role later in the evaluation. 'Participatory' evaluations (that is, those involving substantial collaboration, or wanting to build in advocacy or self-determination among stakeholders) are likely to need to embrace a wide cross-section of these stakeholders, and especially those with lived experience.

Deciding who is to be involved can be challenging, especially where there are particular sensitivities or legacy issues with stakeholders about them. Care and attention here is not only an investment in robust purposing for the evaluation, it can also contribute to utility by boosting confidence and credibility in eventual findings.

Engaging stakeholders in purpose-setting

Choosing which stakeholders are to be involved in scoping purpose needs to go hand-in-hand with careful attention to how they can best contribute. Stakeholder engagement is unlikely to be limited to purpose-setting (this is explored further in Chapter 12). The focus here is specifically on practical, well-fitted ways in which stakeholders can be engaged early with discussions on an evaluation's purpose.

Advocates might see early engagement as a process of co-production of the evaluation. Some caution is needed here. Coproduction would involve open and shared stakeholder partnership aimed at forging consensus and a collective responsibility for setting purpose.[3] While this may be well-suited where an evaluation has a distinctive and strong participatory focus, it may be contra-indicated elsewhere. For example, commissioners who may embrace the value of engagement may be much more cautious about coproduction. They may see dangers in effectively devolving responsibility for purposing, with consequent risks of leaving the door open to widening necessary timeframes, delays to meeting decision makers' needs for evidence, or expanding resource demands.

Even where commissioners and primary users see value in coproduction, this may not be practical. Coproduction will probably need to accommodate a range of competing stakeholder or vested interests, with different power dynamics between them. This may require (considerable) effort and time to negotiate between different perspectives to build something as close as possible to a consensus on evaluation purpose. This may require time that is not available at often intensive preparatory stages for an evaluation. This is not to suggest that coproduction for purposing is impractical; it can be an exciting and empowering process, opening up scoping to greater reflection and innovation. Nonetheless, even where funders support it, coproduction calls for evaluator caution and sensitivity to achieve its potential.

More mainstream consultative or advisory approaches to stakeholder engagement in purposing are more familiar to commissioners and evaluators. These may delegate contributing to scoping discussion to selected stakeholders, but they do not devolve responsibility for a final judgement about purpose. They also involve less risk by working within boundaries for timeframes and budgets. There is also greater flexibility in the approaches that might be taken for purposing engagement (Table 2.2).

Table 2.2: Stakeholder engagement opportunities for evaluation scoping

Scoping through	Typical engagement activities ...
Working or task groups	• Designated working groups with specific tasks and/or terms of reference to shape scope and focus • Progressive (formal) working agendas with (provided) secretariat function and/or facilitation • Designated timeframe; typically meeting on two or more occasions • Invited membership across appropriate diverse; may involve formalised stakeholder representative roles
Small group 'informal' discussions or workshops	• Small group working meeting on one or more occasions to share wider experience relevant to scoping. (Note: May precede formation of a working group (as preceding row)) • Semi-structured, formative discussions to inform evaluation scope and focus • Broad stakeholder composition and 'membership' to provide a necessary breadth of experience/views
Segmented group workshops	• Constituency-based, hosted small groups drawn from common interest groupings (practitioners, sectors, locality areas, and so on) • Useful with multiple 'key' stakeholders' interests (too many for a single forum) or for separating vested interests • Typically meeting once or with very limited frequency • Valuable for extending engagement and/or for breadth of diversity and inclusion in engagement

(continued)

Table 2.2: Stakeholder engagement opportunities for evaluation scoping (continued)

Scoping through	Typical engagement activities ...
Large group discussions	• Engaging large numbers of diverse stakeholders in single events or mediated engagement opportunities • Discussion events usually by invited participation; web- or paper-based opportunities may be open engagement • Specific theme- or issue-based discussions or consultation which may use issue engagement techniques (for example, 'fishbowl' formats)[4]
Piggy-back discussion forums	• Externally hosted segmented workshops or events with engagement negotiated with specific stakeholders • Often 'piggy-back' on planned events where relevant stakeholders are to be involved • Cost-effective opportunity for (intensive) targeted discussions; use presentations/shared issues (for example, conference agenda slots)
Individual stakeholder discussions	• Distributed engagement through selected individual stakeholder discussions • May involve open agenda discussion on wider scoping issues or semi-structured interviews • Offer more opportunity to explore purposing views and issues in depth • Can be used in combination prior to small group discussions to inform scoping/issue agenda or after (follow up)

There are different pros and cons for these approaches. Group methods or workshops provide the opportunity for constructive critical thinking and exchange about evaluation scoping to draw in different perspectives. However, this is demanding of stakeholders' time and set-up arrangements may delay decision-making around purpose. Individual stakeholder discussions offer more depth but at a loss of critical inter-change; they can also extend the evaluation's start-up phase and be resource-extensive for evaluators.

Where 'small' group working is involved, a recurrent issue is just how small? There is a need to balance obtaining a breadth of views, with effective use of time. The author's experience suggests 4–10 individuals as a benchmark (Example 4). Too small, and the purposing discussions will lack necessary diversity or critical mass; too large, and the group may become difficult to organise or manage.

Example 4: HARNESSING STAKEHOLDERS – STAKEHOLDER ENGAGEMENT IN A THEORY OF CHANGE WORKING GROUP

The Gambling Commission, as the regulator of gambling in Great Britain, announced in 2019 its intention to introduce a universal ban on the use of credit cards for payment of any form of gambling. This was aimed at reducing the number of problem and at-risk gamblers building up unstainable levels of debt. Given the many uncertainties about the effective working of the ban, the Commission decided a well-scoped 'theory-based' evaluation was needed, with a cross-stakeholder working group to be set up to help shape a theory of change and use this to set the evaluation's scope and purpose.

The first step was to agree on stakeholders, with the author (as an advisor) suggesting a group of around eight to ten diverse members. The Commission initially suggested seven of its own staff covering a range of policy interests but agreed this underplayed insights from the external perspectives. A subsequent half-day Delphi-style forum was set up internally to explore potential wider stakeholder interests, taking account of the many vested interests. To ensure constructive discussions, it was decided not to include representatives of gambling operators or financial institutions (as card processors) in the working group (they were included in a post-group written consultation).

A working group of eight members was formed: three from the Commission's initial internal list; two from (different) harm minimisation charities; a national debt reduction advisory agency; a debt criminality enforcement body; a researcher with recent field experience; and, the author as facilitator. The group met three times to frame the theory of change. Seven of the eight members went on to steer an external rapid evidence review, set the evaluation objectives and, for continuity, form the subsequent evaluation steering group.

Purposeful evaluation often needs to be creative in stakeholder engagement in scoping while always keeping an eye open for necessary contributions, diversity and inclusion and due process.

Summative or formative evaluation

A final consideration in purposing is whether a 'summative' or a 'formative' evaluation is needed. The differences between summative and formative evaluations cut across the different evaluation types and methods (Chapters 6–10).

A 'summative evaluation' aims to 'sum-up' the results and effects of an intervention. This summation is typically at the end of an intervention's funding or pilot period, or at some other relevant end-point, such as for next steps budgeting decisions. Summative evaluations may start at the beginning of an intervention but can be a fall-back option where the evaluation only starts part way through its implementation. Very intensive interventions may also have little opportunity to offer anything beyond a summative approach. Summative evaluations may provide occasional progress reports on how well the evaluation is progressing, but their findings will be drawn together in a single, one-off composite 'end of evaluation' report.

There is no requirement for interim reporting of findings in a summative evaluation, but a 'formative evaluation' will need to include one or more interval reporting stages. The difference goes beyond how many reports are produced and when to emphasise the utility intended of them. In formative reporting, those interim analyses go well beyond setting out progress to look at how something is working as it is being implemented, usually against preconceived expectations of interim delivery or results. They can be assembled at any stage after start-up, with their timing usually intentionally geared to specific operational stages (for example, post set-up to assess start-up processes and procedures) or at designated funding or other decision points for funders or other interested bodies.

Some of the typical differences between summative and formative process evaluations are summarised in Table 2.3.

Defining the purpose

Table 2.3: Summative vs formative evaluation

Primary user(s)	Purpose	Reporting	Evaluators' role
SUMMATIVE EVALUATION			
- Commissioners - Funders - Policy makers or teams - Supervisory or programme boards - Delivery partners	- Funding (and so on) accountability - End review of performance (against targets) - Policy review - Scale-up or roll-out decision (for example, piloting)	- End of funding period - In-programme critical decision points - End of trial or piloted action	- Independent assessment - External detached review
FORMATIVE EVALUATION			
- Commissioners (finger on pulse) - Fund/accountable manager - Operating providers or managers - Practitioners (modified practice)	- Start-up review (early intended implementation) - Phased or mid-term 'health check' - Trajectory (staged review) reviewing likely end-point - Assessment of performance gaps - Identification of interim improvement	- Staged/interim report(s) - Mid-term report/progress review - Annual review - Key point review (Note: Interim report frequency can be fixed or variable)	- Exploratory to evidence scope for in-programme change or improvement - Quality assurance (against set standard) - External or internal assessment - Independent-impartial review

Source: Author's adaptation; after Parsons, 2017

Although they are different beasts, designed for different purposes, summative and formative evaluations share some common ground:

- They have a developmental emphasis, providing specific evidence to support improvement of implementation (processes) but provide this either only on conclusion (summative) or at intervals and on conclusion (formative).
- They are best conducted independently and impartially, where the evaluation assessment and its reporting are separated from intervention implementation (Chapter 4).
- Their deliverables (findings and implications) involve structured, goal-centred reporting to specific, anticipated, usually fixed points, geared to decision-making.
- They focus on auditing actions, outputs and/or outcomes and other achievements against set expectations and/or a modelled process.

In their different ways, both are also aimed at providing a purpose-based and evidenced rationale, to inform the scope and direction of improvements.

Some purposeful tips

This chapter has shown that purposeful evaluation needs solid foundations for selecting and implementing the 'right' evaluation method. This starts with setting the evaluation purpose to reflect a responsive, prospective use for evidence and through a staged approach to defining that purpose – starting with scoping and followed (in the next chapter, Chapter 3) by translating that into responsive, viable and realistic objectives. Some practice-based insights for this start of the scoping journey include:

- Avoid jumping into the deep end by setting evaluation objectives or points of inquiry at the outset. These will come around soon enough, but judgements on them need to be led by a sufficient consideration of a broad and timely intent for use and utility.

- Take some time (even if there is not much to start with) to give very early attention to the backcloth to what the intervention is about, where has it come from, where it is aiming to get to, and what might underpin its smooth running (and delivery). Evaluators need to have confident foundations for understanding also the 'conditions' for the success of what they are to look at, its situation and what changes are anticipated.
- Paying early and enough attention to the organisational context, culture and perspectives of the commissioning body and other key users. Scoping can be helped greatly with a bi-focal perspective by 'taking a walk in the shoes' of users.
- Stretch thinking about who are the 'key' stakeholders and how to engage them (and when), with the evaluator being prepared to challenge any lack of ambition from commissioners on a diversity of insights.
- Avoid rushed or inadequate attention to the capabilities needed from stakeholders, including their capacities and motivation to contribute to what is not their 'day job'. Purposing needs to regard stakeholders as 'assets' to be carefully managed.
- Foster openness in discussions (among commissioners and with stakeholders) about the evaluation situation and conditions faced and expectations of it; speaking 'truth' is not always comfortable, but it is an essential quality for effective purposing.

A recurrent issue for purposeful approaches is that the necessary clarity and realism on intent cannot always secure a consensus across stakeholders; there may be persisting differences on perspectives between key stakeholders. Where a common view on intent is not possible, the evaluation needs to look to harmonise perspectives across stakeholders of what it will and will not be doing (and why). Not all will be comfortable with what is or is not included, but there will be shared understanding of why those choices were made. Deferring attention to these differences until the evaluation is underway risks at best ambiguity or uncertainty in the purpose and at worst a loss of confidence among some who you need to be engaged. Purposing challenges do not get resolved by 'kicking them into the long grass'.

3

Managing evaluation objectives and expectations

Introduction

There is a lot do upfront if an evaluation is to be purposeful; scoping and setting its purpose (Chapter 2) is only a starting point. Whatever 'close fit' or, hopefully, consensus have been achieved in those purposing discussions, this needs to translate into clear, realistic and actionable objectives to steer the subsequent choices in design and delivery. An evaluation with a statement of purpose but without well-crafted objectives to steer its focus will be rudderless, lacking the necessary levers to shape and control where and how it is going.

Just as purpose-setting for an evaluation involves a managed process, so, too, its transition into sound objectives needs a well-considered approach. In this, evaluators will commonly find themselves needing to come to terms with often unrealistic or inconsistent expectations for what's to be done, further confused by differences in stakeholders' expectations of the evaluation. This chapter explores some of the practicalities for how to get to grips with transitioning purpose to workable objectives and to manage for clear, realistic and deliverable expectations of them to shape a purposeful inquiry focus.

Challenging the ask: from wants to needs

Not all evaluations start with the benefit of careful purpose-setting. This may have been rushed, poorly defined or narrowly forged in not taking account of key stakeholder views. These gaps may not be immediately apparent. Evaluators under pressure for fast starts may only become conscious of these weak foundations some way downstream, leaving them faced with ambiguous, inadequate or unrealistic objectives. Purposeful evaluators will find it prudent to start off with an assumption that funders' or commissioners' 'ask' for the evaluation may be insufficiently considered. This constructive scepticism calls for proactive steps to be taken speedily to review or 'challenge the ask' before confirming the design.

This is not to criticise commissioners. Rather, it is a reflection of the time pressures and other constraints which they themselves also often face. Those specifying the evaluation may be inexperienced or lack the sufficient cooperation from programme managers, policy interests, data providers or potential users. They may also lack the time to engage key stakeholders or be constrained by organisational procedures for involving them.

Whatever the cause, evaluators looking to make design choices from what is, or could be, a poorly placed starting 'ask', will be in a compromised position to plan and make appropriate technical judgements on what specifically to focus on and how. Nurturing a healthy and constructive scepticism will involve interrogating the initial 'ask' to sense-check if the specified 'wants' are what is needed for focus, relevance and viability. This is not about the evaluator knowing better; it is about acting as a 'critical friend' so as to reach the necessary focus. Constructive scepticism is in the evaluators' professional interests; it is also in the interests of commissioners and subsequent users to achieve an end product that is well-placed and useful.

Time for this is likely to be limited, so this post-ask scrutiny will need to be done intensively as well as sensitively. The start-up of the evaluation is at risk if this scrutiny is mishandled, as will be the quality of the working relationships with commissioners and users. A speedy review of programme documentation may help, but of special value will be where a theory of change, or logic chart, sets out the rationale (and perhaps the underpinning assumptions) for the intervention. Not all interventions are (yet) informed by a theory of change, but experience shows the more commonplace logic chart may can substitute as a simpler but still valuable aid to sense checking the initial 'ask' (Example 5).

Example 5: FROM WANTS TO NEEDS – USING A THEORY OF CHANGE OR LOGIC CHART

Some years ago, a review by a governmental auditing body looked at the value derived from commissioned education policy research in the UK. This reported high quality research methods, but raised concerns about the practical, policy-related application of those studies. It also reported a narrow range of university contractors involved across the (then) 121 UK higher education institutions (HEIs) involved in initial and post-qualification teacher training. To improve utility and widen HEI engagement a 10-year Teaching and Learning Research Programme (TLRP) of funded education policy research was subsequently set up by a UK research council and the (then) Higher Education Funding Councils, with a cross-programme summative impact evaluation commissioned.

On commissioning the TLRP evaluation, the research council provided a recently developed programme logic chart along with background information on the funding distribution. The evaluation contractor subsequently attended an inception meeting (of the programme board) to review the workplan, agree start-up communications and stakeholder engagement, and the detailed timeframe.

In discussion, the lead evaluator sought further clarification of possible inconsistencies between the set evaluation objectives and further details of the programme aspiration from the logic chart. The specified evaluation objectives centred on the quality and utility of the funded projects, with no requirement for reviewing the impacts on the scale and quality of policy research capacity-building across UK HEIs, or for new or additional funded research engagement with public bodies. This proved to be an unintended omission, and the objectives (and workplan and resourcing) were modified to integrate the HEI capacity (and capability) impacts.

Not all evaluators will be comfortable with what they (and others) may see as 'second-guessing' what the evaluation needs to be about. There may be a comfort in sticking to the required focus – right or not so right! Such caution is misplaced; challenging the 'ask' is not, and should not be, an adversarial process. It is about identifying and clarifying uncertainties or apparent gaps. In the author's experience, commissioners will not see this unfavourably if done early and constructively, and it can help build confidence that the evaluator is 'asking the right questions'. Some may even invite challenge by building in an early review by the evaluator, of the viability of the scope, objectives or specific research questions as set.

Scrutinising, clarifying and constructive challenging the initial 'ask' is a precautionary principle underpinning purposeful evaluation. However, it needs to be tackled intensively and early. Commissioners are not likely to look favourably on the evaluator deferring such clarifications until the evaluation is well underway. By then, little or nothing might be done to accommodate modifications in the evaluation's purpose, without significant disruption to the method, scope or timing.

From purpose into objectives

A well-scoped purpose is the guiding light for any evaluation. It will set out boundaries, rules for engagement, and broad focus but will not go so far as a specific statement of what needs to be done. The evaluators will need purpose to be drawn out into a statement of intent which conveys an unambiguous understanding of necessary focus, use and utility, typically translating a purpose into prioritised 'objectives'. It is not an exaggeration to say that setting appropriate evaluation objectives is the most critical part of the preparation for an evaluation.

Setting objectives has long been recognised as a cornerstone of systems thinking in planning actions: 'We must learn to look at our objectives as critically and as professionally as we look at our [systems] models and our other inputs' (Hitch, 1960: 19). More than six decades on, Hitch's advice remains pertinent for those shaping evaluations. Objectives are the defining statements for the necessary inquiry focus as well as for managing (stakeholder) expectations and for the decisions to follow on specific lines of investigation and how to address them. Few would take issue with the importance of sound objectives, yet paying sufficient attention to them is easily neglected. Evaluators can find themselves faced with a broad aspiration (goal) but no specific objectives, or half-cast objectives which are vague, ambiguous, ill-fitted to needs or unrealistic. Evaluators may even face misdirected 'objectives' which neglect detail on what they are looking at and what for (Example 6).

Example 6: PURPOSEFUL SPECIFICATION – WHERE THE EVALUATION OBJECTIVES FALL SHORT

A large military heritage organisation, with an extensive on- and off-site educational visit programme for schools and colleges, was to run a pilot to reshape standards and staff training for safeguarding. The programme was to be funded jointly by the organisation and a government sponsored non-departmental public body (NDPB) concerned with cultural heritage. Ahead of the start of the pilot, an open tender was issued for an independent process and impact evaluation of the pilot to assess effectiveness. The NDPB was also keen for the evaluation to assess the potential for transferability of the initiative to other heritage organisations with education programmes. The tender specified: 'The evaluation goal is to assess the effectiveness and effects of the pilot and lessons learned for [the organisation] and to include implications for the roll-out of the safeguarding pilot ...'. It went on to set out specific 'objectives' for the evaluation of: 'Analysing management information [from the operation of the pilot], conducting major stakeholder interviews, a survey of providers participating in the pilot, and providing a small number of provider case studies and reporting with recommendations for improvement.'

The evaluation was later commissioned from a well-established policy research consultancy who, five months later, were 'let go' by the contractor under a breakpoint clause because ' ... they did not sufficiently understand our [the host organisation's] needs'.

In this example, the general aspiration (goal) is broadly set out but the 'specific objectives' say little about the evaluation's intended purpose. They emphasise (rather vague) 'how to' needs (evidence-gathering methods) not the necessary 'what to and for' requirement. They were not time-specified, made no reference to what aspects of use or effectiveness were important, what or whom recommendations were for, or likely utility (that is, host organisation vs transferability for the wider sector). As the tender called for a process and impact evaluation, the objectives also gave no pointers to what impacts were to be investigated, and for whom. We can sympathise with the subsequent evaluator, who had little steer on what the heritage commissioner actually needed.

Examples of objective-setting falling short are not too hard to find. There is nothing wrong with including some method steer in objectives; the problem comes where this substitutes for stating purpose-led requirements, as with this example. Evaluations that lack purpose-centred objectives are not providing necessary foundations for the inquiry to build on. Clarifying insufficient or unsound initial objectives 'downstream' can mitigate this, but this will cause delays, may reduce confidence and risks reduced evidence quality. At worst it can be terminal (as with Example 6).

So, how to go about purpose-led objective-setting? The starting point is with the underpinning rationale, which adequate attention to scoping a purpose should have achieved (Chapter 2) by the time objectives are being cast. Objective-setting casts that understanding into specific, actionable and responsive requirements for the evaluation. Ensuring these follow the well-worn convention of being 'S-M-A-R-T' (Table 3.1) will ensure the necessary precision of the purpose requirements.

The challenge for evaluators is condensing what is 'SMART' into a sharp enough tool for the requirement or specification and for later guiding method choice and delivery. This goes beyond

Purposeful Evaluation

Table 3.1: Setting 'SMART' objectives for purposeful evaluation

SPECIFIC	What specifically is to be done (and when) within the intervention context?	• Precise – emphasising the specific actions, change or aspirations for the evaluation focus • Clear and reflecting the context of the intervention • Unambiguous – clarifying aspects capable of misunderstanding or misinterpretation • Well-defined and reflecting the scope and purpose of the evaluation
MEASURABLE	What is to be dimensioned?	• Quantitative/qualitative dimensioning of target intervention achievements (at end and/or set intervals) • Evidence-based assessment of results through direct or indicative (proxy) 'measures' • Benchmark or comparative requirements within and/or outside the intervention
ACHIEVABLE	Is it attainable within scope and available or anticipated resources?	• Setting clear and appropriate resource-centred boundaries (budget, time, expertise, and so on) • Taking account of data access, quality, suitable coverage, data protection or security issues
REALISTIC	Is it action-orientated and reflecting intent?	• Supporting appropriate evidence-base analysis/understanding for intended purpose/decisions • Proportionate to the intervention circumstances • Complementary to evaluation objectives/intent
TIMEBOUND	When is it to be accomplished?	• Setting timeframe for evaluation component parts relevant to intended use and utility • Clarity on evidence/reporting reference periods or timing (for example, calendar or budgetary years, and so on) • Setting specific dates for receipt of deliverables (progress reports; interim/final reports; and so on)

Source: Author's teaching materials, *Research and Evaluation Project Management*, and *Foundations of Evaluation*, Social Research Association

a technical assessment of what is necessary; it is likely to need to draw on different views about what the evaluation objectives are meant to mean and the purpose to which they are to be put. This may need engagement with those best placed both assessing what will be useful and achievable, and for managing (different) expectations; the next section looks at this.

Managing expectations

Funders and commissioners may have particular expectations of what an evaluation needs, but these may not be shared by others. Different stakeholders are likely to look at an intervention from different viewpoints, and the likelihood of different expectations for its evaluation intensifies in a multi-stakeholder context. These different viewpoints may involve contrasts in emphasis or priorities, but they may also involve conflicting expectations. Whichever is the case, an evaluation which leaves such differences unaired or unresolved risks a subsequent 'road crash' in the run up to, or during, reporting.

Different expectations don't have to be chasms. They may be easily resolved issues, such as differences in a particular focus, for example, how to define: the priority needs groups; the beneficiary age range in scope; appropriate performance measures or comparators; or data or timing boundaries. Others may be more challenging to manage, especially where they involve unrealistic 'asks' of what the evaluation can, or is intended, to do within the delivery or resourcing scope.

Small or large, any contrasts (or conflicts) in expectations need to be faced early and before judgements are made about design and evidence-gathering. Delaying or deferring this risks almost inevitable later disruption to the evaluation's subsequent journey. Purposeful evaluation needs to stay purposeful; getting to grips with unclear, unrealistic or contrasting expectations at the outset may not be the end of expectations management. Legitimate needs for an evaluation can change with circumstances and modified funder or user priorities. They may also face 'mission creep', with calls for more questionable changes to scope or requirements (Example 7).

Example 7: SHIFTING AMBITIONS – MANAGING MISSION CREEP AND DISRUPTIVE EXPECTATIONS

A US-based international development consultant was coordinating the evaluation of a community management

> programme to boost maize yields with the wider aid-funded programme led by a US university. A network of national agricultural research and development centres across 13 countries implemented the activities and had set out a monitoring and evaluation (M and E) framework as part of the programme funding bid. An early activity was design of the data requirements and M and E tools, with the detailed framework and evidence requirements subsequently agreed by a first steering meeting of the 13 country leads.
>
> Mission creep started to occur after that first steering meeting, when the new programme 'technical' lead unilaterally reset the M and E data requirement, substantially extending the evaluation framework. This added new data needs, a further cross-programme survey stage, and an extended baseline analysis to include a cross-13 country study of comparative methods of maize growing. The new requirements went beyond the funded project brief and were described by the data collecting centres as 'not remotely feasible'.
>
> The consequence was a largely unresolved conflict on scope between the consultant (as the evaluation specialist and backed by the steering group) and the technical lead. The result was an unsatisfactory compromise to integrate much of the additionally demanded 'infeasible' data and a concluding evaluation yielding ' ... only a meagre harvest of M&E results'.
>
> Note: Description and quotes synthesied from Archibald, 2019.

Whatever they are and whenever they occur, unclear or misplaced expectations require robust attention to isolate what needs attention, and effort putting into resolving them. Deferring this can leave the evaluator trapped in a straitjacket of ambiguous, conflicting or unresolved misplaced expectations which will almost inevitably compromise the utility of, or confidence in, eventual findings. Timely attention by the evaluator, ideally working with constituent stakeholders, will identify and unpick what is unclear or unrealistic. This may most commonly involve one or more of:

- differences of view of the underpinning rationale for what (and why) the evaluation is being conducted and how it will be used;
- contrasting opinions on what is necessary for the scope of the evaluation and/or its relevant boundaries;
- diverse and often over-ambitious views on what is needed for evidence collection to reflect this or how to go about these;
- different priorities or perspectives on what:
  - processes (or assumptions behind these) within the intervention need to be the focus for the evaluation;
  - which stakeholders are important to engage, how and when;
  - what specific aspects of performance in, or changes from, the intervention need to be looked at, and for whom;
- different views on how evaluation resources should be harnessed, including for the method and evidence mix.

All this calls for constructive critical review of what is vague or apparently ill-placed. Here, well-specified objectives provide the necessary focus for tackling this pre-design, with late onset changing needs, or for expedient challenge of mission creep. They provide a reference framework from which the evaluator can challenge what appears unrealistic or ill-placed by asking how that contributes to the (agreed) objectives. If a case cannot be made by those raising an additional need, there is a reasoned foundation for placing these as 'nice to have, but not our task'. If a case can be made and the added 'asks' are shown to be relevant, then the objectives need to be modified if the evaluation is to continue to be purposeful.

This may all appear a straightforward technical task needing only attention to detail and impartiality. In practice, it also calls for political and relationship skills –which, for most of us, may go well beyond our comfort zone – of crafting and applying methodological solutions. For most evaluators, the biggest challenge of expectation management is consequently our own awareness and confidence to tackle differences of viewpoint and needs.

Those new to evaluation, or inexperienced, are the most likely to lack that confidence. They may be more likely to be subject to pressure (real or imagined) to 'get on with it', have less leverage with users and may not be keen to 'rock the boat'. While caution is a valuable instrument in any evaluator's toolkit, an excess of it in getting to grips with expectations-mismatch risks leaving a ticking timebomb for the evaluation. The purposeful evaluator – new or established – needs the confidence to step outside their methodological roots to be the expectations-mismatch detective, advocate and facilitator for resolutions.

Setting the inquiry focus

Establishing the inquiry focus is the third and concluding stage for setting a deliverable purpose for an evaluation. Here, the evaluator (or those specifying the requirement) engage in a reductive process which moves from the refining the initial 'ask' into 'needs' (scoping into objectives) to the 'must haves' setting an achievable framework for what needs to be answered to meet those requirements. Different evaluators will have different ways of going about setting the inquiry focus, formally or informally, but one way or another it involves:

- scrutinising the objectives to unpick the issues on which evidence is needed;
- setting the necessary 'research questions' to reflect these;
- ensuring a purpose-led fit and viability.

Scrutinising the objectives

There are limitations which even well-expressed SMART objectives can specify for the inquiry. An individual objective will be an amalgam encompassing a range of likely specific issues for inquiry and which will need dismantling (Box 3.1).

Box 3.1: Scrutinising the objectives to set inquiry issues

An evaluation might have set one objective which will require the evidence gathering and analysis to: 'Assess comparative performance and trends of [the programme] for participant impacts over the period [X to Y] taking account of programme aims and the consistency and coherence of provider delivery.'

This is a (more or less) 'SMART' objective, but it would need to be further unpicked to refine the inquiry issues it would need to answer. In particular:

- What 'participant impacts' are expected and are important to assess?
- Are there particular policy aspects within the 'programme aims' which should be priorities for analysis?
- What is it important to compare to (or for) in 'comparative performance'; what comparisons are of special significance for understanding performance or for users?
- Are there particular aspects of 'consistency and coherence of provider delivery' which stakeholders regard as critical to take into account?

Scrutinising what is needed to meet the objectives helps to set out what are the priority inquiry issues and what are the 'must haves' for which evidence will be needed.

As in Box 3.1's (fictitious) example, it may only be necessary to apply a keen eye to the wording of the evaluation to identify where to 'reduce' objectives to specific inquiry needs. It may need a little help from the evaluation commissioners or some stakeholders, but this would otherwise be a simple and transparent way to work through the objectives.

In some situations, scrutiny may need to go further, especially where what is being evaluated takes place in complex cause–effect circumstances. Rittel and Webber referred to these famously and succinctly as 'wicked problems', contrasting these to relatively 'tame', solvable problems in mathematics, chess, or puzzle-solving (Rittel and Webber, 1973). In evaluation, this 'complexity' stems from situation, and specifically, where there is no likely clear, demonstrable (causal) pathway between cause (the actions of the intervention being evaluated) and effect (the desired outcomes or changes sought from it).

In such complexity circumstances, scrutiny of objectives may go back to a theory of change or logic model for the intervention. Where these are to hand, they will already have played a part in purpose-setting (Chapter 2), and they now provide valuable aid to surfacing specific issues for investigation underlying the objectives which may include, for example:

- Delivery assumptions, where there is uncertainty about how sound these are, such as, effective marketing to 'hard to reach' beneficiaries or appropriateness of training for practitioners engaged in the intervention.
- Assumptions about join-up or integration with agencies or others not directly a part of the intervention, but important to final outcomes, such as promotion, recruitment, or referral collaborations with 'external' bodies.
- Attainment of outcomes, where transitional changes are necessary for 'end results' to come about, such as how young, disillusioned participants use new knowledge or skills from an employability intervention to change attitudes or behaviours which had obstructed successful job search.
- High profile risks identified in the theory of change as possible constraints to delivery or achievements, and which might need to be explored, both for if and how they occur and who they affect, and if, and how well, they are countered in the intervention.

This scrutiny might lead to some tightening of the objectives themselves, but the main purpose is to identify the specific issues on which the evaluation should focus its inquiry.

Setting the necessary research questions

With the inquiry focus established, it is helpful to condense it into bite-sized issues for the evaluation's focus. These might be thought of as subsidiary objectives, but are often referred to simply as 'research questions' or RQs. A well-specified objective needs to be broken down into (probably) several specific RQs to provide an unambiguous, tangible, sharp focus for prioritising evidence needs (see Box 3.2).

Box 3.2: Setting the inquiry focus – objectives to 'research questions' (RQs)

Most evaluations will set several RQs for any individual evaluation objective. Some of these may apply to, or overlap, different objectives. RQs are specific inquiry aspects which together inform what is needed to respond to any individual objective.

We may again use the earlier conjectured example of a programme evaluation objective to: 'Assess comparative performance and trends of [the programme] for participant impacts over the period [X to Y] taking account of programme aims and the consistency and coherence of provider delivery'. This might have been cascaded into four specific RQs, set out as:

- RQ 1: What are the quantified differences between programme providers, across recruitment and retention key performance indicators (KPIs), and in participant satisfaction levels?
- RQ 2: Which providers have been more successful in early programme take-up than others?
- RQ 3: How are provider contrasts in early and subsequent recruitment and participation explained? What are the implications for better provider practice in delivery?
- RQ 4: Are there provider contrasts in securing programme-designated beneficiary impacts and what circumstances have influenced better outcomes?

The four RQs would together define the aspects or issues to be addressed to cumulatively respond to the evidence needed for that one objective for the evaluation.

There is, of course, a difference between these sub-objective RQs and more specific 'questions' that might be later set out in evidence-gathering tools. RQs are broader but will later inform the mosaic of questions likely to be 'asked' in, for example, scoping interviews, self-completion questionnaires, participant or focus group interviews. Determining those evidence-gathering questions comes down the line, when the evaluator turns from purposing to the nuts and bolts of designing evaluation tools.

Ensuring fit and viability

With objectives set and RQs formulated, it remains to assure appropriateness and viability. This double-checks that the objectives and inquiry focus continue to reflect the evaluation purpose and are deliverable within the likely constraints of data access and quality, timeframe and available resources.

Is this really needed or is this over-engineering purpose-setting? Double-checking should indeed not be necessary if evaluation purposing has been well considered and has accounted for different expectations, but in the real world, good intentions may not be reflected in sound purposing practice. The formation stage may have been pushed through due to time pressures, or it may be conducted by an individual or team who lack purposing or evaluation experience. Purposing may also have been compromised by power dynamics in funding or key stakeholder organisations (Example 8).

Example 8: EXPECTATIONS REALISM – A CLOSE ENCOUNTER WITH ORGANISATIONAL POWER DYNAMICS IN AN EVALUATION

Early in the author's career, he led a small team conducting an ex-ante impact evaluation of the local economic and labour market effects of the planned development of a new terminal at an international airport. The evaluation was for the airport managing authority, an arms-length body of government, and the team inherited draft evaluation objectives from an initiating project manager (who had left for another job).

One draft objective was to develop plan-based employment projections for on- and off-airport direct job creation with implications for local skills and labour supply. The author was concerned about the viability of this objective, given uncertainties about on/off-airport employer mix, undetermined airport authority decisions on service franchising, and off-airport planning consents. The author suggested instead scenario-based 'whole airport' estimates, but these were rejected by the client as insufficient to meet the needs of a recommendation from the prior public inquiry to the new terminal. The policy research institute employing the author (which had supported his proposed change) subsequently asked the author to comply with the authority (which was a board member of the institute). The author was caught in these power dynamics with no leverage on reforming an unsound requirement.

In the event, the author was rescued by the government department sponsoring the airport authority; they were required to sign-off the sensitive evaluation and raised their own concerns about the viability of projections in an ex-ante review. They pointed out the public inquiry recommendation was for an employment impact review and not for specific labour demand projections. The objective was redrafted, with the final report providing employment and skill 'level' estimates for each of three scenarios.

Situations like this (Example 8) are not uncommon. Sensible caution or advice are not always heeded, and the consequence of proceeding with evaluation objectives (or an inquiry focus) which are not fit for purpose or viable is, at best, an evaluation facing substantial realignment, user-disappointment, delays, and weakening of trust in the evaluation. At the worst, it risks failing altogether.

Sense-checking the goal–objectives–inquiry focus is a not time-consuming precaution to avoid unsound foundations. If power dynamics means those specifying or conducting the evaluation lack the authority to sense-check, it may help to bring in an independent view, perhaps by seeking an expert peer review of the planned inquiry focus.

Some purposeful tips

This chapter has argued for the centrality of well-placed objectives in purposeful evaluation and for avoiding some of the recurrent 'downstream' challenges which face those on less sound 'needs' foundations. Although not a process to be rushed, it can be intensive; here, some helpful tips include:

- Be confident; even where an evaluation's objectives are pre-set, and seem to be set in stone, there is scope to modify expectations through 'on the record' statements of refinement.

- Listen to your 'inner-self' on cautions and uncertainties about the 'ask'. Set and seek out necessary clarifications early; these will not be seen as awkward or disruptive (asking for them when the evaluation is underway will be).
- Push back on unrealistic pressure to 'push on'; even with intensive starts some time can usually be bought for intensive purpose-setting and scrutiny; avoid falling back on trying to make the best of it.
- Value and make time for respecting stakeholder contributions and be attuned to your personal bias when taking them into account.
- Do not leave it to others to resolve expectations-mismatch; be prepared to be proactive in raising clarifications, advocate for solutions, and negotiate compromises.
- Make sure there is coherence between goal and objectives; moving from the general (goal) to the specific (objectives) can lose aspects of intent (or introduce others that are not consistent with a goal).
- Avoid ambiguous or unclear RQs; what is asked for in the inquiry must be answerable and language matters in clarifying boundaries, focus and avoiding misunderstood needs.
- Use ToCs or logic models (if available) to reflect on the detail of what is being asked; are (important) things missing in the objectives or the coverage or expression of RQs?

Sound purposing is 'considered' purposing. This needs early emphasis and attention but is an ongoing process needing a watching brief for mission creep, changing dynamics (such as key staff changes), or circumstances likely to affect needs. Evaluations take place in 'real time', so circumstances may change, and legitimate expectations need to reflect that so as to avoid a widening gap between what is being done and what is purposeful.

4

Managing the ethical dimension

Introduction

Evaluation judgements for scoping, objective- and inquiry-setting, and delivery are interwoven with ethical dilemmas. These occur for any form of evidence generation and use, but in purposeful evaluation identifying ethical risks and resolving them have a particularly important role to play. Carol Weiss cautioned: 'Evaluation has an obligation to pay even more attention to ethical questions than most other kinds of social science research' (Weiss, 1998: 92).

Ethics have attracted considerable interest among academic and other researchers, although with less attention to the enhanced challenges within evaluation. This has generated an extensive international literature and various derived codes of practice-setting principles and competencies for evaluators, including some of the earliest guidance in the 'professional code' of the American Evaluation Association. Implementing such guidance in practice can be challenging and Guillemin and Gillam (2004) helpfully separated these into 'ethical procedures' (clearance and professional standards) and 'ethical practice'; this chapter's focus is on the practice. Later, Chapter 13 includes a review of managing ethical procedures.

What is the ethical dimension to evaluation?

For some commissioners and evaluators, especially for medical, health and social welfare interventions, consideration of ethics can be reduced to managing ethical clearance of a methodology. Clearance may also be mandated in other fields by some delivery organisations, notably for university teams, but elsewhere organisational or procedural needs for ethical clearance are patchy. These requirements are considered in more detail later in the book (Chapter 13), but with or without a need for ethical clearance, a lot of judgements need to be made about applying ethical practice in evaluation.

This ethical dimension looms especially large in evaluation, because of whom, and what, it is about and for. Evaluation will be dealing directly or indirectly with people (beneficiaries, delivery practitioners, stakeholders or agents), their actions and consequences. The findings drawn from, or about, them will be intended to influence decision-making which will have the potential for real consequences for them or others like them. This inherent context for any evaluation raises inevitable ethical issues not only for what evidence is collected, from whom and how, but also for the treatment of that evidence, its interpretation, scrutiny and communication of findings.

The American Evaluation Association, which was an early proponent of embedding ethical practice across evaluation judgements, most recently reflected in its principle that evaluators should: 'Abide by current professional ethics, standards, and regulations (including informed consent, confidentiality and prevention of harm) pertaining to evaluation' (American Evaluation Association, *AEA Guiding Principle D2*, 2025). There is a lot that lies behind ensuring 'informed consent, confidentiality and prevention of harm', and the ethical challenges will be intensified when evaluators find themselves focusing on interventions aimed at individuals who are disadvantaged, vulnerable or otherwise at greater risk of harm. In this, tackling ethics in evaluation may seem little different from similar challenges in social research, but Simons (2006) suggests important differences. These stem from the inherent 'political' dimension for evaluators in providing evidence to inform some aspect of decision-making which is a less commonplace feature of social 'research'. The political context intensifies the responsibility for action, and transparency, by evaluators for addressing ethical considerations, in particular for:

- identifying needs and applying well-informed practice to embedding ethical principles and practice within that process;
- how to make and communicate fair judgement across the evaluation process from purposing through to communication of findings.

Although interdependent, the two considerations merit separate considerations as in the next two sections.

Embedding ethical principles into practice

For an evaluation to be, and be seen to be, ethical requires a demonstrated commitment to a number of underpinning principles. Setting down robust principles for ethical design and delivery of evaluation almost inevitably invites controversy, depending on what 'ethical' is seen to constitute. Some might argue evaluation utility is an ethical consideration. While crucial to purposeful evaluation this book takes utility as the starting point for making ethical judgements based on five 'bedrock' principles:

- avoiding harm in the collection of evidence
- voluntary engagement guided by informed consent
- respecting capacities for engagement
- protection for the evidence contributors
- protecting the data assembled from contributors

These are drawn from the common ground of various ethical guidelines. Although each is considered separately here, these principles are complementary, together providing for the evaluation process to be (and to be seen to be) based on sound 'ethical' judgements.

Avoiding harm

'Do no harm' is a widely recognised and deep-seated ethical foundation for how evidence is collected and used. It impacts on all method choices, through to how the evidence is assembled, communicated and used – an issue we return to later. It means what it says; judgements for evidence collection (and use) will be predicated on assumptions that selection, sampling, engagement, collection and focus will avoid known risk of causing social, physical, psychological or any other harm. It applies to any individual providing evidence about themselves, their practice, their service provider or employing organisation, as well as to those gathering the evidence.

In practical terms, this is about keeping risks to an absolute minimum and conditioning those that cannot be avoided. Some possible harms will be self-evident risks. This might include, for example, a loss of opportunity or gain from those which a sampling strategy excludes from engagement for comparison or control purposes (Chapters 8 and 9). Other risks may be less easy to anticipate, such as the controlled evaluation of a new drug or therapy. To mitigate these, participants need to give informed, conscious consent (see the next section) to what they are engaged with any potential risks (as well as benefits and support).

Voluntary engagement and informed consent

Some evaluations may not need direct engagement of participants in collecting the evidence they need. Most, however, will and an underpinning ethical principal is that they should engage voluntarily and consciously:

- 'Voluntary participation': Evaluations need an individual's engagement to be at their choice, with them free to opt in or out at any point (with no obligation to continue). They will not need to provide a reason for not committing (or leaving) and will know there will be no repercussions from doing so. Voluntary participation inevitably risks some dislocation or disruption to the scale or quality of evidence, but the effects can be mitigated. For example, the evaluation can offer alternative forms of participation, such as optional telephone interviews instead of completing a questionnaire survey.
- 'Informed consent': To make a conscious choice about participation (or not) potential participants need to be aware of what they are committing to. This usually takes the form of an informed consent process combining an appropriate written and/or oral briefing with an authority to confirm their engagement.

A consent briefing in writing (or perhaps oral) is integral to individuals being able to make informed decisions about

Table 4.1: Indicative information for a pre-participation consent briefing

What is the evaluation about and for?	• The evaluation's focus, scope (for example, coverage, timing) and origins • Who is it for, for what intended purpose and who funds • Who is conducting it, their involvement and any relevant interests
What engagement is needed and why?	• Statement of voluntary participation and any timelines for involvement • The required form of their participation and what this will involve • The aims, procedures and benefits of participation (and options/alternatives)
Any known disadvantage or risks from participation?	• Statement of possible risks or negatives to participation (and likelihood if known) • Countermeasures to be put in place to minimise risks (for example, security of data)
What (if any) harm mitigation support is available for participants?	• Statement of available support processes available for minimising harms • Clarity on access to support processes
What arrangements are in place for query handling?	• Contact point and access for queries or further information about participation

participation. Typically this will set out information on what they are being asked to commit to (Table 4.1).

Respect for capacity for engagement

The evaluation cannot assume all being asked to participate will have equal or appropriate capacity to do so. Some will not be legally or practically able to provide informed consent, for example those below the legal age of consent,[1] adults with learning disabilities, or those with low levels of literacy. Some of these may require proxies or helpers to provide for consent safeguards, others may need translation to other languages (or an interpreter) or different modes of briefing (such as those with visual impairment) if they are to have all the information they need.

Respecting capacity to engage does not end there; minimising the potential for participant duress is also an ethical issue. Duress can occur when what is asked of participants is unfair or unreasonable or risks embarrassment. For example, in a past impact evaluation (led by the author) of a multi-channel helpline for young people, a well-intentioned team member assembled a schedule for follow-up interviews with 16–19-year-olds estimated to need 80–90 minutes completion time. Although very comprehensive, the draft expected far too much of their likely attention span; it would have, in effect, placed interviewees 'under duress' (we reduced it to priority questions and 20 minutes).

Protecting the contributors

Evaluators have an obligation to protect participant rights, and this will often need identity protection. Although a common ethical requirement, it is also a sensible approach if participation is to be optimised. This often centres on protecting participants' identities, either by a commitment to anonymity or confidentiality. Both offer a non-disclosure guarantee, although anonymity and confidentiality have different implications for how identity is protected in the evaluation, and who from:

- 'Protection through anonymity': Anonymity means those conducting the evaluation will not record the identities of participants or identifiable data collected from them (for example, names, phone numbers, email/IP addresses, photos and other personal identification information). Where it is not possible to fully anonymise data (for example, if a telephone number is needed for arranging or conducting a telephone interview, or an email, for web-access to an e-survey), this may require data 'pseudonymisation' to obscure the identifier.[2]
- 'Protection through confidentiality': Confidentiality is a halfway house which means the evaluation team will know who the participants are and be able to link them to 'their' data, but those outside the team will not. Knowing whose survey return or interview transcript it is may be crucial for cohort surveys, non-response survey reminders, or follow-up interviews. Confidentiality nonetheless protects participants from being identified in the presentation of data or any aspects of reporting.

To be ethically compliant, pseudonymisation or confidentiality needs attention to detail. For confidentiality, it will mean not only names or other obvious identifiers are absent from reporting but also any implicit identifiers. In another example, drawn from the author's experience, in an evaluation of impacts on smaller firms of an innovation programme, a colleague hoped to ensure confidentiality by removing a case study firm's name in the concluding report, instead describing it in the text as '… an owner-managed automotive engineering supplier established in [a specific city] in 2010'. The author pointed out that probably only one such firm had been set up in that sector and city at that date and as such, it was identifiable to those with local knowledge (the draft and final report dropped the establishment date and replaced 'city' with a region location).

Protecting the data

It is not only identities which (often) need protection, the evaluator will have an ethical (and likely legal data protection) obligation to ensure the safety of participant data. This will also include security of that data (digital or 'hard copy'), appropriately limited access, and steps to ensure data security. This is not the place to describe these measures in detail, but typically it needs robust attention to secure storage, appropriate firewalls, encryption and cyber-security systems as well as safe (usually encrypted) transport or digital transfer for any off-site team access or transfer).[3]

Most of these ethical considerations relate to the interactions with and about stakeholders and participants, but they also affect how an evaluation supports those collecting evidence and analysing it (Parsons, 2017). This needs to ensure:

- Practitioners are free from any relevant (undeclared) potential conflicts of interest;
- Appropriate steps are taken to provide evaluator safety online and in the field;
- Practitioners follow professional standards and requirements and ensure high standards of integrity and honesty through the evaluation process;
- Evidence and data gathered are supported with appropriate intra-team security for data protection, storage and transmission;
- Practitioners are free from coercion, including for evidence coverage, representation or exclusion.

A final ethical consideration is that evaluators have a responsibility to commissioners and engaged stakeholders in effective communication of process and evidence. This centres on, but does not end with, reporting and, for all evaluation deliverables, evaluators have a responsibility to help communicate the findings and to assist in exploring implications. This is explored later (Chapter 14).

Making and communicating fair judgement

The responsibility on purposeful evaluators to provide sound evidence-based findings cuts across the practice of ethically principled design and delivery. To speak 'truth' to users calls for providing positive, use-orientated findings as well as those likely to present unwelcome news to stakeholders. Providing balanced positive and negative findings calls for evaluator confidence (and freedom) to do so, as well as stakeholder confidence that the judgements on what to prioritise, and how, are just and fair. Both evaluator and stakeholder confidence place an emphasis on:

- ensuring independence and impartiality across evaluation choices and application;
- applying integrity and honesty across the evaluation process;
- assuring fairness in evidence-gathering, interpretation and communication.

Independence and impartiality

To have freedom to provide negative (as well as positive) findings, evaluators need the shelter provided by independence and impartiality. There is no lack of professional discourse on what it takes to achieve independence and impartiality but in essence:

- 'Independence' refers to the condition where the evaluator (as an organisation, individual or team[4]) is free from outside control in setting a workplan, delivering it and reporting without undue influence from external parties.
- 'Impartiality' involves the avoidance of bias when, for example, weighing-up method choices or evidence requiring freedom from conflicting interests or judgement influenced by personal

opinion. Impartiality ensures evaluator judgements will treat the parties or competing interpretations equitably.

Independence is, arguably, a pre-condition to impartiality and both are necessary for an evaluation's ability to be seen to 'tell it as it is'. Stakeholders may have greater confidence both conditions[5] are met, when an evaluation is conducted externally to the funding or delivery of the intervention evaluated. But what of an evaluation conducted 'in house'? Internal evaluators risks being seen as 'marking their own homework'. Even here, steps can be taken to demonstrate functional independence by robustly separating evaluation responsibility from intervention delivery. This may go some way to fulfilling the ethical dimension, although it will still risk difficulty in persuading all stakeholders that those arrangements are genuinely free from internal influence or bias.

Integrity and honesty

Independence and impartiality count for little, if the evaluators do not consistently act with integrity and honesty. The American Evaluation Association sets one of its five core 'ethical' principles as: '… evaluators behave with honesty and transparency in order to ensure the integrity of the evaluation'. This links honest judgement with transparency of process, with these qualities being demonstrated by the evaluator across the whole evaluation process. Where either is flawed, integrity will likely be doubted, undermining the credibility of findings and any recommendations.

Fairness in evaluation

Fairness is a vaguer concept but one that is nonetheless important in ensuring ethical judgements are reflected in objectivity. Fairness is value-based, creating differences in what is seen as 'fair' (or not) between evaluator and stakeholders, and perhaps between different stakeholders. Making 'fair' judgements touches all aspects of evaluation, but especially in setting a workplan, evidence prioritisation, the quality of engagement and how evidence is interpreted and communicated (Chapter 14), and where some of the principles underpinning fairness are set out, as in Table 4.2.

Table 4.2: Demonstrating fairness across the evaluation process

'Fairness' in evaluative practice	Applying fairness by ...
Valuing difference	• Identifying diversity and heterogeneity in the population of interest • Recognising cultural and intersectional considerations and engagement potential • Adapting delivery to accommodate situational contrasts for engagement
Respecting stakeholder interests	• Recognition of different motivation and capacity to engage within stakeholder 'community' • Identifying diversity across stakeholder interests and what is most important to them • Respect for the legitimacy of different viewpoints, including decolonising values • Adjusting engagement and communications to stakeholder diversity
Demonstrating cultural competency[a]	• Sensitivity to intercultural differences affecting engagement in the population of interest • Proficient adaption of design and delivery to other cultural environments • Self-awareness (by evaluator) of cultural influence on evidence interpretation and presentation
Open and transparent communication	• Collectively informed 'upward' and 'downward' communications aligned to evaluation intent • Timely communication of necessary information, including emerging risks or situational change • Transparency and full disclosure, including aims, process, engagement options, and limits of findings/interpretation
Right of reply	• Integrating a 'right of reply' to evaluation judgements • Incorporating fair exchange of different perspectives (for example, for stakeholders affected by 'negative' findings)

[a] See for example: Fox et al, 2017: 31

Of course, fairness does not end with those considerations. It needs to be situated within what is being evaluated, why and for whom, and where stakeholders will be important in positioning 'fair' judgement.

Ethical engagement and inclusion

A cross-cutting issue for evaluators in applying ethical principles and making fair judgement is managing for diversity. Purposeful evaluation needs evaluation designs to take all necessary steps to optimise confidence in findings; in many settings, this places a premium on inclusion of diverse perspectives and experiences. For evaluations in social and community settings, robust attention to inclusion may be essential to credibly reach and secure evidence from marginalised or hard to reach individuals or communities.

How diversity is addressed will depend in part on the evaluation model being followed; a strongly participatory or developmental evaluation (Chapter 6) will require a deeply embedded approach to diversity. For others, robust attention will still be needed but its intensity will vary with circumstances and ambition. Steering an appropriate pathway through necessary inclusion issues involves evaluator sensitivity for, especially:

- purposing and planning, including contributions to design assumptions;
- governance, guidance and steering across the evaluation journey;
- implementing the approach and integrating culturally appropriate methods;
- analysis and reporting.

Purposing and planning

Inclusion issues to be considered in these preparatory stages most commonly include early judgements about engagement with stakeholders. This needs to reflect and value both the range of diversity in the population and communities of interest to the evaluation[6] as well as intersectional influences on outcomes from empowerment, disadvantage and discrimination. These inclusion dynamics relate to participation and priority groupings in or affected by the intervention, as well as to representative bodies and users.

A sufficiently thorough effort in the early purposing of the evaluation will help to identify some of the constituent issues and needs around whom to engage with to bring sufficient insights (and lived experience); these might not otherwise be available during the planning stage. Evaluators are well advised here to bring in a substantial degree of humility to recognise that their own perspectives, however well-meaning and informed, will be socially, culturally and experientially limited. Insights gained from tapping these needs and potential at this early stage can help to shape more inclusive objectives and to condition the inquiry focus.

Resourcing and required expertise

Sensitivity to inclusion should also, ideally, be reflected in how an evaluation team is put together to draw on different social, cultural or other perspectives. Obviously, there are practical limits to how much diversity can be accommodated in usually small teams, but inclusive capacity can be aided by external advisors with important cultural or inter-sectional experience. The guiding premise is which aspects are of most significance to the credibility of what is being evaluated and why, and for any specific challenges anticipated for evidence-gathering (including access and cooperation), analysis and representation.

Some evaluations may go further by using 'emancipatory approaches' (Mies, 1993), where evidence collection is by individuals recruited to the 'team' from lived experience and/or from specific inclusion interests. Although these approaches evolved largely from social research traditions, they have value for evaluations where participation challenges are anticipated for alienated or hard-to-reach participants and where participant engagement may be improved by an inclusive, cultural or linguistic affinity. One notable evaluation in the UK, for example, focused on the service experiences of homeless people 'living rough'; this recruited, trained and employed former homeless people as interviewers with considerable success in gaining access to, and the confidence of, this 'hard to engage' group.

Steering the evaluation

Depending on their scale, evaluations may variously involve high level governance, steering, advisory or working groups to shape and steer the evaluation journey. Chapter 12 considers some of the options; here we are looking only at how diversity is an issue for the quality (and credibility) of inclusion and 'intercultural communications' (Fox et al, 2017: 37) in external scrutiny or guidance. Again, there are practical limits which call on sensitive advice from evaluators, although this may be constrained by commissioners resistant to casting the net too wide.

Inclusion issues in steering an evaluation raise added challenges for evaluations in international development and aid programmes. Most evaluation methodology has been shaped from euro-centric traditions (North America, Europe, Australasia); evaluation steering which focuses on and engages with the Global South needs to provide appropriate authority and representation in the composition, and dynamics, of those steering the evaluations. Decolonising evaluation has a strong intersectional dimension. It deserves more attention than can be provided here and goes well beyond an issue for design and delivery of evaluation involving low-income countries; in particular it may also be key to the credibility of community-specific evaluations elsewhere.

Implementing the approach

This is where the evaluation will be looking to integrate socially and culturally sensitive methods and harness them for the quality of evidence, as well as for confidence in findings. This will shape technical choices to respect critical 'inclusion' of identity-based evidence and experience so as to optimise mass, and minimise bias, for groups at risk of being over- or underrepresented. This may be limited to diversity-sensitive sampling or stratification of evidence-gathering or go much further to balance inclusivity gains with contributory and participation burdens for key groups. Here, purposeful evaluation will guard against over-simplifying social and cultural dimensions and the risks of treating cultural or marginalised groups as homogeneous. Ethical considerations will also reflect heavily where the evaluation includes vulnerable people, and especially when focused on qualitative evidence-gathering among vulnerable groups (Mauthner et al, 2002; Armstrong et al, 2014; Bashir, 2020).

Analysis and reporting

The common thread through this book is that purposeful evaluation optimises the use to be made of its evidence by decision-makers. A litmus test for this is in the attention paid to inclusion and diversity in the approach to reporting. This may have a particular bearing on confidence in the evaluation among community groups and others engaged in or with vulnerable and disadvantaged groups. Many evaluations will be looking at actions aimed at improving the situation of people in those groups, so the attention to inclusivity in reporting will have a special bearing on the confidence and credibility – and use – of such evaluations. Chapter 14 looks more broadly at these issues, but for inclusion two issues will be of special importance:

- 'Language and cultural sensitivity': Careful attention needs to be paid, through the reporting, to the use of insensitive or poorly judged terms or expressions. The evaluator may not be in the best position to recognise these, but their use can have a disproportionately negative influence on confidence in the evaluation – and in the evaluator. For example, do not make the mistake, as the author once very nearly did early in his career, of describing the influence of a particular action group as a local 'crusade' (it was knocked out at drafting, thanks to a colleague with middle-eastern heritage). The term was meant to be a vernacular description for a single-issue campaigning body, but would have been interpreted differently by some community groups.
- 'Incautious use of evidence examples or illustrations': Reports will often make extensive use of evidence highlights or specific examples through participant quotations, profiles or perhaps mini-case studies. Some may also use visual illustrations, such as photographs. Selection and presentation of these needs to be sensitive to balance (such as, too many male/female examples; not enough young person illustrations; too few/no minority group cases). Examples are used to highlight particular features of findings; while they are not intended to be representative of all participants, some cultural sensitivity is needed in what is chosen to be represented. Caution is also needed to ensure that the way examples and illustrations are presented and used, does not inadvertently perpetuate stereotypical perspectives or risk stigma for those featured.

These are specific considerations for the quality of inclusivity in reporting, to which needs to be added the more mundane, but equally important aspect, of how data is represented, and the classifications used to reflect diversity aspects.

Inclusion in practice: the example of the gender dimension

Different intervention circumstances will require an evaluation to make judgements about what is appropriate for inclusion against the diversity dynamics, and their intersections to interpret findings. Making choices about what is appropriate to genuinely reflect what is needed for inclusion can be one of the more challenging aspects of evaluation design. This is illustrated here with an example of gender dimensions as (just) one marker of diversity.

Respecting intersectional influences means that neither gender, nor any single inclusion marker, should be treated in isolation from other aspects of diversity. Nonetheless, choices will need to be made about inclusion priorities, and gender provides a useful illustration of some of the practical judgements likely to be involved. As Fletcher observes: 'Gender affects everyone, all of the time. Gender affects the way we see each other, the way we interact, the institutions we create, the ways in which those institutions operate, and who benefits or suffers as a result of this' (Fletcher, 2015: 19). A starting point for 'ethical' inclusion is the evaluator avoiding ethnocentric or predetermined views on what needs to be 'included' and how to go about this. Gender illustrates how perspectives on what it constitutes are culturally influenced and can change over time. Gender in many cultures has been seen as essentially a biologically determined distinction, but this binary distinction is now widely, but not universally, challenged. As Fletcher again cautions: '… there is no one accepted way to understand what gender is'. If and how gender is to be considered in an evaluation will need the evaluator to be sensitive to often differing stakeholder and situational perspectives. In this, tackling gender along with other inclusion dimensions is not likely to be as simple or straightforward as it may appear.

As with other diversity markers, gender is commonly seen through the prism of differences in 'fair' or equitable treatment, or outcomes. To be inclusive, interpreting those differences needs to respect culture influences on how they are expressed. For gender, this need to reflect: ' … the roles, behaviours, activities, and attributes that a given society at a given time considers appropriate for women and men' (UN Women Gender Equality Glossary[7]). Gender-based inclusion in an evaluation might simply focus on contrasting results across different societal contexts between 'men' and 'women', as well as exploring intersectional influences on those differences. This takes a data-led approach to categorising gender, usually as an independent variable for analysis to identify, explore and characterise contrasts.

A category-led approach may satisfy some inclusion requirements, but in other circumstances it may be necessary to take a different culturally sensitive approach to understand diversity in an intervention's performance and effects. Gender differences, for example, may need to take a broader view of human interaction (in an intervention) being intrinsically 'gendered'. This would go beyond biological categories to explore how gender contrasts to emphasise are shaped by underpinning values, stereotypes and norms of what constitutes 'masculine' and 'feminine' regardless of birth-determined sex. Table 4.3 provides an illustration of how these different inclusion models for approaching 'gender as a (data) category' and 'gender as a process' would affect an evaluation, its scope and likely focus.

This distinction between a simplified category-led or process-led gender approach is echoed for other diversity markers. Both approaches can be relevant and involve an ethical choice on which is most appropriate for an evaluation to be purposeful and responsive to circumstance. For gender, evaluators have traditionally regarded gender from the 'category-led' focus, reflecting the ease of handling gender from this perspective and also, in the author's experience, the requirements and expectations of those commissioning evaluations. This will continue to be at the heart of many purposeful evaluations, but relying solely on a category-led emphasis risks neglecting an understanding of the consequence (and changes needed) for beliefs, perceptions and pre-suppositions in gendered situations. As a programme manager for one of the devolved governments in the UK once observed to the author: 'Putting targeted effort and resources into promoting positive gender actions will get us better results [for women] … [but] will that be sustained if the attitudes behind the problem in the first place don't actually change.'

Some purposeful tips

Tackling the ethical dimension of an evaluation effectively is challenging. It needs clear and shared intent on what is to be

Table 4.3: Contrasting gender dimensions in an evaluation

	Gender as a category	Gender as a process
Intervention focus	Programme to increase women's recruitment and retention on construction trades training	Programme to increase women's recruitment and retention on construction trades training
Intervention perspective on gender	Gender is seen as a descriptive category for participants (managers, tutors, course applicants and entrants)	Gender understood as a process affecting all
Constituent objective (Note: There would be others as well)	To assess the comparative programme impact on men and women entrants 18–21 years of age on uptake, retention, attainment and post-course (>26 weeks) transition into construction employment/self-employment	To assess admission and course tutors' views on trainees' attributes for entry to construction work and extent to which attitudes influence their in-programme decision-making on selecting entrants, in teaching and learning support
Desired impact	Increased entry of women to construction training and subsequent skills-based work	Reformed application and admissions processes for construction trade courses based on gender-neutral practitioner views and decision-making
How will successful impact be assessed (what for and in what circumstances)?	• Increased proportion (against baseline) of women entrants to programme (regardless of sexuality, ethnicity, and so on) • Raised retention of women entrants (against pre-programme benchmark) • Increased entrant numbers within 26 weeks of completion (pre-programme benchmark) of women entrants to craft-level construction employment or self-employment	• Change from baseline in tutor attitudes and perspectives on work entry attributes • More tutors holding gender neutral views by the end of the programme • Tutors applying gender neutral judgements in admissions, teaching and learning support processes

Source: Author's teaching materials; after Fletcher, 2015

done (and not done) and how it is sensitively situated to avoid pitfalls. Some of the practical tips which might help to anticipate and avoid the more likely risks include:

- Avoiding overconfidence (or neglect) in the evaluation team about comprehending and addressing the less tangible dimensions of cultural and other differences across participants or stakeholders, or for vulnerable people.
- Adopting a whole team approach to understanding, ability and willingness to acknowledge ethical practice, but within this giving one team member a distinct role for ensuring ethical practice across the evaluation.
- Encouraging whole team proactivity to anticipate ethical risks and prioritising early response to any emerging issues with rigorous 'just in time' responses to avoid deferring necessary design or delivery adjustments.
- Fostering caution when relying on intervention gatekeepers for decisions about participant engagement or recruitment and putting in place well-defined roles and responsibilities to avoid 'external' disruption to ethical practice.
- Ensuring integrity of participant consent processes (and briefing) to emphasise comprehension of what they are consenting to and managing the process by putting one person in the team in charge of mechanisms, documentation and compliance.
- Ensuring also clear separation of functions, to avoid risks that those collecting evidence in social settings may confuse their role in evidence collection with offering advice or guidance to individuals. This is a 'compassion risk', especially when working with disadvantaged or vulnerable people, but risks evaluators becoming agents of change in what they are investigating.
- Care and close attention to the hidden risks of incautious or ill-advised communication or reporting of evidence which breaches identity safety commitments for anonymity or confidentiality.

To this can be added the fundamental issue of robust engagement with whatever ethical competence processes may be needed in the evaluation team (Chapter 13).

PART III

Choosing the right method

The mechanic that would perfect his work must first sharpen his tools.
Confucius

5

Understanding the choices

Introduction

A few of the very many ways to conduct evaluation are relatively new, but most are long-established. Those with a longer track record are more likely to be seen as tried and tested – and are highly likely to have more currency among commissioners than others. Nonetheless, all have potential. All are right for the right circumstances, and the duty of evaluators is to ensure the most appropriate fit of method choice to the circumstances to which it is to apply.

In finding the 'right' fit, the early roots of systematic evaluation in 'scientific' and value-free inquiry have seen great emphasis placed on evidence quality, conventionally choosing between those offering optimal rigour. This primacy of evidence quality in method choice serves many evaluations well, but this book suggests purposeful evaluation needs to adopt a modified 'primary' perspective led by intent for application. This is certainly not to sideline rigour. Evidence quality remains important, but as an issue supporting utility and optimising methodology within a purpose-driven approach.

Placing intent and utility at the forefront of choices builds on the early efforts of commissioners and evaluators to set a tangible and appropriate purpose (Chapters 2 and 3). This chapter focuses on what follows to provide the best chance of making the right choice and fit of method to purpose.

Starting points: evaluation types, approaches and methods

As design choices and techniques in evaluation have multiplied, so too has the terminology used to describe them. This 'Babel confusion' as referred to by Patton (Patton, 2008) has great potential for baffling all but the most experienced evaluators. This is intensified by different disciplinary legacies and national traditions, and compounded by practitioners' often contrasting use of terminology.

Where the language of methods is not used consistently this has the real and present danger of muddling those translating evaluation purpose into best-fitted method choice. A recurrent demand on purposeful evaluation is for the evaluator to not take as read that the terms used by others are consistent with their own understanding. Without this any evaluation risks starting off with a potentially deep misunderstanding of what is being expressed as a requirement.

If the muddled lexicon of evaluation methods is not enough, pressure to get an evaluation underway can risk choice of what method (and mix) is 'right' being insufficiently considered. Even where there are pressures of time or urgency, it pays to take a little time over this, and a practical starting point is recognising differences between:

- Evaluation 'types': as we will see, there are only four types and deciding which best fits the circumstances is the starting point for 'method' choice.
- Evaluation 'approaches': these are the (many) available techniques which make up the broad options within each type of evaluation.
- Evaluation 'method': where a choice of type and a relevant approach leads to solid foundations for deciding just how to go about the chosen approach through a well-honed method mix (methodology) to address the evaluation's specific inquiry focus.

Decisions about fitting method (and appropriate terminology) to purpose start not at the end of this simple typology but by taking a sequential approach through these levels of refinement. This commences with some basic but essential considerations about which 'type' is appropriate, and with that clear then progressing to the wider range of technical choices for a suitable approach. Only with type and approach clarified can judgements be confidently made about what method expression is needed to deliver the intended purpose and circumstances.

Adopting this sequential approach to progressing to the necessary method mix may add very little time to planning, but it can help synthesise and navigate the choices to be made. This avoids the risks of following a first thoughts pathway based on a pre-selected or preferred approach or specific technique which may be insufficiently conditioned to circumstances, use and utility.

Unpicking choices through this type-approach-method sequence can be explicit or implicit. It will be *explicit* where the requirement has yet to specify an anticipated approach or method. Here, the evaluator will be leading on assessing and agreeing first type, then approach, before moving to the appropriate method mix as a preferred approach, or justified options before seeking sign-off.

In some circumstances, the evaluator starts with pre-set (commissioner) expectations of approach and, perhaps, method. Here, they can *implicitly* apply the same sequence to sense-check that expectation. The author was recently tasked by a national regulator to evaluate a diversity programme which had a pre-set requirement for an 'economic' evaluation emphasising social capital. Sense-checking with the type–approach rubric suggested this did not reflect programme aspirations, with commissioners subsequently emphasising a mainstream impact evaluation emphasising socialised outcomes.

The sequenced approach is intuitive and need not be burdensome or incur significant delay to commencing the evaluation. Using this simple reductive sequence to translate purpose into an indicative method mix can be the difference between underpinning good method choice, or a more presumptive method-led approach risking undermining it.

Understanding evaluation types

Evaluation approaches can be loosely clustered into four broad groupings, which for convenience are referred to as 'evaluation types':

- process evaluations
- economic ('value for money') evaluations
- impact evaluations
- meta-evaluations

Each has a distinctive scope and likely evidence focus as outlined next. Each also encompasses a range of technical options – approaches – which can deliver what is needed. For example, an impact evaluation is a 'type' whereas an 'individual randomised control trial or i-RCT' (Chapter 8), or a 'synthetic control design', or 'difference in difference' comparator (Chapter 9) are specific approaches (among many) to deliver it.

Some have made a case for differentiating other types. A persuasive case has been made for example, for regarding 'developmental evaluation' as a distinct type (Patton, 2011); others might argue for managerial, implementation, experimental or theory-based evaluation being distinct types. Condensing this to these four evaluation types does not negate other ways of describing the many methodological opportunities. It offers instead a simplified characterisation for the preliminary choice of a purpose-led and broad type of an evaluation which is easily grasped by stakeholders, and which is separate from the many different possible delivery approaches (methodological pathways).

Table 5.1 headlines the main contrasts between the four types followed by a brief description of focus. The subsequent chapters provide a lot more detail and also set out a range of different 'approach' options within each type.

Process evaluation

This is often the type of evaluation which new evaluators may be first involved with. They are likely to be less conceptually demanding than economic and impact evaluations, but nonetheless involve a lot of choices in how best to go about them. As the label suggests, process evaluations focus on the constituent mechanisms of an intervention and (usually) their interplay against expectations and on assessed direct results. Table 5.1 shows that process evaluations share a common purpose, in evidencing how an intervention has been implemented, compared to the

Table 5.1: Purpose and focus for the four types of evaluation

	Purpose ... to provide for:	Focus ... to provide evidence for:
Process evaluation	A review of the intervention process for accountability and/or learning for implementation improvement	• Compliance and/or effectiveness of internal procedures and mechanisms • Nature and quality of delivery of constituent actions and activities • Achieved performance from delivery (outputs) • Critical appraisal of what worked well for whom, in what situation, and so on
Economic evaluation	An appraisal of the quality of use and value gained from the resources underpinning an intervention to justify use or intended further use	• How effectively interventions' resources have been used; could they have been more cost-effective? • What monetary or proxy value has been achieved from the gains? • Whether the value and/or utility of the gains achieved outweighs their costs?
Impact evaluation	An assessment of observed changes (outcomes and impacts) from, and contribution by, the intervention to inform design improvement and/or transferability	• Consequential changes (positive and negative) produced by an intervention • Direct, indirect, intended and unintended changes and how achieved • Level or quality of attribution of the intervention actions to those effects
Meta-evaluation	A structured comparative analysis of past studies to inform intervention design and implementation	• Identifying past relevant experience to guide (new) design • Transferable experience and lessons from past practices • Implications for planned or intended (new) policy and practice

expectations, and to what extent (and how) it produces what it does (Chapter 6).

Novice evaluators, and stakeholders, may be confused between process and impact evaluations, especially where an assessment of impacts needs to dig deep into issues of process to explain how observed impacts come about. The difference is that the performance review aspects of a process evaluation will stop short of looking at the wider consequences of what happens after activities and outputs from them occur. As we will see, outcomes and impacts are focused on 'consequential changes' which come about (or do not) as a result of outputs being achieved. So, a process evaluation of a new training course might well look at recruitment, drop-out rates, attendance, grades, certification or qualifications achieved; it will not go as far as to assess whether a new qualification led to (a consequential change) for those securing them, such as higher earnings in work linked to the acquired certification, knowledge or skills from the output (the completed course).

Economic evaluation

Here also labels can confuse. There is a current tendency to refer to an 'economic' evaluation as a 'value for money' evaluation. There is some risk in doing so, since economic evaluation can assess 'value' in many ways and with different interpretations and aspirations regarding what constitutes 'value' from stakeholders. Economic evaluations are important where decision-makers focus wholly, or mainly, on the costs of interventions and the value of returns from them.

Table 5.1 summarises how the heart of any economic evaluation is the interrelationship between costs (the resources put into the intervention), and the 'net' benefit gained from those resources being utilised. Its end result will be some approach to determining whether or not the costs outweighed the benefits. These can be relatively simple designs (looking at cost description to see if resources used were applied to what was expected) or much more complex. A full cost-benefit evaluation, for example, will involve extensive efforts to *monetise* the value derived and set this against a range of costs, including taking account of substitution and other effects and the disbenefit of lost opportunities. They may also look comparatively at alternative uses of resources for generating greater cost-benefits.

Impact evaluation

This type of evaluation is concerned with the journey towards and the achieved end gains from an intervention. As touched on previously, this goes beyond looking at intervention activity or outputs, to focus on what happens as a result of them – the *consequential changes* taking place after those activities/outputs. Decision-makers may be keen to review direct results (for example, from a process evaluation) but are likely to be especially concerned with how well the intervention has got to grips with tackling the problem, or opportunity, which it was set up to address. In the example given earlier of a new education course, this would focus on the changes occurring from people securing the 'new' qualification; did they get a job, promotion or better job; more wages or a higher salary; more security or better prospects, or did employers see more skills flexibility or better productivity?

Impact evaluations are not just an extension of process evaluation to look at end gains. A direct link between what the intervention does and what its consequential changes are will likely be influenced by many factors outside the intervention. Getting that 'better job' from a new qualification, for example, will be influenced by the individual's job aspirations and motivation; the state of the labour market; their quality of job search; and, employers' selection processes, among many other things. To get an accurate assessment of impact performance, an impact evaluation needs to find ways to discount non-intervention influences, to see what actual contribution the intervention has made. Getting to this 'attribution' can be challenging and is looked at here and for different method options in Chapters 8 and 9.

Meta-evaluation

This is a systematic examination of, or across, other evaluations and/or research studies seen as relevant to the target intervention (Table 5.1). Meta-evaluations harness evidence drawn from other relevant, usually data-based, inquiries. There are various approaches which can be used in meta-evaluation (Chapter 11). All centre on a structured approach to the selection of what is relevant to look at, and comparative review across those selected topics to draw out common messages or learning.

These descriptions only scratch the surface of what each evaluation type is about: Chapters 6 to 11 provide more detail and a roadmap of the different approaches which can be adopted within each.

Horses for courses: making the 'right' choice

Choosing 'type' is more than putting a label on the evaluation; it is about setting off on the right journey to picking a suitable approach and translating that into a cost-effective methodology. Making the right choice can be self-evident if the relationship between forging the evaluation and the development of the intervention has been considered and fruitful. Too often, however, this is not the case, and more may need to be done to choose type.

How straightforward the choice of type is will depend on the starting point. In fact, the type may have already been defined, where a lot of forethought, combined with some well-placed stakeholder input, has gone into what the evaluation needs to be about. This forethought may have come from solid purposing foundations (as outlined in Chapters 2 and 3) or from a previously (well) conducted evaluability assessment.

In either case, this should have secured a (hopefully) clear view (and also stakeholders' acceptance) of purpose, scope and limitations of the inquiry. It may have gone as far as objective-setting and pre-determining a 'type' to reflect a necessary inquiry focus. In these situations, it remains for the evaluator to be comfortable with the type proposed, by assessing if a pre-set 'type' reflects:

- the nature and circumstances of the intervention, including its state of play;
- the status, significance and value of the intervention, including the level of innovation in what it intends to do and who for;
- how the evidence is to be used and the scope for decision making to use the findings at that time;
- the expectations for credibility and confidence in what the evaluation does.

Such sense-checking is precautionary. Commissioners may lack necessary knowledge or may be under pressure from others with (not always well-placed) pre-determined expectations. Sense-checking may endorse a pre-set requirement but, if not, a purposeful evaluator will need to (again) play 'critical friend', in seeking clarifications for an earlier judgement and/or proposing alternatives.

A final consideration is that opting for a single type of evaluation may not fit all circumstances. Looking at these types as distinctive options helps to focus the aspiration for what the evaluation needs to tackle and, subsequently, for more specific judgements on mode and method choices. However, these do not have to be stand-alone choices, where the evaluator makes a conscious, purpose-led choice about which is the (only) right approach within which to work. The more ambition, innovation, complexity or value intended in an intervention, the more likely these types of approach may need to be mixed.

Combining types to better meet an evaluation's needs involves a 'pluralistic' approach. These combinations can also make up for any limitations of pursuing any one specific type. For example, an impact evaluation often needs to include substantial elements of a process evaluation, if the evidence of how much impact (what for, for whom, when, and so on) is to be explored, for improvement potential. Here, process evidence will dig into how impacts came about, for example: unpicking the circumstances; why there were differences between participants and providers; what actions were involved; what were the constraints; and, if and how these constraints were overcome?

Similarly, pressures on programme or service budgets, as well as cost-effectiveness, may mean both process and impact evaluations are expected to include a basic 'value for money' assessment. Pluralistic evaluation may be a useful 'right' choice for larger-scale, longitudinal or more complex evaluations, but inevitably ratchet up the challenges involved for method choice and proportionality (Chapter 12).

Unwrapping cause and effect: tackling attribution

All four types of evaluation will be looking at some aspects of the level and distribution of the effects of an intervention (outputs or outcomes). Most will also be making some attempt to assess how those effects come about, as well as disentangling cause and effect. This raises particular challenges for impact evaluation, where getting to grips robustly and purposefully with cause and effect requires a 'deep dive' into confronting attribution.

Assessing attribution calls for an impact evaluation to produce credible evidence of how much and/or how the intervention contributed to its observed effects (outcomes and impacts).

There are few situations where all observed effects will be wholly attributable to the actions of the intervention; many will come from, or be affected by, influences from outside the intervention. Tackling attribution will help to disentangle the interventions contribution, by separating out gross and net effects:

- 'Gross outcome and impacts' are what is observed of the desired 'consequential changes' from an intervention. These will not be limited to the end gains which may be longer-term and may include early outcomes, such as improved beneficiary motivation, self-esteem, confidence or knowledge about something.
- 'Net outcomes and impacts' are where the 'gross' consequential change observed can be confidently attributed to the actions of the intervention itself. These will discount any outcomes or impacts resulting from the action or influence of non-intervention influences.

Decision-makers will see 'net' outcomes or impacts as a more useful indication of what has actually been achieved by the intervention – what they have actually achieved from the resources put in. However, assessing attribution in the real world is complicated by the often complex and compound influences from outside the intervention.

Attribution is unquestionably a methodological headache for an impact evaluation and the practical challenges mean some may be tempted to conclude: 'if you cannot reliably assess attribution, better to not attempt it at all'. The author has no sympathy for this view; it is a counsel of despair which greatly compromises the reliability and utility of the evaluation. Assessing attribution is not a 'nice to have' adjunct for a purposeful evaluation; it is an integral part of what is needed to evidence the necessary approach. If this is neglected, the evaluation will be reporting only headline (gross) impacts with no indication provided for the level of success or effectiveness of the intervention in contributing to them. This will be an incomplete and possibly wholly misleading picture for decision-makers.

Attribution is consequently a bullet that needs to be bitten. Purposeful evaluation will look to fitting method choices for assessing attribution, as close as possible to the evaluation's circumstances; there are two main pathways to do this:

- experimental approaches to measuring or estimating the level of 'net' impact;
- non-experimental evaluation, which assesses the likely contribution to observed impact and digs deeper into causal inference.

Experimental evaluation

Attribution has traditionally been addressed through statistically led approaches forged through a scientific or 'experimental' lens. Here, the evaluation design sets up a conditional 'experiment' to isolate separate intervention and non-intervention situations, typically using either fully or partly (quasi) experimental approaches:

- Fully experimental approaches provide for two strongly comparable and controlled participant groupings – one taking part in the intervention and the other (the 'control') as an active part of the inquiry and evidence-gathering but separated from involvement in the actions of the intervention. These so-called randomised control trials (RCTs) are designed as laboratory-style experiments, conducted (usually) in social or community settings, and as Chapter 8 shows, there are various options for how to go about these.
- Quasi-experimental designs (QEDs) replace the carefully selected non-intervention 'control' group with a comparator. The comparison group is not an active part of the intervention but is carefully selected from an external situation. The comparator will provide for a close, point of time benchmark, to what and where the intervention is taking place and for which participating groups.

There are numerous facets to both fully and quasi- experimental designs; evaluators have long relied on these to quantify and statistically demonstrate attribution. In this, fully experimental methods are widely regarded as the gold standard although (as Chapter 8 shows) they have limitations in the practical situations in which many evaluators find themselves. They also face considerable challenges in managing ethical consideration and avoiding snags in the quality of 'proof'.

There is a third set of possibilities, which offers much less robustness but greater flexibilities and lower costs. We refer to these as 'constrained experimental designs', including weaker comparator designs such as 'before and after' methods (Chapter 9). While these may be a fall-back option for where RCTs or QEDs are not possible, they are much less reliable in measuring attribution.

For this chapter, this is as far as we are going in exploring the constituent techniques. The background to control and comparison approaches, and methods options for each, are unwrapped in Chapters 8 and 9 respectively.

Non-experimental evaluation

Fully and quasi- experimental methods have been a part of evaluation for a very long time. The idea of non-experimental approaches has a much shorter history but is now emerging as an alternative set of possible designs for tackling attribution in complexity circumstances. Here, evaluators face a situation of multiple, perhaps volatile and/or (some unknown) non-intervention, influences and a complex association of impact cause and effect. Control, or comparator (QED) methods, are often not well-placed to address such situations.

Non-experimental approaches move the attribution focus away from robust, generalisable measurement to a largely exploratory emphasis. This looks to unwrap how internal (actions in the intervention) and external influences come together in a conjunction of influences to cause (or constrain) impact achievements. This is not to say they are not concerned with measurement, but they emphasise an in-depth assessment of the cause–effect interplay to better understand the impact journey. This involves deconstructing often complex causal mechanisms, perhaps against a background of uncertain influences and interactions and where evaluators can now harness a plethora of possible approaches and analytical methods (Chapter 10).

It is only fair to say that not all evaluators, commissioners or users will yet be comfortable with any change in emphasis from experimental to non-experimental evaluation even for complex causal situations. Early exponents anticipated this caution (Pawson and Tilley, 1997) and, nearly 30 years on, many commissioners remain cautious about their use or are otherwise committed to precise measurement of attribution, even when this is not suited to the particular cause–effect eco-system. However, the author, among others, has seen a significant shift in the attitudes of many intervention funders and evaluation commissioners towards the usefulness of non-experimental methods – in appropriate circumstances.

Causal inference and the counterfactual

How to go about disentangling cause and effect (of an intervention) within a larger system of influences calls for an evidence-based exploration of causal inference. Experimental, quasi-experimental or non-experimental approaches give the evaluator a lot of choice about how to go about this, but with corresponding challenges for making the 'right' choice. This commonly relies on quantitative measurement or estimation, but qualitative evidence can also help by unwrapping the causal processes behind causal inferences. Whatever choice is made; it will usually call on collecting evidence to provide a 'counterfactual'.

Thinking about the practical uses for a 'counterfactual' case or argument goes back a very long way, even if the term was first used more recently (Lewis, 1973). For the evaluator (and researcher), it refers to an evidence-base built into an inquiry, which compares observed results (in evaluation usually 'gross' outcomes or impacts) to those that would be expected if an action (intervention) had not been implemented. In this way, it sets out evidence for '… what would otherwise have happened (to observed effects) if the intervention had not taken place' (Parsons, 2017: 107).

The idea behind a counterfactual is simple; the practice is not. A counterfactual is seeking evidence for a hypothetical situation but in a context where the intervention being looked at (which is happening or has happened) is very real! Nonetheless, counterfactual evidence is needed to demonstrate attribution, and it can be achieved in two very different ways:

- a systematic counterfactual, or
- a logical counterfactual

Systematic counterfactual

The control group of an RCT, or the carefully selected (external) comparison group of a QED, are both systematic counterfactuals.

They are ways of collecting quantified evidence to provide for a credible demonstration of what would have happened without the intervention. The RCT control group provides the purest expression of this; for example, in a vaccine trial, it would show the difference in outcomes for a group of volunteers who had an injected dose of a specific compound (the intervention group) and those who were also in the trial but had a placebo injected (the non-intervention group). The non-intervention group would provide counterfactual evidence; an external QED comparator would play a similar role.

Logical counterfactual

These are also quantified counterfactuals, used where it is not possible by circumstance, timetable or resources to construct a systematic counterfactual. The alternative is to put one together by constructing one logically. This most commonly involves using an agreed baseline as a proxy for 'what would otherwise have happened'. Commonly, this might be data on the starting point for participants, before they engaged with the intervention and where there was confidence that the starters' situation would have remained the same without the intervention. That baseline would then represent a logical counterfactual. Logical counterfactuals can be much simpler to construct, but should not be seen as a ready substitute for a systematic counterfactual. Their reliance on readily available data means they can only be used as estimates for attribution.

The search for an appropriate counterfactual can be exacting, and systematic designs can be quite challenging. Counterfactual designs may consequently end up as compromises between what would be ideal but impractical, and what was the best that could be put in place. These are challenges that nonetheless need to be faced if the results for assessing impacts are to be credible and purposeful. As we have seen, avoiding assessing attribution would leave users of the impact evidence in the dark; they will not know the 'real' contribution of the intervention to an effect.

Some purposeful tips

This chapter has started to introduce the rich field of technical possibilities open to evaluators, each with different merits but also drawbacks. Purposive evaluation is built on an expectation that method choice will be conditioned by well-reasoned use and utility, where all methods will be right for some circumstances but not others. There are some common pitfalls to making the 'right' choices which some forethought can often avoid:

- Start with clarity about the basics and avoid pressure to rush judgements about type and approach or defer necessary issues of clarification on utility. Effective judgements need absolute clarity on what the evidence will be used for and how.
- Harness the methodological continuum in guiding method judgements: type–approach–method, where the starting point is well-prepared groundwork on 'purposing'.
- Tap your own reflective capacity from past practice, and the knowledge of others, to be a critical friend to judgements needed, or scrutinised, on the method pathway.
- Have the confidence to challenge predetermined judgements (by commissioners or others) on 'type' or 'approach' to identify any apparent misalignment between needs and method choice.
- Be confident that whatever the challenges, a purposeful compromise can be achieved to provide counterfactual evidence. Avoiding any assessment of attribution is not a solution; some (well-cautioned) causal inference is better than none at all.
- Avoid falling back on 'oven-ready' counterfactuals such as relying wholly on evidence from 'before and after' effects. Choose these only where there are no other practical choices and, if unavoidable, manage (down) user expectations of them.

None of this is radical practice; it is about valuing the time put into understanding the choices – by evaluators and others – as being time very well spent for (subsequently) making the best-fitted method choices. This does not take too much time, but if under pressure to fast track these choices, it pays to remember that time is a solid investment in getting to a purposeful evaluation.

6

Process evaluation

Introduction

Any concern with an intervention's resource inputs, effectiveness and performance (outputs) is likely to need at least some consideration of how they came about. This goes well beyond what might typically be done through monitoring activities and engagement, and calls for a more rounded assessment if decision-makers are to draw sensible conclusions about what has resulted against their expectations. As the title implies, this focus on intervention mechanisms, their effective working and performance is the bedrock of process evaluation.

To be purposeful, process evaluations go deeper than results to probe interplay between individual and organisational dynamics for an intervention. The nucleus will always be with assessing how an intervention has worked against expectations (or targets), both overall and for specific constituent parts of it. Those dynamics, and the intervention aspirations and mechanisms which fuel them, are the prism through which the evaluation disentangles how, and how well, the intervention has or is working – its underpinning processes.

What 'processes', why and when to evaluate them

Process evaluations are a long-established, and still important, part of the evaluator's armoury. They can be stand-alone inquiries or may involve pluralistic approaches (Chapter 5) within an impact-focused or theory-based evaluation. For simplicity, this chapter looks at process evaluation as a distinct approach, but the principles and practice set out can be applied equally when combined with, or as an embedded part of, another type of evaluation.

The domain of a process evaluation can be wide but has some limitations. Figure 6.1 sets out the essential sequential parts that characterise any intervention; process evaluation is concerned with only the first parts of this sequence. Typically, this is some combination of the *inputs* that 'kick start' what is being evaluated (funding, timeframe, partnerships, procurement of provision, and so on), the actions and *activities* that result from inputs (what the intervention is delivering), and the outputs resulting. This chapter will not go so far as to look at outcomes or impacts which are the territory of impact evaluations (Chapters 8, 9 and 10).

The distinction between outputs and outcomes is crucial to setting boundaries for a process evaluation, but this can be confusing to less experienced evaluators and many stakeholders. Outputs are the direct result of the intervention activities; outcomes are what happens after them. For example, in a new skills training programme, outputs might be numbers recruited, tutors or teachers trained to deliver or assess it, retention levels, module engagement levels, qualifications or attainment levels achieved. In contrast, outcomes for someone graduating from the course might be securing a new or better job, gaining a promotion, securing better pay, more job security or contributing to filling an organisational or local skills shortage. Put more simply, outcomes are the consequential changes resulting from outputs; process evaluation stops short of looking at the much more challenging area of outcomes.

Early in the author's career, process evaluation dominated most commissioned evaluations, sometimes looking at little more than different aspects of intervention performance against set delivery targets. Much has changed since, but this focus remains commonplace for programme-focused inquiry but with different purposing ambitions, the most common being:

- 'Accountability process evaluation': Here, the focus is on if and how the resources (broadly defined) that went into what is

Figure 6.1: Component parts of an intervention

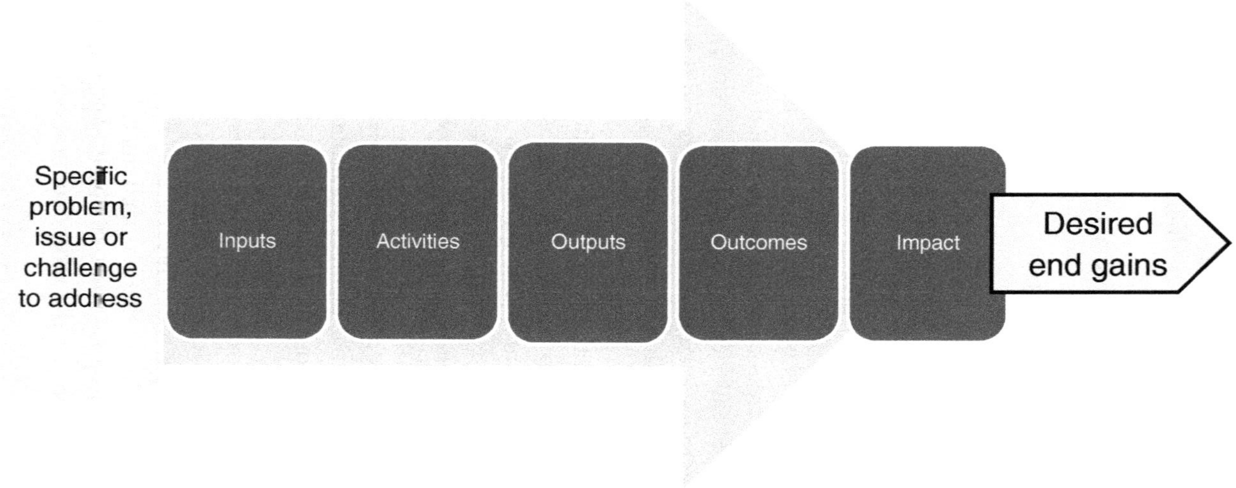

Specific problem, issue or challenge to address → Inputs → Activities → Outputs → Outcomes → Impact → Desired end gains

being evaluated were applied as expected, and if and how they were harnessed to produce results. Accountability-based process evaluations were an early evaluation emphasis and remain important to funders as well as for scrutiny regarding, for example, use of charitable or public funds. They may also be used by compliance or regulatory bodies to assess quality and other standards to monitor or discipline intervention processes and procedures.

- 'Improvement process evaluation': The driving purpose here will be applying what can be learnt from intervention processes to improve effectiveness or inform future designs. This could be conducted in real time to inform ongoing developments, at the intervention conclusion, or at a decision-making breakpoint (for example, when the next phase of funding might be being agreed).

Accountability and improvement focuses do not need to be mutually exclusive, and may be combined. However, the need for ongoing evidence to review successful progress means process evaluations now more commonly go beyond accounting to better understand how accountable performance (or lack of it) came about, and what can be learnt from that. This greatly extends the review of process to assess how well the cogs and wheels of an intervention (for example, resourcing, marketing, recruitment, functionality) or wider implementation (for example, stakeholder engagement, partnership working, monitoring, management, data and communications exchange) serve necessary performance and identify 'choke points' or blockages to effective working. For improvement, process review should also be looking for if, and how, any blockages were addressed and how those responses might guide improvements.

This introduces another area of potential confusion, the difference between 'summative' or 'formative' process evaluations. Accountability evaluation is characteristically summative, 'summing-up' results in a one-off report at the conclusion of the evaluation. Summative reporting (see Chapter 2) may also involve more frequent progress reports, setting out where the evaluation has got to against its workplan but not going as far as preliminary findings.

Improvement process evaluations may also be summative, especially where short evaluation periods are involved. However, they are now more commonly 'formative' evaluations, providing one or more interim reports for findings so as to critically appraise how something is working as it is being implemented, often suggesting ongoing improvements. This is the 'real time' approach outlined previously, where a formative assessment is usually benchmarked against some pre-conceived expectations of the intervention's early and subsequent delivery. Formative reports can be delivered at any point in an intervention but usually at user designated points for progression, interim funding or other decision points.

Purpose drives the emphasis for a process evaluation (and other types) and whether it is to be summative or formative, but it also informs how best to go about it. The approach to a process evaluation needs to suit the particular purposes intended for it, with choices to be made between (or in a combination of) four likely emphases:

- achieved performance and the intervention;
- evidence to inform intervention development or for transactional purposes;
- assessing the intervention for effectiveness and efficacy in delivery processes;
- achievements or compliance in the quality of processes and outputs.

Each involves a different emphasis and inquiry focus. For simplicity, this chapter looks at each separately.

Evaluating performance

This is probably the closest to the main, or only, focus of an accountability-based process evaluation. It reduces the inquiry to an evidence-based assessment of what the intervention achieves for the resources put in. Those achievements will usually centre on pre-determined ambitions for the intervention including, but going beyond, just the end results. Funding or budgetary requirements for the intervention will usually have set out activity as well as output targets, perhaps as key performance indicators (KPIs). A performance evaluation may be limited to those but may also include other delivery or output yardsticks (Table 6.1).

Table 6.1: Likely inquiry issues for a performance process evaluation

Performance issue	Input, action or process	Output or 'result'
What budgetary or 'core' resources were harnessed over the intervention; how were they distributed?	√	
What discretionary or supplementary resourcing was achieved (for example, matched, co-finance or funding in-kind)?	√	
What planned actions/services were offered over the intervention, by whom?	√	
What was the distribution of offered actions or services over time/geography?	√	
What specific performance 'results' were achieved from actions or services? Was/where was this optimal?		√
What was the distribution/take-up of achieved results? Was/where was this optimal against expectations?		√
How do results compare to budgetary/other requirements, KPIs or targets?		√
How did the distribution of actions and/or achieved reach compare to intended priorities or targeted 'needs' groups?	√	√
Where were (any) performance gaps or contrasts between funded partners, providers or other delivery agents?		√

Looking across these issues (and perhaps also others more distinctive to a particular intervention) puts together a grounded picture of what was achieved over a specific timeframe against intervention expectations. As Table 6.1 shows, there will be a mix of 'input', 'action', 'process' and 'output' performance issues. Outputs are likely to be particularly important and will likely go beyond end results:

- entry-level 'results' (for example, applications, registration, recruitment, entry or starts);
- process achievements (for example, participant retention, renewals, progression across intervention actions);

- end-of-action achievements (for example, targeted behaviour changes, achieved qualifications, job entry, heath or welfare outputs).

Only the simplest performance-based assessment will be limited to aggregate data. Most will need to explore differentiated dimensions, to look at (and learn from) what resulted in different parts of an intervention's delivery or for different needs groups. This might separate out different geographies, providers, or economic sectors, or look at different client demographics, their situation (for example, economic activity, education level) or contrasts between priority or particular needs groups. In this, purposeful process evaluations are designed to have a sharp focus on responding to policy makers' interest in how results from a particular innovation contrasted within it. Decision-makers may also be keen to see an external comparator showing whether achievements out-perform past practices or similar actions.

A process evaluation needs to go a lot further than a differentiated assessment of what was achieved against the over-arching needs of the intervention, delivery or contracted targets. If it is to be purposeful it will need to anticipate, and provide for, a credible platform of evidence for:

- Likely subsequent funder or partnership responses to findings and any policy or development priorities. This will most likely draw on the use and utility aspirations from preliminary 'scoping' discussions with funders and stakeholders. Where those priorities change, evaluation will rely on subsequent dialogue about key evidence needs.
- Emerging evidence on efficiency and change implications for the intervention, or for parallel practice, from performance discontinuities, process blockages or constraints and any effective responses.
- Observations of better practices in delivery aiding performance where these have implications for future or enhanced practice.

The evidence to inform the inquiry focus will be primarily quantitative, but where KPIs are more loosely set, it may involve qualitative evidence to assess issues, such as quality of responsiveness, working relationships, better practices or enhanced service innovation. Where the evidence comes from will depend on the situation of the intervention and, in particular, how much of performance evidence needs was anticipated when designers set requirements for monitoring or management evidence. This might include an appropriate mix of:

- available documentation (for example, provider or intervention management phased reports to funders);
- additional data requests (for example, specific data breakdown) or client/funder interviews;
- performance measurement data (for example, against KPIs for the delivery agents);
- finance or activity monitoring information.

Performance process evaluations will lean heavily on these (and other) available sources, but it would be unlikely if the evaluation could collect all of its required evidence from monitoring, documentation or other available sources. There will be evidence gaps and additional information needs, which are likely to require some (and possibly extensive) primary evidence collection. For a purposeful focus it would be unusual if this did not place a particular emphasis on the 'lived experiences' of those taking part in the intervention and from the groundwork of delivering it.

Transfer or developmental evaluation

Both transfer and developmental evaluation are principally concerned with informing the transformation of intervention design or practice, either for the target intervention or perhaps to inform design of a parallel prospective initiative. Although they share a similar aspiration for evidence-use, there are important differences between 'transfer' and 'developmental' approaches:

- 'Transfer evaluations' follow a specific, usually narrow, policy or budgetary-geared focus for evidence, often to inform next steps for an intervention. Well-placed, this can be a valued tool for decision-makers in evidencing anticipated change.

- A 'developmental evaluation' (DE) directly engages with adaptation across an intervention, through an evolving evidence focus which provides (near) real-time guidance on changes to focus and delivery. The openness of DE is its unique selling-point, but it may be resisted by commissioners requiring a more predictable pathway.

Transfer evaluations

Many evaluations will have a sense of using evidence to improve responses or practices within an intervention; transfer evaluations target a specific aspect for how that evidence is to be used for decision-making, involving one of two transfer directions:

- 'Internal transfer for a next steps decision', such as renewed resourcing or scale-up for the intervention being evaluated. This might be to inform which (and whether) activities are worth replicating or improving in a renewed action, which might anticipate modifying, streamlining, expanding what is being done or rolling it out to parallel situations. For example, an internal transfer evaluation of the set-up and delivery of a biodiversity management support programme in a pilot area of heathlands might be asked to recommend what practices would be transferable to other areas with similar habitat and land use.
- 'External transferability of evidence to inform other interventions', where the process evaluation commonly focuses on ongoing or planned actions in other situations. This investigates transferable potential of process evidence from the situation being evaluated to other contexts. For example, it might include assessing an in-custodial (prison) counselling service for offender resettlement to see what aspects have improvement potential for modified information, advice and guidance for non-custodial offenders or others on probation in the community.

External transfer approaches are likely to need much wider information. Cartwright and Hardie (2012) describe these as 'support factors' to evidence if it is reasonable to suggest successful processes in one evaluated context have transferable potential to another that is different, including:

- which of the effective aspects of the evaluated intervention were transferable, for whom and under what conditions;
- what adaptive change had relevance;
- if intervention scale mattered (as replicated programmes are likely to be conducted at a different scale);
- whether there is sufficient situational equivalence (social and economic), including for any 'political' stakeholders (for example, partner engagement and working arrangements).

Both internal and external 'transfer evidence' will be essentially summative in its emphasis, although this summation may refer not to the end of an intervention but a point of time when the transfer evidence is to be used. Some years ago, for example, the author with colleagues undertook a 40-month long evaluation of a large-scale, five-year teacher and tutor development programme in post-16 vocational education. The 'final' report of the evaluation was required 14 months before programme funding concluded, so as to inform further budgetary decisions in the UK government's periodic (usually five-year) Comprehensive Spending Review. In some countries or regulatory regimes, similar set periods for 'post implementation reviews' (PIRs) may also be set for review of new standards or legislation.

Developmental process evaluations

Developmental evaluations (DE) are not restricted to process evaluation, with differing theoretical considerations (not considered here) about where DE is positioned within the panoply of evaluation options. It is looked at here as 'process evaluation' from the practical standpoint: DE is heavily centred on assessing and guiding evolving ambition and delivery processes for an intervention. DE-type approaches may have been practised informally for years, but their genesis as a distinct and strongly purpose-led approach stems from the work of Michael Quinn Patton, a former President of the American Evaluation Association.

DE reflects Patton's long-established concern with utilisation-focused evaluation (Patton, 2011). It might be characterised as applying adaptive, action research principles in contexts of innovative actions where design and delivery face uncertain or chaotic situations which need adaptation evidence from emerging experience: 'Developmental Evaluation supports innovation development to guide adaptation to emergent and dynamic realities in complex environments. ... [where] A complex system is characterized by a large number of interacting and interdependent elements in which there is no central control' (Patton, 2011: 1). Evidence to inform adaptation may be a feature of many process evaluations, but in DE this takes a distinctive, heightened dynamic and embedded approach (Patton, 2006). This anticipates an ongoing and often radical approach, going beyond the usually staged, formative approach of conventional improvement-centred process evaluation. DE remains firmly evidence-based, but its influence, and that of the evaluator, for a purposeful approach is deeply embedded in the practice of an intervention. The approach is well-suited to situations where stakeholders have different, and perhaps conflicting, views on focus or how to proceed.

The application of DE uses adaptive methods which are modified or introduced to reflect changing circumstances and emerging needs. These are guided by some broad principles of practice, as summarised in Table 6.2.

DE goes beyond informing innovation; it leads it, and this calls for a very open and agile approach to what the evaluation focuses on and does (and the resourcing for it). These approaches can be very powerful where the intervention needs to optimise innovation in both what it does and for whom, and where its funders are open to active direction and engagement by the evaluators. Not all commissioners will be keen on the openness and flexibilities needed. Even if they are receptive, commissioning and funding processes may not be conducive to an open resource commitment, with no clear (or a changing) evaluative framework, or an objectivised end point. Nevertheless, in some situations, a strong case can be made to justify this optimal flexibility for evaluation of problem-centred social innovations in uncertain environments.

DE may have rising currency for policy makers keen to speed up how evaluation can be applied to decision-making settings

Table 6.2: Principles of method choice for developmental evaluation (DE)

DE 'design' feature	Method choice and delivery by ...
Dynamic approach and structure	• No fixed direction • Aims to adapt and use an evidence focus to nurture adaptive learning by those developing and delivering an intervention
Responsive to (evolving) situation	• Highly responsive to circumstances and change within what's being evaluated • Adopts a real-time focus to adjust to what is happening and the environment within which it takes place
Formative feedback of evidenced implications	• Emphasises user-friendly, frequent and opportunistic review of emerging evidence • Evidence feedback geared to the intervention adapting to emerging issues and circumstance
Optimised multiple insights (and sources)	• Involves diverse sources of (multi-mode) evidence which are likely to change as evaluation leads adaptation • Method application will be inherently participative
Constructive co-production	• Evaluation actions (and adaptation) coproduced through embedded creative and critical thinking • Coproduction reflects closeness to delivery and direct engagement with intervention design and delivery teams[1]

Source: Adapted by the author from Patton, 2006 and 2011

and placing a premium on fast evidence feedback. The author is conscious of a growing interest among policy makers in the use of fast response 'test and trial' methods for policy and programme development, where conventional evaluation methods can be seen to lack the flexibility and feedback for very intensive, progressive evidence of what works and implications for revised design or practice. DE may have much to offer here, certainly in early micro- or small-scale 'test' stages of policy development, before perhaps moving onto more extensive and robust evaluation-based 'trials' with more confidently based larger scale applications.

Evaluating effectiveness and efficacy

Decision-makers harnessing public or charitable funds and those in resource-constrained environments will be especially concerned with cost-effectiveness in an intervention. In some situations, this might require a more specialised approach, within economic evaluation (Chapter 7). Elsewhere, resources constraints are a key driver for taking account of intervention efficacy and efficiency, as well as results. Like an internal transfer evaluation, an efficiency-focused evaluation will need to explore deeply how well something works, but with a different, usually formative, focus on efficiency improvements. It shares with developmental evaluation an aspiration for continuing adjustments, but involves a more impartial, predictive and structured focus.

Evaluating effectiveness purposefully is not a simple, binary distinction, where something is effective or it is not. The point of departure for such a process-centred evaluation is a credible definition of what dimensions of 'effectiveness' need to be assessed. These will likely include key mechanisms and their interactions, perhaps including external interactions of an intervention with, for example, inward referral of participants or outward signposting or integration to specialist support. It will also need to take account of any points of leverage by funders, stakeholders or providers on efficiencies. Exploring these component parts may result in an overall assessment of effectiveness, but it is based on a fine-tuned approach to unpick what makes up 'efficiency' and whose focus is informed by stakeholders.

As an illustration, well-positioned recruitment of unemployed young people vulnerable to long-term unemployment into an employability-enhancement programme does not of itself ensure that that programme will be effective. In this case, achieving the outputs aspired to (early or subsequent job-entry) will need to review efficiency precursors including, for example, selector comprehension of well-articulated eligibility criteria, entrant screening and branching to different support mechanisms, effectiveness in post-entry retention, beneficiary engagement and motivation, segmentation, and capacity for personalised support. Effectiveness for this programme, as elsewhere, will be made up of a number of interwoven influences.

Effectiveness for purposeful evaluators consequently needs to articulate and dig deep into influencing processes on efficiency. Where evaluators are confident that they are familiar with the intervention area, the challenge being addressed and the likely context of beneficiaries, they may have enough information to guide both commissioners and users on what efficiency 'facets' to consider. This will provide the necessarily more granular focus on the different components of what constitutes effectiveness. Where they lack this confidence or sufficient insights, early discussions or more formalised scoping work will need to be able to pin down the expectations and needs of effectiveness influences. Some of the more likely component parts for a review of efficiency are set out in Table 6.3.

Table 6.3: Common issues for 'granular' assessment of effectiveness

	Cause	Effect
Set appropriate start-up foundations (for example, engaged partners and providers, working/collaboration protocols, standards, data sharing)	√	
Secured the anticipated resources at start-up and through the intervention period	√	
Appropriately defined and communicated the eligible/target population and how to reach them (including for any segmentation of delivery)	√	
Appropriately defined the stakeholder interest, including for any integration issues for service delivery	√	
Applied provided resources appropriately for design, development and delivery and within any ring-fencing of reach/key activities	√	√
Engaged (and retained) eligible participants and (any) priority groups, including with any segmented services or actions		√
Implemented activities/services delivery as anticipated by funders/policy makers and to specified standards	√	√
Identified processes which have held back or constrained achievements and implementation, or where the anticipated model is working less well		√
Made appropriate and responsive delivery adjustments to intervention constraints where necessary		√
Achieved planned outputs within specification and to any service-level requirements		√
Achieved additional outputs (unintended/supplementary to service requirements)		√
Engaged appropriately with stakeholders and/or partner organisations in the delivery arrangements		√

Including both cause and effect avoids a focus which is too narrow and positions what is needed against what the intervention did or did not put in place for 'efficiency' to come about. For example, an evaluation might show that there had been poor effectiveness in the engagement of a particular needs (priority) group (effect), but this might be explained, not as a 'results failure', but because 'appropriate' eligibility criteria to define that needs group had not been sufficiently clearly outlined at the outset, or communicated to providers (cause). Table 6.3 has illustrated the more common effectiveness considerations. Not all will be relevant to specific interventions, and others will probably need to be added for specific situations to reflect particular expectations of effectiveness.

A well-developed theory of change for the intervention is a highly valuable aid in scoping what effectiveness issues are important. Views about what constitutes a solid theory of change vary greatly among commissioners and evaluators (returned to in Chapter 10), but there is a consensus it should explicitly set out the mechanisms by which change is supposed to happen (Funnell and Rogers, 2011). This provides a framework for surfacing important (and sometimes implicit) issues for success within the delivery model (Example 9).

Example 9: ANTICIPATING INFLUENCES – USING A THEORY OF CHANGE TO ANTICIPATE 'HIDDEN' INFLUENCES ON PROGRAMME EFFECTIVENESS

In preparation for an evaluation, the author was retained to advise a cross-agency partnership developing a pilot programme to support economically inactive 'over-50s' to return to work. A theory of change (ToC) was developed to help focus the programme evaluation through staged 'theory building' partnership workshops to set and scrutinise the likely outcomes, assumptions and risks behind the pilot.

Among the more tangible assumptions (for example, effective branding, cross-partnership marketing, referral mechanisms, functionality of services, and so on) were some less clear but important likely success factors. In marketing alone, for example, the ToC defined the need for segmented marketing to meet the different motivations of those aged 50+ who were seen as 'close' to the labour market (for example, recent leavers, qualified, with relevant skill sets) and those further away (such as those demotivated by long periods of past ineffective job search).

Achieving this segmentation was built into the inquiry focus for the subsequent evaluation, as a condition for effective marketing. Other pilot mechanisms were seen to be underpinned by less obvious, but important, 'effectiveness' assumptions which were also 'surfaced' by building the ToC. Without the ToC, this segmentation issue, along with a number of other 'hidden' effectiveness assumptions, could have been missed in the evaluation, and in understanding service effectiveness and integration.

Evaluating quality

A process evaluation may call for a particular focus on the assessment of quality. Delivering an effective intervention is not just about how it worked to deliver an expected level, or distribution, of outputs; it also concerns delivery quality. Quality review in a process evaluation is likely to go beyond an intervention's quality control or assurance processes to take account of stakeholder aspiration for what makes up necessary quality for its delivery. This provides nuance and understanding which might otherwise be neglected in favour of more readily assessed measures.

Getting to grips with this quality dimension can be challenging for purposeful evaluation if user-aspirations on what constitutes 'quality' differ or are vague. To cut through the possible issues to consider, it can help to start with any ready-made quality indicators or standards, such as set out in a programme quality plan, provider service-level agreements, or contractual obligations referencing regulatory or other standards. This may only be a starting point; the quality dimension may need to further refine, or add, what needs to be measured.

Finding and prioritising less tangible quality requirements may open the door to very different views on what needs to be 'quality' among stakeholders. As an illustration, in the ToC workshops for the 50+ job re-entry pilot (Example 9), there was a 'lively' discussion among stakeholders over 'quality jobs'. Some stakeholders felt a high 'quality' bar could adversely affect participants' self-confidence and employability motivation and so job re-entry. Others felt 'quality' should exclude casual work, short-term contracts, jobs paid below a 'living wage' premium or job locations which were inconvenient for re-entrants to get to. A compromise was eventually agreed for a less demanding 'quality' yardstick, but this example shows that quality requirements for what needs to be evaluated have to be framed within the context and ambition of stakeholder views about the intervention aims.

Table 6.4 sets out a generic rubric that can be used to identify necessary quality dimensions with some of the likely indicators which might be relevant.

The inquiry will need to look at what quality was or was not achieved in order to explore contrasts between higher and lower quality delivery, and their causes. As with other emphases for a process evaluation, a lot can be learnt for intervention improvements from exploring delivery differences between different delivery circumstances, providers and participant groups.

A final practical consideration is that quality is likely to need to go well beyond a 'yes' or 'no' assessment of whether explicit standards are met. Quality needs to be viewed from the experiential perspective, drawing on any contrasting insights from participants, providers and engaged stakeholders. This will also help with confidence in the findings, especially where stakeholders have different quality aspirations (as in the employment re-entry example cited here).

Participative process evaluation

Participation in purposeful evaluation is certainly not limited to process evaluations, but here it is a crucial element in shaping

Table 6.4: Some pointers to determining 'process' quality indicators

	Clarification issues for purposing ...
Engaged quality plan or quality assurance process	• Is a quality plan or quality assurance process put in place? • Who is responsible for quality management/compliance? • Are there/what are relevant compliance processes/indicators?
Relevant external referred standards	• Are there/what are referred relevant quality requirements most likely to condition intervention processes or outputs? • Are there/what are intervention-relevant external standards or benchmarks from regulatory or other bodies?
Mandated quality yardsticks	• Have any intervention-specific quality requirements mandated in service-level agreements for providers/service agents? • Do (any) mandated requirements set specific criteria or other yardsticks for quality?
Quality confidence yardsticks	• Are there/what are internal/external quality requirements critical to the credibility, confidence in or continuity of the intervention?
Quality performance risks	• What/where are the most likely internal/external quality compliance gaps (perhaps identified from a theory of change)?
Quality or compliance failure consequences	• What knock-on consequences for the intervention if quality requirements are not being met? • Are there/what are any of these consequences critical or highly sensitive for the intervention?
Quality and ethics	• Are there ethical compliance issues which should be added as essential quality yardsticks?

method choice and use. Participative approaches are given fuller consideration in Chapter 12, but there are some special considerations for participation in process evaluation.

Reviewing intervention 'process' needs to go beyond looking at a series of mechanisms and how they work together to interpret evidence from the (different) experiences of those designing, delivering and engaged in the processes. The extent to which proportionate participatory evaluation methods should inform and interpret intervention processes remains an issue of substantial controversy. This book does not seek to add to what can be entrenched attitudes about participative methods among evaluators, but suggests that two broad but mutually exclusive directions for process evaluation are:

- 'directed participation', which takes a well-honed and selective approach to whom to engage in participation and how; and
- 'embedded evaluation', which places 'participants' centre stage in design, conduct and interpretation.

Directed participation

This approach values the contribution to be made by those outside the evaluation team, but it is essentially pragmatic in how this is harnessed and with whom. It is likely to be highly selective in who is engaged, how and when. In addition to any stakeholder engagement in early stage purposing and steering, its participative focus will be on evidence contributions and mixed-mode insights, often through participant self-assessment or creative methods (Kara, 2020), such as individual story-telling, participatory forums, change-mapping. Directed participation may also harness structured participatory methods of analysis, such as 'Most Significant Change' or 'Outcome Harvesting' (see Chapter 10). Participation is likely to be selective across these possibilities, determined by the evaluator and available resourcing.

Embedded participation

This increases the ambition for participation and effectively devolves much of the evaluative judgements to participants themselves. Here, participants are likely to be directly involved in scoping, design (for example, of evaluation tools), shaping evidence mix and critical assessment of findings and implications. This draws heavily on longer standing traditions from participatory action research (PAR) and it provides opportunities for process evaluators to put stakeholders and beneficiaries at the heart of what is done and who with. This places evaluators in the position of supporting and facilitating participation and taking their lead from participant-led, collective and self-reflective inquiry (Kemmis and McTaggart, 2005; MacDonald, 2012). It provides a radical alternative for process (and other) evaluations, although many commissioners may be cautious, seeing its benefits as being outweighed by risks and a lack of control over focus and rigour.

However they are applied, participatory methods are especially important to process evaluation, opening up different experiences, lines of inquiry and interpretation which might have otherwise remained obscure or unrealised. For purposeful evaluation, they have added-value for the credibility of the evaluation, especially within a voluntary or community sector, or public policy environment.

Some purposeful tips

Process evaluations may not involve the many conceptual challenges of economic or impact evaluations, but they have their fair share of pitfalls and judgmental traps. Some practical issues to consider (or to mitigate) these include:

- Placing judgements on process emphasis and priorities within a firm understanding of the intervention context, including how situational circumstances, complexity and likely volatility may affect intervention agency and delivery processes.
- Paying attention to how the intended delivery processes were forged, including considering delivery assumptions (implicit and explicit) in intervention planning and design, ideally harnessing a theory of change.
- Identifying and seeking resolution on (any) uncertain or unresolved key stakeholder differences on process priorities and use for evaluation timing and improvements. Clarity here will steer a formative or summative approach as well as emphasis.
- Looking under the skin of what is likely to influence process effectiveness and quality, taking account of potential for leverage by decision-makers, reflecting this in appropriate granularity in evidence-gathering and analysis.
- Providing analysis which digs deep into process contrasts within the intervention and their causes. This anticipates well-placed independent variables in evidence-gathering to explore lack of homogeneity in participation and/or uniformity in provision.

Sound judgements will also be needed on the ambition for cross-evaluation participation. Beyond broad aspirations for, perhaps, seeking appropriate stakeholder and beneficiary engagement, commissioners may be vague about these needs, with the evaluator needing to determine what is necessary, appropriate and achievable. This will also need to manage likely different and even conflicting stakeholder expectations of participation. There are pitfalls to be avoided here for balancing achievable aspiration with practicalities (including available resources) and the implications for the credibility and confidence in findings.

7

Economic evaluation

Introduction

Many evaluations will be looking for evidence of what returns there have been for the investment or resources put into an intervention. Fulfilling users' appetite for this is not the exclusive preserve of economic evaluation. A capable process evaluation can show accountabilities for those resources, and an impact evaluation can go further to explore how efficiently allocated resources delivered expected benefits. However, neither are well-placed to demonstrate robustly to decision-makers whether achieved outputs and outcomes justified the resources that went into them; economic evaluation looks to fill that gap.

Evaluators who are not economists, or lack that insight, may be cautious about tackling economic evaluation; that caution is well-placed. Even a rudimentary grasp of economic theory will show the challenges faced in robustly demonstrating if an intervention's costs outweighed its benefits or if there were 'more economic' ways of achieving those outcomes.

Not all of the economic 'asks' of an evaluation will be so demanding. But where there is greater ambition, this calls for an approach chosen from a highly specialised domain; here, however, the language of economic analysis can hold back making sensible choices for what is 'purposeful'. This chapter seeks to demystify much of the terminology, as well as set out possible pathways and how best to make choices between them.

What is 'economic' in economic evaluation?

If the evaluator places themselves in the policy makers' or users' shoes, they will see that the importance of the economic dimension of evaluation stems from a combination of (likely) scarcity of resources and the need for an intervention to make the best of what is allocated or available. This is about value for money, and some prefer to call economic evaluation just that – 'value for money' (VfM) evaluations.[1] VfM has a very specific meaning in economic analysis (see later) and not all economic evaluations need to consider this; so, to avoid confusion, this chapter stays with 'economic evaluation'.

Terminology can be challenging in many other ways. Unpicking this is important for making the choice of an appropriate approach, so a useful starting point is with some of the core economic terms, and in particular the concepts of 'cost', 'value', 'value for money', and 'utility':[2]

- 'Cost' assessment in economic evaluation is not limited to a direct costs or budgetary allocation for an intervention. Economic cost needs to dig deeper and look at both tangible and intangible costs underpinning provision: that is, cost to participants and to cooperating delivery bodies (for example, referrals). For delivery, this will include, for example, fixed and variable costs (of delivery), sunk or unrecoverable costs (those with no continuing exchange value), marginal costs, and average costs. For participants, it will include any entry costs (for example, registration), materials, travel costs, or other costs for engaging with the intervention. Not all will be relevant to all intervention contexts, but some will be. Added to this, opportunity costs, which represent an allocated cost from a loss of gain or opportunity from engagement (in an intervention), have special importance to some economic evaluations (see later).
- 'Value' in economic terms can be interpreted in different ways depending on how we look at 'price' in terms of use and exchange. In evaluation, the focus is usually on economic value which is concerned with the benefit of the intervention (or parts of it) as provided goods or a service. This is different from

value for money (see later), although VfM is also important to many evaluations. Value is usually 'monetised' by expressing this as currency which involves inevitable challenges for evaluators when looking at things that cannot be readily converted to a money value (looked at a little later).

- 'Value for money' (VfM) involves an assessment of whether the resources put into something (that is, the intervention) are being used effectively to secure anticipated benefit. VfM can be determined in comparative ('better' or 'best value for money') terms if the evaluation looks at comparative utility (see later). In evaluation, VfM may be more likely to be seen in more absolute terms – do the actions and their achieved benefits constitute value for money or not?
- 'Utility' is also a common way for economic evaluation to assess an intervention and may contribute directly to a VfM assessment. This is seen differently for utility maximisation and comparative utility:
  - Utility maximisation recognises that, as resources are not infinite, it is likely to be important to relate scarcity of resources to decisions made about them and their use. This assumes resource management for an intervention can be optimised by efficient decisions and allocation to achieve the most favourable outputs or outcomes.
  - Comparative utility sees 'value' of an intervention as relative to how resources might have been better used. Decision-makers will often be concerned to know if an intervention represents 'best value', needing comparative evidence of how the same or a similar level of resource might have been used more (or less) effectively in a different way.

Any approach to assessing economic utility will need to consider 'opportunity costs' arising from the evaluated intervention. The concept can be difficult to put into practice but involves allowing for the value of foregone (lost) opportunities or benefits resulting from participation in an evaluation. It means that to assess the true value of what was achieved the gains from observed benefits need to be counterbalanced by placing values on 'lost opportunity'. This is the cost of not enjoying a benefit that would have occurred if there had been no participation or if alternative choices were made. For non-economists the idea of 'opportunity costs' may appear a little esoteric; it should not be (Box 7.1).

> **Box 7.1: A hypothetical example of opportunity costs**
>
> A modular training course has been set up following accreditation of a new qualification to improve digital competencies of technicians providing plumbing, heating and electrical maintenance services. The course is aimed at sub-contracted and self-employed people transitioning to domestic heat pump, solar and related technologies.
>
> Self-employed participants in the course were expected to gain measurable 'economic' benefit from taking part. An economic evaluation would be expected to assess the value of direct benefits, including: securing more work or recommendations; higher customer retention; raised charging rates; or better rewarded contracts.
>
> In taking part in the course to secure those benefits, the participants may have foregone other things. This might include loss of earnings (from foregone 'paid time') while travelling to and attending the mandatory modules, and for course assessment. Lost earnings would be an opportunity cost (and there may be others) to be set against the direct benefits to provide a more rounded assessment of the true economic value derived from the course.

Understanding some of these core concepts and their implications for an economic evaluation will be important to commissioner, user and evaluator alike.

Economic evaluation, value and monetisation

Tackling the economic dimension by applying quantifiable measures to some of these concepts will need to translate key elements for inputs, outputs and often outcomes into a readily analysed and standardised[3] metric. This usually involves setting a monetary valuation on different costs and benefits: 'monetising' them.

Monetisation has underpinned cost-benefit analyses for decades, although with some differences among economists about the relative use of different approaches such as market price, transfer costs, or abatement costs. For economic evaluations, monetisation is a recurrent practical challenge and poor judgement here is the most common cause for error, or lost confidence in, their findings. Monetisation can be straightforward where intervention elements have a clear tradeable value (for example, fixed labour costs). It is much more difficult with 'social' values (for example, raised self-esteem) which are described as 'intangibles'; here, credible proxy measures need to be developed.

The challenges of a purposeful economic evaluation do not stop with determining monetary values. They include making appropriate judgements about what elements are critical to take into account, gaining consensus on those (and their valuation), and securing appropriate data for monetising them. Reducing the analysis to what is more readily monetised or applying monetary values which lack stakeholder confidence falls well short of what is purposeful, objective or credible. All this needs care and attention to, in particular:

- identifying and reducing varying costs and benefits to a common unit;
- choosing that unit (usually currency) so that it is comparable across the intervention;
- ensuring that valuation is a fair and sound reflection of the intervention's value creation.

Experience shows considerable attention needs to be paid to monetisation of 'social' costs and benefits. In the earlier example of the self- employed person with a new qualification, the gain from additional or higher paid work can be quantified through valuation of net additional revenue gained or anticipated (for future gain) from projections of market wage rates or inflation adjusted past rates of received earnings. But if they subsequently chose to work less hard because they now earn at higher charging rates, what value might be placed on added leisure time? Quantifying such 'social value' relies on setting proxy values (a 'shadow price') for the gain.[4] This will be more prone to misjudgement (valuation errors) or omission (not including things that should be valued) so, for purposeful evaluation, the anticipated social values will need to be credible to stakeholders.

Valuation errors can also affect more tangible elements if the value applied does not provide a true reflection of the value of a good or service. However, the risks are much greater for intangibles, especially where social value is multi-faceted, for example with interventions aimed at improving biodiversity, greater amenity use, enhanced well-being, or improved safety. Where it is possible, using 'plug-in' values, perhaps from past research, may be helpful or the evaluation might look to external expertise or stakeholder discussions to produce estimates which can be confidently used.

Monetisation also often needs to take account of externalities or 'extension values' to quantifying the value of outcomes for individuals (or service providers) not directly involved in the intervention. Many years ago, the author led an evaluation of a new adult guidance initiative, funded by the European Commission, to reduce risks and duration of long-term unemployment. It was able to estimate value from levels of achieved post-initiative paid employment and average hours worked (for different occupations and localities) at market wage levels. However, it also built in extension values, including from estimated cost-savings from unemployment subsidies and reduced costs in public employment services.

However much economists try to make this an exact process, economic evaluators can rarely aim to provide perfect and comprehensive valuation. Judgements that are made are best set out early, explicitly and subjected to scrutiny perhaps through peer review of stakeholder engagement. 'Sensitivity analysis' is also an important scrutiny tool, and can be one-way or multi-way (Drummond et al, 2005):

- One-way sensitivity analysis can show how sensitive an analysis is to often small changes in the tested key elements. This contrasts results by varying the values of the selected element, one at a time, to show how much the tested value of a cost or benefit would have to rise or fall to 'tip' the overall cost-effectiveness or cost-benefit analysis. This is useful where there

is fixed, stable or confident demand for the intervention, but less well-suited where there is uncertainty.
- Multi-way sensitivity analysis takes a different approach, often using scenario-based analysis to demonstrate the vulnerability of findings to different situations for the intervention. This is useful where interrelationships between (different) costs and between costs and benefits are complex, with greater stakeholder uncertainty about them or volatile demand within or from the intervention. It can be used ex-ante or ex-post by putting together a small range of alternative scenarios for the intervention circumstances (for example, high, moderate, or low demand in different demographic or market circumstances). Each scenario is then harnessed to adjust, for example, assumption values, consistent with those circumstances and tested for variations in the cost-benefit analysis results for those different scenario circumstances.

Sensitivity analysis cannot test for everything, and judgements will need to be made about what to test, what scenarios (if any) may be appropriate, and how to frame them. Again, for purposeful evaluation it is strongly advisable for the rationale for those choices to be open to scrutiny; this rationale will usually be presented with reporting of an economic evaluation.

Options for economic evaluation

Monetisation and sensitivity analysis are key components of methodologies; but what methodology options are open to economic evaluation? In most circumstances, this will come down to making a purpose-driven choice between four broad approaches:

- cost-description evaluation
- cost-effectiveness evaluation
- cost-utility evaluation, and
- cost-benefit evaluation

Any of these economic approaches can be applied ex-ante or ex-post. As in other evaluation types and approaches, an ex-ante economic evaluation is conducted before an intervention starts, as a prospective analysis of likely costs and benefits. This may be useful as part of a funding or business case, for more detailed budgetary planning, or for fine-tuning intervention design. An ex-post evaluation takes place at the conclusion of the intervention (and occasionally at a mid-point for decision-making) to assess how resources have been used; it is usually a summative assessment of costs and benefits and value for money.

Of these four broad approaches, cost-benefit evaluation is much more complex than cost-description evaluation, but the contrasts between the approaches are more than their intensity and sophistication. They represent different solutions for addressing different aspirations for the evaluation's scope (Table 7.1).

The choice of which pathway to take is consequently driven by purpose. Looked at this way, economic evaluation can offer a narrow and fairly simple assessment, limited to costs of the intervention's start-up, subsequent inputs and (probably) delivery, or it can be much more ambitious and requiring higher levels of sophistication. Clarity of purpose (and terminology) is crucial; commissioners asking for a cost-benefit evaluation may only be looking for a process or impact evaluation which takes some account of incurred direct costs and tangible benefits, not a fully monetised cost-benefit analysis.

Table 7.1: Scope and coverage of the main types of economic evaluation

Economic evaluation approach	Intervention elements ...				
	Design and delivery inputs	Activities and processes	Performance (outputs) and achievements	Outcomes	Impacts
Cost-description	√	√			
Cost-effectiveness	√	√	√	?	
Cost-utility	√	√	√	√	?
Cost-benefit	√	√	√	√	√

Source: After Parsons, 2017

The more complex the approach, the more its design and use will need to engage with (and resource) the more challenging aspects of economic evaluation. The rest of this chapter looks at the four economic evaluation pathways, and important practical issues in choosing between (and applying) them.

Cost-description analysis

Table 7.1 shows how cost-description has the narrowest focus for an economic evaluation. It may be conducted as a stand-alone or integrated within a process or impact evaluation. However, the modest scope of these evaluations is not necessarily reflected in the simplicity of their analysis. They will need to reflect a range of actual incurred and net costs which may be more or less tangible, as outlined in Table 7.2. Those costs will often then be set against costs proposed (usually budgeted) to identify or project cost savings or over-run.

Table 7.2: Costs to be considered in a cost-description evaluation

Nature of costs	Likely scope	Example
Fixed costs	Costs constant over a specific period of time (for example, annual or financial year) irrespective of volume of activity	Rental or mortgage repayment costs for premises; property taxation; fixed maintenance contracts; contracted staff wage/salary costs
Sunk costs	Costs incurred for start-up that are not apportioned to fixed costs	Adaption or conversion costs to premises; professional registration fees; provider certification
Variable costs	Costs which vary within a specific time period or according to the volume of activity	Costs for casual or sessional staff (where there is no retainer fee or other fixed cost); marketing; non-contracted equipment or maintenance costs
Semi-variable costs	Costs which include a fixed and variable element	Sessional staff costs where including retainer fee (fixed); sessional staff costs according to time engaged (variable)
Step costs	Costs that do not change steadily with changes in activity or volume, but at discrete points	Costs of facilities or premises fixed to a frequency/level of use which will rise when capacity is exceeded, or where additional facilities or premises are needed

Cost-description evaluation typically starts with a long list of in-scope costs (and data needs). Some may later not be included where evaluation (or data) resources are limited, or a trade-off is needed between the effort needed to collect cost information and its importance to the evaluation where: 'It is not worth investing a great deal of time and effort considering costs that, because they are small, are unlikely to make any difference to the study results' (Drummond et al, 2005: 57). Streamlining scope and data needs is not just about relative cost levels; it will involve judgement about 'what difference' a cost could make to outputs or outcomes. For example, staff training may be a relatively small part of staff costs, but in a cost-description approach it may be a key 'cost' consideration as undertrained staff could impair intervention quality or results. Conversely, including equipment depreciation costs or stationery loss costs may not justify the data efforts needed in collecting this. Other considerations are:

- Inclusion of indirect or marginal costs of set-up, product or service delivery.
- Apportionment of irregular costs, such as for senior management or specialist input (for example, HR, IT, legal) where they are mostly employed on other (non-intervention) tasks. Here, their input may be small, but (possibly) higher salaries and on-costs may make them significant in overall costs.
- An appropriate (usually longer) time period for cost collation to avoid distortion by unusual events (for example, professional fees for start-up recruitment; seasonal staff cover).

Cost-description evaluation might also involve a comparative look at resourcing costs of similar activities. These have been referred to as 'cost-minimisation evaluations' since their ambition is primarily to contrast incurred costs with something comparable elsewhere to optimise cost efficiencies.

Evaluating cost-effectiveness

Cost-effectiveness (CE) evaluation goes much further than cost-description, although without the intensity of a data and analytically rich cost-benefit evaluation. It sets out quantified

Economic evaluation

Table 7.3: Cost-effectiveness and CE–EC ratios

	CE/EC indicator	Example
Cost-effectiveness ratio (CE)	CE = Cost per individual unit of effectiveness (Note: Output or outcome)	The costs in an active labour market programme for an individual participant (unit) subsequently securing paid work after a fixed period from leaving the programme
Effectiveness-cost ratio (EC)	EC = Effectiveness per set unit of cost	The numbers of people securing paid work per designated unit of expenditure (for example, $10,000; £1,000)

input–outcome relationships (or more occasionally input–output), relating the costs of implementing and delivering the intervention to what is generated. The approach is more flexible than cost-benefit evaluation and can be useful where there is limited resourcing for the evaluation (Rossi et al, 2004). It can also be used prospectively for an ex-ante evaluation or to assess ongoing or concluding cost-effectiveness as an intervention progresses (or concludes).

Table 7.3 summarises two main options for representing cost-effectiveness (although these may be used in combination).

'Unit-cost' ratios are binary and can be applied, and readily compared, for all sorts of different activities. They are usually used in combinations of selected unit-cost metrics which are chosen to reflect the intervention context and its delivery priorities (Box 7.2).

Box 7.2: Setting purposeful metrics for a cost-effectiveness evaluation

A hypothetical programme might be centred on improving life-chances for disaffected young adults at or over 18. The actions of the programme would aim to motivate, guide and support these young adults' return to existing post-compulsory vocational or other work-related education or training. Focusing only on a ratio for programme costs set against each successful re-entry to education or training would provide a headline cost-effectiveness ratio but too little understanding of different aspects of cost-effectiveness.

Looking at the ambition of the overall programme, evaluators working with stakeholders might agree a range of cost-effectiveness metrics (ratios), to include, for example:

- cost per applicant (that is, total incurred programme costs/number of received applications)
- cost per admission/entrant
- cost per concluding entrant (full-term participation)
- cost per new qualification (or certification level) achieved
- cost per further education/training course entrant (up to +26 weeks)
- cost per paid job starter (up to +26 weeks from completion).

Those chosen would need to be assured of sufficient data to make calculation possible. These would be cost effectiveness (CE) ratios; the same unitised focus could be used for an effectiveness-cost (EC) metric.

A particular value of unit-cost methods for purposeful evaluation is that as simple unitised ratios they are readily grasped by evaluation users. Data which shows it costs X amount of money to get one of Y (CE ratio) is easily comprehended, and so more likely to be trusted as an indicator of added-value. However, this places a particular obligation on the evaluator to ensure both careful selection of appropriate metrics and reliable data to calculate them.

This simple representation has drawbacks. It requires a breadth of costs data to aggregate overall costs and robust quantification of the output or outcomes units. This may not be available, or sufficiently robust, for the preferred metrics. Cost-effectiveness will also not be taking account of some of the more complex valuation issues (such as opportunity costs) and may not be able to confidently account for intangibles or social value.

Cost-effectiveness ratios can also be segmented to look at contrasts in added-value for different parts of the same programme, perhaps for different geographies, time periods, participant groups (such as, by age), and/or different participating providers. More ambitiously, where evidence allows for a counterfactual assessment, it is possible to move to contrasts of programme effectiveness against past or alternative actions.

Cost-utility evaluation

'Cost-utility (CU) evaluation' is a specialist variation on cost-effectiveness methods. Researchers have used utility to explain what motivates individual behaviours in areas such as criminology, labour market and human capital studies, but its use as an economic indicator by evaluators has remained largely confined to health and welfare, or social programmes. Nonetheless, it has particular value where an intervention concerns non-market goods or services or for social value outcomes.

This approach sets 'utility' as a quantifiable value (usually to an individual unit) in terms of the total satisfaction experienced by a consumer of goods or services, or to a change in their well-being. It has been used to better understand the relative value of new medical treatments, moving away from traditional output measures such as lives saved or extended years of life, to a patient-centred view based on quality of life. One such metric has been the Quality of Adjusted Life Years (QALYs), another is the 'healthy day equivalent', both expressed as money values. For QUALYs, for example, the measure quantifies a money value for 'quality of additional years' in representing extended life expectancy.

Cost-utility evaluation can be used in different ways, including for multiple potential outcomes perhaps combined into 'single attribute utilities' in a composite assessment. CU can be used comparatively, to assess utility values for a range of attributes, perhaps by using proportional scoring and comparative ranking on a common scale or combined with allocating a relative 'importance' weight for each attribute. One limitation is that in most uses, cost-utility (unlike cost-effectiveness or cost-benefit evaluation) provides the evaluator with little (or no) discretion in choosing the utility measure. How the utility is selected will need to closely reflect the evaluation purpose; this usually involves robust stakeholder engagement to ensure confidence on the utility focus and, critically, its valuation.

As with any economic evaluation, the robustness of this approach will depend on the accuracy (and sufficient breadth) of the costs data used to define attributes. A cost-utility approach best centres on intervention situations, where there is a strong causal association between the action and the effects for which utility is measured. This can mean it is not a confident assessment of utility unless it can demonstrate the quality of causality, perhaps using a sensitivity analysis.

Others have long observed that cost-utility could have wider application in evaluation (Ovretveit, 1998). There have been some developments in this area, such as costs of criminality on the victims of crime and for addiction management programmes, but outside health, these methods are, as yet little used in policy and programme evaluation. In the author's judgement, if stakeholders can be reassured of its value, there is scope for intelligent application of cost-utility evaluation in other areas such as welfare, well-being, mental health optimisation, and other programmes aimed at social value.

Evaluating cost-benefit

Cost-benefit evaluation draws on a long legacy of cost-benefit analytical methods, especially from public programmes. When well-designed, they offer a comprehensive, complexity-sensitive and sophisticated assessment of added-value which can be used ex-ante or ex-post. However, while analytically rich, the data and resource demands mean cost-benefit is not always an appropriate choice. Anyone making choices of an economic evaluation approach needs to be fully conscious of the inherent data and analytical complexities of cost-benefit evaluation if it is to be well-placed and purposeful.

Put simply, cost-benefit evaluation is a framework approach to set total resourcing costs of an intervention against the costed benefits. This is expressed as 'net present value' (NPV) of costs to the NPV for benefits (or vice versa). While it shares common ground with cost-effectiveness and cost-utility methods, cost-benefit goes much further in situating the analysis, its depth and reach to extensively (and effectively) monetise tangible and intangible costs, alongside accountable benefits. Costs and benefits are reduced to a consistent and comparable value metric (usually a common currency unit) to put together an overarching assessment of the net cost-benefit associated with the programme.

This concept may seem quite straightforward, but it is a substantial and demanding ask for a purposeful (economic)

Economic evaluation

evaluation. Cost-benefit evaluation requires a rigorous, multi-faceted and often incremental approach. Judgements will need to be made, across a range of issues, about the particular intervention circumstances and how the evaluation of it is to be used. This in turn will be fuelled by substantial data from and about the programme, and perhaps external comparisons. Put simply, cost-benefit evaluation is not for the incautious.

The core content of what a cost-benefit evaluation needs to cover, compared to cost-effectiveness and cost-utility evaluations is summarised in Table 7.4.

Cost-benefit evaluations often need to go beyond these core elements. Depending on the circumstances of the intervention, and the purpose of the evaluation, it may compare the intervention's cost-benefit NPVs with what might be achieved in alternate

Table 7.4: Comparative (indicative) content of economic evaluations

	Cost-effectiveness evaluation	Cost-utility evaluation	Cost-benefit evaluation
Identify contributory (direct and indirect) resourcing and costs	√	√	√
Determine (and justify) focus for analysis reduction to most significant variables	√	√	√
Quantify monetary values for agreed (currency?) unit for intangible costs	√	√	√
Assess intervention outrun (tangible and intangible benefits) and convert to monetary values (Note: Proxy values where needed)	Limited to select tested benefits	Limited to target benefit utility	√
Conduct sensitivity analyses to validate assumptions (for example, intangibles valuation); adjust NPV correspondingly	Unlikely (limited scope for assumptions)	√	√
Provide reasoned adjustments to benefit values, to account for any opportunity costs	–	–	√
Determine and adjust for cost-benefit influencing externalities	–	–	√

forms of delivery. This may be relatively straightforward where comparative NPVs are readily available from suitable alternatives. If not, external NPV comparisons substantially extend data needs with practical challenges for identifying (and justifying) what alternative delivery is reasonable and relevant, and where stakeholders may have contrasting views.

Cost-benefit evaluation provides a point of time analysis but may need to allow (discount) for any erosion in the duration or value of costs and benefits over time. A common discount will be to allow for inflation, so as to reflect diminishing value of future costs or returns. Other discounts may be less easily accommodated (Rossi et al, 2004). For example, the author advised on a recent complex evaluation of the effects of a new regulatory ban on credit card payments for gambling on unsustainable debt built up by problem and at-risk gamblers. This needed to 'discount' for the likelihood that early debt reductions might reverse over time, as persistent gamblers found substitute forms of accessible credit and borrowing.

All of this will commonly need to be backed up with appropriate sensitivity analysis (as discussed earlier) to justify assumptions. This is especially important to a purposeful cost-benefit evaluation if it is to demonstrate what has conditioned analytical judgements. Without such transparency, cost-benefit evaluators may find users have limited confidence in the overall analysis. In the author's experience, the more complex the analysis, the greater the need to bring prospective users with you in understanding what went into it.

Compared to a cost-effectiveness analysis, cost-benefit evaluation can provide a much more rounded assessment of what is being evaluated. Well-placed and resourced, it can provide for a sophisticated, multi-factor, sensitised and adjusted analysis accounting for tangibles and intangibles to provide for a 'full-frame' picture of the net balance of costs and benefits.

Some cost-benefit inquiries apply adjusted methods of assessing net value including for the use of 'social return on investment' (SROI) analyses. SROI evolved in the US, but has gained currency elsewhere, especially in the third sector. As the name suggests, its focus is on (usually) intangible 'social' value involving, in essence:

- a highly participatory focus to setting and scrutinising a valuation framework;
- a focus on valuing less tangible social and environmental impacts;
- strong multi-stakeholder engagement through the process;
- a theory-guided assessment, often based on a theory of change;
- a sharp focus on valuing priority inputs and outcomes (that is, that are most material to the intervention purpose).

SROI integrates the logic of cost-benefit analysis but modifies this by using seven specific underpinning SROI design principles. Others have written guidance on applying the principles, specific SROI techniques and practice (Nicholls et al, 2012).[5] Their application (and related training) is guided by members of the Social Value UK network (formerly the SROI network) or by guidance on social valuation or SROI in specific areas of application (for example, sports).

Whatever specific approach is put together for cost-benefit methodology, it is going to amount to a tall order, needing significant evaluation resources, extensive direct or proxy data, time, and suitable experience for the necessary rigour, as well as paying particular attention to justifying this type of analysis. Cost-benefit analysis will have great significance to decision-makers where they are confident in the process and findings. Where the intervention is data-rich, with few intangibles (or having pre-existing valuations to apply to them), this may not involve a complex and intensive process. More commonly, it is analytically demanding, requiring caution and extensive consideration for sound monetisation and other judgements if it is to avoid the risks of producing misleading evidence, or findings based on questionable or disputed assumptions.

Some purposeful tips

There is no shortage of pitfalls waiting for the incautious in economic evaluation, with a particular risk that evaluators may be swayed by over-ambition by commissioners for what approach is needed. In purposeful economic evaluation, the evaluator is consequently likely to face an immediate need to better clarify expectations against realism and utility ahead of confirming the necessary approach. Clarification questions also need to be asked of those seeking the work (and providing data) as well as the evaluators, of themselves, for their capability to meet what might be exacting needs. Beyond these broader issues, some practical tips for constructing a purposeful economic evaluation include:

- Be very clear about the evidence (data) potential for meeting the anticipated approach, including reviewing if intervention management information (or other available data) can meet the likely extensive data needs, coverage and consistency.
- Establish (and agree) clear and realistic analytical and evidence boundaries for the scope, and valuation, of constituent costs and benefits, with particular attention for specific priority considerations for decision-making.
- Critically appraise needs and expectations for any external comparative dimension, focusing on situational relevance and data potential.
- Be realistic about the resources needed for collation and manipulation of available data and/or collecting supplementary data to fill gaps with appropriate expectations management with stakeholders.
- Engage stakeholders in making necessary judgements about wider scope and especially for priorities for indirect or variable costs, intangible benefits, and likely externalities for discounts; this is crucial for credible valuation of social benefits.
- Rehearse with stakeholders any technical options for identifying and adjusting for value conditioning factors, including for integration of opportunity costs (for cost-benefit evaluation).
- Consider relying on value ranges rather than absolute values in any reporting of evidence to allow for uncertainty about valuation or conditioning assumptions.

Underneath the precision of economic evaluation approaches lies (a lot of) judgement about what assumptions to make for their analyses. These demands intensify for cost-utility and cost-benefit evaluation, but if any economic evaluation is to be purposeful it will need an open and engaging approach at forging those assumptions. Given some of the technicalities involved this may not be easy and may take time. However, it is crucial to avoid risks not only in the quality of analyses, but also confidence in them.

8

Fully experimental impact evaluation

Introduction

Impact evaluation has a choice of approaches for assessing effect and confronting how much of that change could be due to the intervention being evaluated (attribution). This returns us to the territory of the counterfactual (Chapter 5) where, among the many ways for tackling this, fully experimental methods – that is, randomised control trials (RCTs) – continue to be seen as the purest expression.

Those seeking evidence may refer to hierarchies of evidence quality for counterfactual designs, and these consistently place RCTs at the top of the list as the 'gold standard' (Cook and Campbell, 1979). But, RCTs do not lend themselves to evaluating all situations, and there is a persisting debate and controversy about where they best fit, as well as how much design flexibility is possible without compromising validity. Nonetheless, they have a major role to play in purposeful evaluation as a prospective preferred choice for evaluators.

The appetite for RCTs among many commissioners and users is undiminished and will remain so. However, their enthusiasm is not always grounded in a recognition of their resource and other demands or limitations on effective practice. From time to time, most evaluators will likely face situations where they need to educate and guide funders and users on more realistic aspirations of RCTs alongside alternative options (covered in Chapters 9 and 10).

RCTs and the gold standard

Without taking any credit away from Dr Lund and his maritime experiment for preventing scurvy (Chapter 1), RCTs have rather less deep historic foundations. Their roots are set in the combination of treatment and non-treatment (control) groups, robust management, and randomisation and appropriate 'blinding' which can be traced to the start of the 20th century in the US.[1] Others followed later, notably in medicine, where RCTs became the required standard of proof for clinical and drug trials.

Medical interventions within clinical settings were often favourable to collecting precisely structured, comparable treatment and control data in stable environments. Such RCTs are called (fully) experimental designs, because the evaluator can anticipate the intervention and its influences to set up an 'experimental' inquiry modelled on those which might be used by scientists in a laboratory. RCTs for evaluation in community-based or social settings came much later and are referred to as 'field experiments', differentiating them from RCTs in clinical or other controlled conditions.

This distinction is about a lot more than where a trial is carried out. RCTs conducted in a lab or clinical setting have more scope than field experiments in their set-up, design precision, stability of implementation, and control for non-intervention influences. Applying RCTs to 'field' settings often has much less favourable conditions. Trials for clinical settings can put a lot of time into pre-trial planning (for funding approval), recruitment, organisation and necessary clearances, with this effort carried out well ahead of commencing the trial. In contrast, the start-up of a field experiment is more likely to encounter limited timeframes, pressure for the evaluation to start, or not enough time for necessary set-up planning. Starting an RCT when the intervention is already underway will be especially challenging.

Even with sufficient time and resource for pre-planning, field experiments commonly face greater situational challenges for ensuring the necessary internal and external validity:

- 'Internal validity' refers to the extent to which an observed difference between the two constituent groups of the RCT (the one 'treated' by the intervention and the one not) can be correctly attributed to the intervention. It is about the quality of proof and trustworthiness coming from identifying and demonstrably tackling challenges for assignment, randomisation, and the treatment of disturbances to establish valid 'net' impacts. An RCT with compromised internal validity is likely to under- or overestimate an intervention's 'net' effect(s) and risks misleading decision-makers and users on an intervention's value.

- 'External validity' looks outside what is being evaluated, to the transferable potential for trial findings to other situations. This 'generalisable' potential for RCTs has long been questioned in non-clinical 'field' settings (Guba and Lincoln, 1986; Pawson and Tilley, 1997). This thinking suggests that a well-planned and designed field trial can evidence only that a particular intervention had a particular effect, at a point in time and in specific (usually controlled) circumstances. Since RCTs in social settings face often inherent challenges to isolating tested, usually singular, cause–effect relationships from other non-intervention effects, they commonly face acute challenges to generalisability.

Planning circumstances and validity are not the only considerations in the potential for RCTs Recently, a debate has been started about the merits of RCTs in an era of rapid advances in data science where 'big data' opportunities could revitalise the scope for observational studies over RCTs (Fernainy et al, 2024). This remains a controversial viewpoint, but one with relevance especially where data advances in public and other health systems have led some to question the centrality of RCTs in clinical settings. This is given added currency by any consideration of 'equipoise' as part of ethical justification of an RCT when balancing the potential benefits of a trial with uncertainty about the relative effects of the intervention for participants (discussed later).

Whatever the merits of RCTs vs big data, where clinical trials take place, these can have scope to better allow for challenges to validity by constructing controlled environments in which an RCT takes place. In social settings this is much more difficult; where an RCT attempts to do so (for example, artificially sheltering the RCT 'units' from non-intervention influences), this risks a knock-on effect, distorting internal validity and generalisability. These application constraints are not endorsed by all; enthusiasts for RCTs see allowing for causal complexity or confounding variables as largely a matter of effective randomisation and trial design.

These different positions on the fit and utility of RCTs especially in field settings can understandably confuse many new to the evaluation community. They can also harden the perspectives of those more experienced. This should take away nothing from RCTs as the pinnacle of the evidence hierarchy, but the considerations touched on here emphasise the high bar set for its situation, planning and validity. A purposeful evaluation approach will acknowledge RCTs as a gold standard, but only where its design can be well-placed (Oakley et al, 2006; Moore et al, 2015). Where they are not, evaluators need the knowledge and confidence to argue and opt for other modes.

This chapter has only so much scope to consider details of RCT design. Looking along a path well-trodden by others suggests common ground that, to be purposeful, RCT designs should be applied with rigour and robustness to ensure in particular:

- the approach to randomisation is strong and well-conditioned;
- the choice of control groups and assignment is relevant and reliable;
- the design choices and implementation have ethical integrity;
- there is initial and persisting attention to the integrity and validity of the design.

There are other considerations in the confident fit and design of RCTs[2] but these four areas are cornerstones. The principles behind these, and their necessary combination, are simple. The practice is not, and each is looked at in the rest of this chapter.

Randomisation in practice: units and designs

As experimental methods, RCTs rely on fixed designs to provide for:

- Recruitment of an appropriately large number of eligible participating units relevant to measuring the intervention effect

(what is 'appropriate' for scale and appropriation is discussed in the next section).
- Division of units for treatment and non-treatment (control) groups with probability-based, randomised assignment to the two groups so one mirrors the other.
- Introduction and management of the intervention to the two assigned groups over an appropriate timeframe, where both the treatment and non-treatment groups are actively managed as part of the overall trial.
- Setting agreed design, management and application protocols for the trial to ensure influences (beyond the intervention itself) which might affect outcomes are minimised (and if they occur, are identified and adjusted for in the analysis).
- Uniform collection (and analysis) of appropriate outcome(s) indicator evidence and conditioning data to statistically contrast (and validate) the different effects for the intervention and non-intervention groups.

There is no lack of literature on trial design and set-up. One of the more accessible is the so-called 'nine-step' approach to design, implement and adapt an RCT as summarised in Figure 8.1. This puts considerable emphasis on the inputs and sequences needed to start the design through careful positioning (stage 1), foresight on focus and boundaries (stage 2 and 3), attention to detail in anticipating necessary scale for its integrity (stage 4), and the requirements and practice for setting-up two active parts of the evaluation – the treatment group, and its counterpart, the non-treatment group (stage 5). There are various RCT designs for how to go about this (Boruch et al, 2009); making an appropriate choice among them is at the heart of the robustness of their use.

The 'units' engaged in the trial are its participants – often people, but perhaps other units (such as social or commercial enterprises) or geographical units (such as defined plots or fields in an agricultural trial). A trial recognises that, however well unit involvement is defined, those engaged will almost certainly not be homogeneous. Engagement in a trial involving 18–25-year-olds in mental health advice and counselling, for example, may well be consistent in their age group eligibility, but will have many other differences. These might include different conditions and

Figure 8.1: The 'nine-step' approach to an RCT

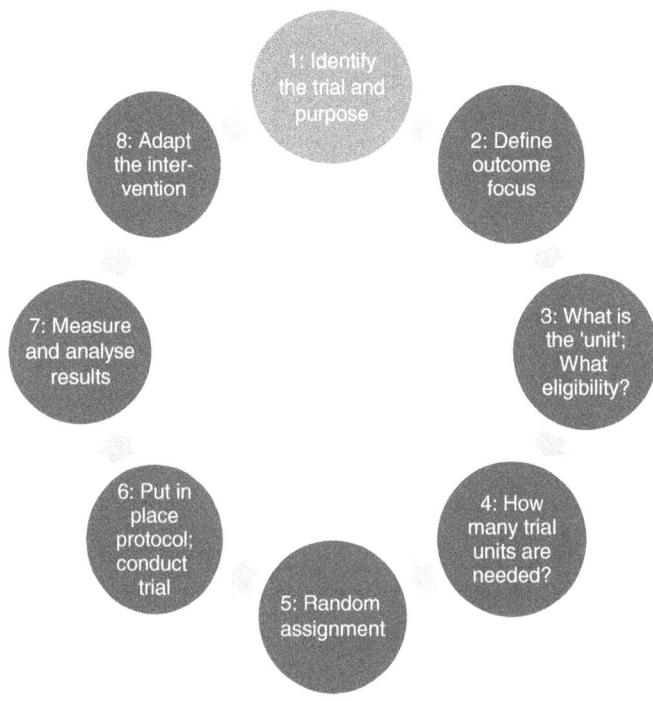

Source: Adapted from the Behavioural Insights Team model produced for the UK Cabinet Office

incapacity from their current mental health, ability to access other support services (locally or functionally), previous experience of mental health illness or support, and values affecting expectations and willingness to engage. This will be alongside the plethora of demographic and socio-economic characteristics which might in some way affect their quality of engagement and use of what is being tested.

Without sufficient attention, these differences may also be differently distributed between the treatment and non-treatment group; this will risk compromising the quality of the RCT. The risks of such bias are inherent to any RCT; avoiding (or mitigating) them is at the centre of good design. Randomisation is the key tool for this in the assignment of units into treatment and non-treatment groups to, in effect, construct each as models in miniature of each other. Randomising means any individual unit will have an equal chance of assignment into the intervention or its control group. Done well, this means inter-group differences will be equally distributed within each group, minimising selection biases. The quality of randomisation consequently needs to be given robust and appropriate[3] attention for the internal validity of an RCT.

There are different ways to approach all this. In social settings, two of the most common, involve either:

- 'Individual RCTs' (i-RCTs): This is a simple and commonly used approach involving parallel assignment, with randomised selection for each individual engaged unit of participants to the treatment or control group.
- 'Cluster RCTs' (c-RCTs): In c-RCTs, the unit of selection is not single individual participants, but a cluster group of them. For example, a trial of a new school attainment programme might see assigned units as a whole entry cohort, class or tutor group, not individuals. This can be useful where there may be ethical constraints to selecting individuals (for example, those under the age for individual consent) or if data for randomisation is best collected in groups.

Other assignment choices can be used in more complicated intervention circumstances:

- 'Cross-over designs': These are a version of a 'factorial design' which is useful where the intervention may be made up of several constituent activities. To use an RCT here, units in the intervention will be assigned to different individual activities in a sequential manner, where only the order of intervention (who does what and when) is randomly assigned. This 'cross-over' will mean each participant will act as their own control for when they are engaged, and when they are not. These can be useful for formative evaluations, although breaking up the intervention group into these necessarily smaller activity groups may reduce overall reliability. Cross-over designs are consequently often combined with a separate summative and aggregate 'follow on' trial of a final version of the intervention.

This adds time and cost, which may not be available in many evaluation circumstances.
- 'Step-wedge designs': These are a pragmatic response, where the intervention does not provide for simultaneous treatment of some participants. For example, the intervention may be a phased design, applied at small-scale first in some areas, and gradually rolled out to others. The 'step-wedge' copes with this by engaging participants in different cohorts or 'waves' across the different sites or with these usually staggered (stepped) across the intervention. These are another form of cross-over design, where those not initially involved will act as the control for those that are, but where the cross-over will be in one direction, usually from control to intervention.

This is not an exhaustive list of randomisation and assignment choices. Other variants of RCTs also exist (Shadish et al, 2004) for interventions in social settings, all relying on this quality of randomisation.

Control groups, assignment and blinding

Randomisation cannot control for all forms of bias, or misrepresentation of outcome effects, in an RCT. Technical guidance on designing RCTs gives this more detailed consideration than is possible here, along with some domain specific reviews, such as in education (Torgerson and Torgerson, 2008a). Instead, we focus on four of the more common issues to be allowed for:

- appropriate sample size applied to the trial baseline
- sampling considerations to avoid 'chance bias'
- management of participation attrition
- blinding and allocation concealment

Trial size

RCTs need an appropriately large sample size to guarantee adequate precision. With enough 'statistical power', this credibly concludes the scale of the causal effect of what is being tested, with an acceptable degree of confidence (from statistical testing) that the results can be applied to a similar population. This precision is likely to decrease with small samples, especially where the effect size is small (Example 10). If sample size is insufficient, the trial is not in a position to say one way or another whether the intervention has or has not worked and decision-makers will regard the trial resources have been wasted.

Example 10: SMALL 'N' RCTS – SMALL SAMPLE SIZES MEAN LITTLE OR NO CONFIDENCE IN PROOF OF EFFECT

An RCT was conducted in a central European country to assess health effects of high daily diet levels of flavonoids. These are naturally occurring compounds in many plant products with antioxidant properties. Clinical evidence shows that individuals who have had heart attacks or strokes can reduce future risks by consuming high levels of flavonoids. The trial aimed to demonstrate if this effect could also reduce cardio-vascular risks in a healthy population.

The RCT used clinical measures of cardio-vascular health (CVH) as an outcome proxy for future propensity; improvements in CVH were taken to indicate reduced future risk of heart attack or stroke. The RCT recruited eligible volunteers randomised to treatment and non-treatment groups, each taking baseline and post-trial clinical CVH level tests. The trial set a protocol for a specified daily consumption level and frequency of supplied dietary juice; the treatment group citrus fruit juice had high levels of flavonoids and the non-treatment a vegetable juice with minimal levels. Both groups were 'blinded' (that is, they were not aware of their allocation group), and observed through self-completion checks for any changes in behaviour or non-compliance.

At its conclusion, the post test showed the treatment group had an average effect in aggregated CVH measures of +4.7% over the non-treatment group. The sample size for both groups was, however, just 51 people each; the results were not statistically significant. The RCT consequently could not show if flavonoids did or did not impact cardio-vascular health.

The costs of an RCT will always put pressure on reducing the sample size to an effective minimum. Optimum size will depend, in particular, on the likely (anticipated) effect size from the trial,[4] trial design (for example, clustered or not), and the logistics and complexity of the intervention. It will also be influenced by the data breakdowns needed, such as separate results for different parts of the country. Making the choice of sample size needs an RCT design to carry out power calculations,[5] usually drawing on pre-trial data or past research (or evaluations) to show the optimum sample size required to detect the likely effect.

Chance bias

The best planned RCTs may still encounter allocation or selection mishaps, and these potential biases can creep into designs unnoticed. While end-of-trial adjustment might be possible, 'chance bias' risks the RCT's internal validity and are better countered before they become problems. More sophisticated sampling (for selected characteristics) can go some way towards this. This might use allocation stratification based on 'prognostic factors' of those features of the participating population most likely to be associated with the intended outcome not being achieved if there was no intervention (Box 8.1).

Box 8.1: Using prognostic factors to reduce risks of 'chance bias'

The earlier example of the flavonoids RCT might have reduced the risk of chance bias by stratifying assignment to the treatment and non-treatment group through prognostic factors. Hypothetically, they might have identified participants with low incomes, as a prognostic factor. This would anticipate those on low incomes would be less likely to have improving indicators of cardio-vascular health had they not participated, due to high-priced fresh fruit and vegetables. These would then normally be underrepresented in their usual diet.

With low income as a prognostic factor, and if their sample size had been much larger, the RCT could have stratified the allocation-based on income strata (for example, low, medium and high) for both treatment and non-treatment groups. This would avoid the 'chance' that (unstratified) this could become a bias in the trial.

This RCT might not have stopped there. Complex stratification can allow for several prognostic factors, although with the consequence that the overall sample size will need to be greater.

Attrition

Most trials lose some participants as they go along; the longer the duration of the trial, then the more likely attrition will substantially erode participation. Attrition is not likely to be evenly distributed, so by the trial end it will lead to a delayed selection bias. This will be intensified if loss rates (and characteristics) are different between the treatment and non-treatment groups. The best approach to tackling attrition bias is to avoid it as much as possible by motivating continuing engagement, encouraging attendance at any end of trial (post) tests, and applying this evenly across participation. If the scope for minimising attrition is limited, evaluators can anticipate the need to adjust by carrying out (baseline) pre-test equivalence comparisons of key participant characteristics of both groups and subsequently contrasting the erosion.[6]

'Blinding'

'Blinding' aims to counter risks of 'unconscious bias' in the trial, where participants may change behaviours (and distort outcomes) if they are aware of whether they are in the treatment or a non-treatment group. For example, participants in a novel service or therapy trial might be more likely to be motivated to engage constructively, when realising they are recipients of whatever is being innovated, than those in the non-treatment group receiving 'standard' service or care. Outcomes from the treatment group could then be inflated (or conversely those for the non-treatment group depressed), distorting the accuracy of the counterfactual.

Blinding may sometimes need to involve both participants and any practitioners working with them. It is easier to achieve in clinical than in social settings, especially in situations where it will be inevitable that participants know whether or not they are subject to the treatment. A control group for a trial of a new education programme may be very well aware that they are not receiving the intervention – and vice versa. Where 'blinding' is not possible, it does not mean an RCT is not possible, but there will need to be a robust approach to pre-trial allocation concealment. This falls short of comprehensive blinding, but it will mean neither providers nor participants will be aware if the next eligible participant will be receiving treatment or in the control until that participant is ready to receive the intervention.

Ethical integrity and evaluation of participation risk

Ethics in evaluation requires the appropriate design and proper conduct of the inquiry to take account of cultural norms, practice and professional ethical standards. This needs to be a feature of any evaluation design (Chapter 4), but the nature of RCTs means ethical demands are intensified. One overriding consideration in trial ethics merits particular attention – the assessment of justifiable utility, risk and benefit to the participants and how these are balanced in the design for:

- pre-trial (and pre-approval) assessment of justifiable utility;
- consideration of the risk of harm to and the safety of those involved;
- embedding appropriate consent procedures, to provide ethical integrity;
- compliance with ethical oversight at design and through implementation.

Justifiable utility

Because an RCT is being asked for, or appears to be technically possible, this does not mean it is ethically justifiable. Before setting up, and often as part of the ethical approval process, it may be necessary to assess whether it is ethical to conduct the evaluation as envisaged. This exercise may need to justify 'equipoise'[7] to demonstrate whether the potential for harm (as next section), especially to participants, can be justified by its utility. This might consider, for example, if a similar trial had been conducted in the recent past and, if so, would an alternative non-trial approach be better placed? It might also need to look at the specific design issues, such as ethical assignment and randomisation, and the implications for denying access to what is being trialled to some participants.

Risk of harm and safety considerations

Chapter 4 has set out that avoiding identified harms to those taking part is a key ethical consideration for all evaluation. For RCTs, in particular, risks of harm may be intensified because RCTs' design will deny access to some participants to actions within the intervention that might otherwise benefit them. This will require consideration of what harms might arise – for both treatment and non-treatment groups, sharing these with funders, partners and prospective participants (as next sections) and setting these out (with mitigations) to the ethical approval process. The trial will also build in a monitoring mechanism, to identify any additional harms or unacceptably high frequency of adverse events which might result in the early closure of the trial.

Consent

In some situations, RCTs may not require individual (or proxy) consent from participants, but most will. These arrangements need to be uniform and consistently applied. They must also provide sufficient information to those asked for consent so individuals are able to make an informed choice to be involved (or not). This much is common to any evaluation, but RCTs may have additional ethical considerations, for example, the need for, and implications of, the assignment process and randomisation may need to be explained.

Ethical oversight

An external assessment of ethical compliance starts but does not end with an ethical approval process. RCTs are well-advised to integrate external oversight, throughout their conduct (and reporting). Such oversight may be supplementary to any steering arrangements and will support decisions to be made during implementation, such as what is appropriate (or culturally sensitive) to ask in evaluation questions, what protocols are needed for compliance, and what in-trial monitoring is in place to identify and manage emergent harms.

RCTs are at greater risk of ethical complications than other evaluation methods. The evaluator may not always be able to determine what processes are put in place to mitigate these, especially where the commissioners have set procedures. However, they have an obligation to go the extra mile, in working within any required process, to ensure ethical integrity for their own professional standards and to safeguard the evaluation against likely reduced confidence in its findings, or failure, if ethical considerations are neglected.

Managing threats to validity

Social settings for RCTs will mean that 'good' design cannot anticipate all threats to validity, but it can go a long way towards this by building in responses to the more common threats:

- inappropriate responses to the high costs of RCTs
- trial management and integrity
- unintended outcomes
- confounding factors – 'Hawthorne' and 'John Henry' effects

Inappropriate responses to the high costs of RCTs

All evaluations face challenges to 'cut the cloth' of what's done to fit the available budget; for RCTs, these can be acute. Trials have considerable resource demands to ensure necessary scale, quality management and integrity, and are often at greater risk of (inappropriately) cutting corners to meet budget pressures.

Reducing sample sizes to save costs, for example, may mean that confidence to estimate effect sizes is impaired, as might be the trial's ability to identify effect contrasts in different populations. Both will greatly constrain utility. The solution lies with articulating and negotiating trade-offs to manage expectations of users downwards: 'If we reduce sample size by X, we will save Y, but will not be able to provide breakdown data to show differences for A and B.'

Trial management and integrity

RCTs are fixed designs guided by well-set delivery and management arrangements, but the best planned trials cannot avoid some risks to compliance or disturbance. They consequently need ongoing, sound management to identify and counter integrity risks. This starts with minimising integrity challenges and bias by avoiding as many as possible in the first place, through putting in place a robust trial protocol which is:

- comprehensive in anticipating likely implementation risks;
- thorough, accessible and well-expressed to provide for consistent application;
- pre-briefed to those implementing the RCT to ensure understanding.

A 'good' protocol is unlikely to eliminate all risks to non-compliance, so trial management needs to put in place early identification for dealing with non-compliance as the trial progresses and for appropriate adjustments. Excluding non-compliant cases is a common adjustment, but evaluators should take care this does not introduce other internal validity biases, such as assignment imbalances between treatment and non-treatment groups.[8]

Unobserved and unintended outcomes

RCTs put a lot of effort into identifying and defining the outcome for the focus of the trial (factorial designs might define more than one). This precludes taking into account unobserved or unintended outcomes. While the sharp focus enables a robust assessment of the (singular) effect, it may present a misleading picture of impacts of an intervention, which in social settings may be much more diverse and not all of which will be positive for the effectiveness of the intervention.

Making no allowance for unconsidered effects is not a risk to internal validity and may be completely consistent with commissioners' focus on specific intended effects. However, it fails to provide a more rounded assessment of impacts and as such further weakens the external validity. This need not be the inevitable result of the trial precision. The RCT could be complemented by a more plural approach, perhaps accompanying it with qualitative 'nested' work, separate from the trial participation to identify other outcomes. Another alternative might be to add a post-test survey of participants, to identify outcomes that were not a priority for the trial, or unintended effects, to estimate other consequences.

Confounding factors

Any impact evaluation is likely to be affected by influences beyond those intended in the intervention on the outcomes assessed. These 'confounding factors' are a persistent headache for analysis but have particular significance for RCTs because, as fixed designs, they look at what they are targeted to assess not outcomes influences beyond those. RCTs are consequently not well-placed to take account of confounding variables, making it difficult to establish a clear causal link between intervention and outcome.

Confounding variables come in all shapes and sizes, and may well operate unevenly across the trial population, affecting participants with particular situations or characteristics more or less than others. Most trials in social settings deal directly or indirectly with people, who are heterogeneous and likely to behave in different ways to the same stimulus. Confounding variables are consequently often different behavioural responses and where 'Hawthorne' and 'John Henry' effects have long been recognised as illustrations (Example 11).

Example 11: CONFOUNDING VARIABLES – THE EXAMPLES OF 'HAWTHORNE' AND 'JOHN HENRY' EFFECTS

The Hawthorne effect

This is named after an early use of experimental methods in the 1920s and '30s reviewing productivity enhancements at the US Western Electric's plant at Hawthorne, Chicago. Various RCTs, led by Elton Mayo, observed the impacts on assigned panels of employees of specific tested changes to physical workplace environments (for example, raised shop floor lighting levels). The RCTs showed consistently significant improvements to productivity in the intervention groups and also some gains to other unintended consequences, such as reduced absenteeism.

Much later analysis, however, demonstrated the need to control for confounding variables. At the Hawthorne plant, initially untested behavioural influences showed the major effect on productivity had not been changed working conditions, but motivational enhancements and raised workplace morale. This resulted from enhanced drive and self-direction, consequent on worker perceptions that management was concerned about their workplace conditions and was engaging them in the process. This has come to be known as the 'Hawthorne effect' which encourages experimental methods to set the individual in a social context to allow for confounding factors such as behavioural influences.

John Henry effect

The John Henry effect refers to an experimental bias from self-awareness of participation exclusion or disadvantage (in control groups) leading to unintended effects. It is named after a railroad 'steel-driver' and Black-American folk hero of the mid-19th century, who was engaged in a competition to contrast machine–human performance. The effect accounts for his response to hearing his rate of work was being compared with that of a steam-powered machine drill; he then worked so hard to outperform the machine that he subsequently died of a heart attack. If the consequence for John Henry was extreme, the effect is named after him as an unintended motivational consequence from knowledge of the control assignment.

As with unintended consequences, a picture of confounding variables and their effects on the intervention can be built up by post-RCT qualitative work, to assess non-intervention influences on outcomes.

Some purposeful tips

There is no shortage of potential pitfalls to befall incautious (or unlucky) implementation of RCTs. Some may come from poor preparation or from risks of snags occurring that had not been planned for or anticipated. Forewarned is forearmed and some of the more purposeful tips to avoid pitfalls include:

- Ensuring a well-purposed and precisely defined primary outcome is set as the trial's targeted (measurable) effect. Appropriate outcome measures are not always self-evident, and these should be guided by stakeholders' discussions, scoping research and practical considerations of what measurable effect is most appropriate to target.
- Providing an appropriate timeframe for the target outcome (effect) to be achieved and resisting pressures for (too) early assessment. Outcomes may have long lead times and trial timeframes need to reflect this for effect size to be realistically measured.
- Reflecting the necessary scale and composition of the trial in adequate budgetary provision over the trial duration to minimise risk to 'forced' realignment or reduction from later budget limitations and consequent threats to validity and confidence.
- Avoiding overconfidence about the expertise or skill-mix needed. Some evaluator humility is well advised to meet the

exacting demands of RCT design, management and analysis, combined with harnessing experience from outside the evaluation team.
- Paying close attention to the groundwork needed for robust randomisation and allocation to avoid validity threats from compromised 'population' data on participant units, inaccurate or incomplete sampling, or inappropriate adjustment for selection bias.
- Paying particular attention in cross-over or similar designs to overlapping issues which might also threaten allocation or selection biases, or introduce overlapping influences from current (or past) practice.
- Ensuring continuous, protocol-guided attention to detail within the trial conduct to anticipate, identify and respond early to any integrity challenges (for example, attrition; non-compliance) and providing for transparency about these in analysis and reporting.

Perhaps the greatest pitfall to using an RCT, is a forced fit to circumstances where they are not appropriate. For RCTs to justify their place at the top of the evidence hierarchy, they have a lot of application and integrity conditions to satisfy; a 'good enough' design is not good enough for the level of effect proof demanded of an RCT. Many interventions in social contexts will not fit all of these requirements, so rather than attempt to fit a square peg into a round hole, the evaluator has many other method pathways to look at as either combinations (with an RCT) or as alternatives.

9

Quasi-experimental impact evaluation

Introduction

The gold standard of applying fully experimental methods is not open to all, or many, impact evaluations, especially in social settings. Where there are barriers to RCTs, it is widely possible to use quasi-experimental designs (QEDs) applying well-chosen comparison groups instead of control groups. As their name implies, quasi-experimental approaches are not as rigid as RCTs in their requirements and set-up. With fewer constraints to the circumstances where they can apply, they offer much greater choice and flexibility for purposeful evaluation.

Making that choice, however, comes with a need for sound judgement across the many QED options open to impact evaluators. QEDs may lack the counterfactual precision of fully experimental methods, but sound choice and application of a robust QED approach can offer a level of proof of effect sufficient to satisfy many user demands for quantifying attribution. In practice, different options present different trade-offs between flexibility, simplicity and reliability, and contrasting pros and cons. This chapter introduces many of those options, their merits and challenges to help evaluators make a 'best choice' of this high-utility approach to counterfactual insight and analysis.

What are 'natural experiments'?

QEDs are sometimes grouped together as 'natural' experiments. This term cannot cover all QED options, but it serves to separate the constructed 'controls' (that is, non-treatment groups) of RCTs, from the use of available 'natural' comparators, often adopted from outside an intervention. An evaluation asked to look at the effect of a pilot intervention on a disadvantaged group in one location might look for a comparison from a similar needs group in a close-fit 'comparator' geographical area where the intervention was not taking place. To be sufficiently robust, the chosen comparator would need to be closely matched to the pilot area in socio-economic and other characteristics: it would be a 'natural comparator'.

Ideas about quasi-experimental techniques have been developing in the six decades since their potential in social policy research was proposed (Campbell and Stanley, 1963). Various options for exploiting them have emerged, sharing a common feature of setting findings for outcomes in an intervention population against the same outcomes in a (usually) concurrent comparator. The contrast between control groups (in RCTs) and selected comparators in QEDs goes further than terminology. A control group in an RCT is an active part of the trial itself and provides an *embedded* counterfactual through a direct measure of what would otherwise have happened if the intervention had not taken place. In contrast, a comparator is drawn typically from *outside* the intervention so is not an active part of it. It is a proxy for 'what would otherwise have happened' and not a direct control: 'A control group [in an RCT] is actively selected and is an active part of the evaluation of the intervention; a comparator is also actively selected, but is only a passive part of the evaluation' (Parsons, 2017).

This difference is fundamental but, unfortunately, the lexicon of impact evaluation is used inconsistently. Some commissioners refer to control groups when they mean comparators; some merge the two referring to more and less robust controls. This loose use of terms is not helpful for those new to impact evaluation; a control is what it is, and a comparator is something different. Each has very different implications for method, the eventual reliability of a counterfactual, and for meeting the intended purpose of findings.

Using natural comparators in impact evaluation has the great advantage of much greater application flexibility than control approaches because of three main practical considerations:

- They do not require randomisation. The intervention being evaluated is open to eligible participation and does not need a constructed approach to assignment (or randomisation); the comparator group(s) will harness existing (natural) evidence and is also not randomised.
- They can readily be used to look at multi-activity interventions where the constituent actions combine to make up the whole intervention. Those actions may not be applied evenly over time or across participants, perhaps with some targeted at specific needs, eligibility groups or participant circumstances. QEDs focus on the whole intervention, irrespective of how many actions it constitutes. It is unlikely to quantify attribution effects of separate actions within the whole intervention but will collectively assess effects across them. Exploration of separate action effects may be possible from well-aligned supplementary qualitative methods.
- The focus of QEDs on quantifying effect (and attribution) can readily accommodate an explanatory element using qualitative evidence because they are not constrained by blinding participation. Those receiving the intervention in a QED will likely recognise they are taking part, so there is no impediment to involving (some of) them in parallel case studies or supplementary interviews, to probe for how and why effects come about.

Although more flexible, QEDs are not a substitute for RCTs. They come into play where RCTs are not workable, eligible (ethical considerations), or appropriate, but that flexibility comes at a price. Using comparators outside the intervention, and non-randomisation, means they cannot offer the strength of proof of a well-placed RCT.

Nonetheless, QEDs are valuable alternatives, especially where purposeful evaluation calls for the inquiry to assess effect measurement and also understanding (Chapter 5). There are various QED pathways for the evaluator to explore – and choose between. These options offer different approaches to constructing and using comparators, each with different merits and limitations; some have wide potential for use, others are more restricted to very specific intervention circumstances. To avoid confusion between the choices it helps to simplify the differences by grouping the main QED options as:

- concurrent matched comparators
- difference-in-difference designs
- eligibility cut-off regression discontinuity designs

This loose categorisation is not comprehensive and a case could be made for including parallel time series, although potential and space mitigates against this here. Other comparator approaches are not 'natural' comparators and are considered separately for 'synthetic control designs' and constrained designs, referred to here as 'fall-back comparators' for reasons which will become clear.

Matched comparator groups

These are a mainstay of quasi-experimental designs offering a flexible approach to selecting one or more external comparators to what, where and for whom the intervention is being applied. Some of the more useful 'matched' comparator methods include:

- matched variable comparators
- phased comparators
- intermittent application comparisons

Each involves different ways of selecting a 'natural' comparator; some with higher reliability than others. For all, quality will depend largely on the energy and effort to pick the 'best' comparator. In purposeful evaluation, this will need at least some negotiation with funders and users, on comparator appropriateness to circumstance and utility.

Matched variable comparators

This common comparator approach can be used where the intervention takes place in just one (or a few) specific geographical area(s), as is often the case for programme or policy pilots. Choice of a suitable comparator sets the key features of the intervention area and/or group against those of possible comparators to demonstrate the quality of a match, although this need not be restricted to a single choice. In situations where there may be some risk to comparability, it may increase the evaluation quality (and reduce risks) to select more than one comparator.

Typically, the variables used for matching may include demographic, socio-economic, spatial or other intervention-relevant characteristics, usually involving multiple variables. This needs evaluator time to determine the variable mix, source and put together the matching data to then identify close matches. That data then steers choice of comparator(s) and perhaps demonstrates the quality of what is proposed to advisory or steering groups. An illustration from a past evaluation led by the author is summarised in Example 12.

Example 12: QEDS AND MATCHED COMPARATORS – SELECTING GEOGRAPHICAL COMPARATORS USING MATCHED VARIABLES

Example 3 (Chapter 2) set out the evaluation planning for the UK 'super casino'. For the intended quasi-experimental approach, this needed an appropriate socio-economic geographic comparator to the location (Leeds). For the necessary quality of 'matching', this needed to take into account demographic contrasts (for example, density, trend, ethnicity and age structure), labour market and social characteristics, gambling activity (prevalence), levels of 'at risk' and 'problem' gambling, as well as possible sourcing and quality of the data needed at sub-region and metropolitan level.

Data on these variables came from a range of national sources (Office of National Statistics), local government data (for example, deprivation indexes), and from two national surveys of gambling activity which included prevalence and 'problem' gambling data (where sample sizes provided for comparisons between UK metropolitan areas). A total of 27 matching variables were selected (and agreed with the steering group) and data put together, to contrast the Leeds distribution to the comparative distribution data for each for all eligible urban areas.

Unsurprisingly, no single other urban area provided a precise match on all 27 variables. Matching was then subject to a distribution variance assessment for each variable. A 40pp 'matching' report to share selected 'close match' recommendations was shared with the steering group and five closely matched urban areas were selected as suitable for weighted comparators for the QED. The whole matching process took five weeks.

Pre-participation group

Interventions are not always applied simultaneously across the intended application for logistical or resourcing reasons. They may be phased-in for different start times, localities or circumstances through successive participation 'waves' (cohorts), often with 'pathfinder' areas preceding wider roll-out. Where this occurs, a comparator can be drawn from a close-match pre-participation area. This is similar to a cross-over RCT without the randomisation of the pre-participation group. Such comparators are suitable where what is being implemented rolls out but does not change over time, and where expected outcomes occur on a relatively short timescale (that is, before the comparison joins any wider roll-out).

With sufficient attention to the quality of match, these are probably the more robust methods for selecting QED comparators using matched variables. Other possible matching approaches, where internal validity may be constrained, include:

- 'Phased interventions', which may roll out planned activities to different areas over time and where a pre-participation area may provide a 'non-intervention' comparator. This can be useful where the intervention circumstances, and activities involved, do not change over time.
- 'Intermittent application', which may see interventions involving usually short-term phases of 'on-off' activity with actions taking place at different times in different areas. Here,

QED methods could match 'quiet' areas at a specific point of time with active areas.
- 'Voluntary opt-out comparators', which might select a unit which chose to opt out of engaging with an intervention, especially where reasons for opting out are known and can be adjusted in final analyses.
- 'Parallel modality comparisons', where a concurrent comparison group is selected from a diversified intervention (or a parallel intervention) where the actions have very similar goals, but different delivery modalities.
- 'Administrative or close match eligibility comparators', where comparators may be selected from a 'near' age or status group, not eligible to take part in what is being evaluated, but very close in its characteristics.

For very small-scale (small-n) evaluations, it may even be possible to use matched pairs (that is, an individual beneficiary with a non-involved 'twin'), although the statistical power of such comparisons will be limited. Table 9.1 summarises some of the strengths and limitations of different matching options.
Obviously, the weaker comparator designs will not be a first choice but will come into play where more robust alternatives are not possible. They will have lower internal validity and poor generalisable potential, but they may offer a better fall-back choice than 'constrained comparators' (looked at later). Opting for lower strength comparators will have implications for user confidence so, for purposeful evaluation, the QED choice will need explaining and justifying to funders and key stakeholders.

Difference-in-difference

Difference-in-difference (DID) is a highly credible QED design – and possibly a first port of call for such a design, where suitable comparisons and data can support it. Its value for purposeful evaluation lies with its more reliable quantification of counterfactual effect, bringing together matched comparator approaches (as discussed in the previous sections) with a 'before-and-after' analysis. This combined time and spatial comparisons so is sometimes referred to as 'double difference'. This econometric

Table 9.1: Options for matched comparator designs

	Strengths	Limitations
Matched variable comparators	• Strong capability, especially for pilots or single-site interventions • Can use multiple variables to optimise comparator quality • Credible and easily comprehended by users	• Not suitable with national or wide intervention coverage • Needs high-quality data for matching • User endorsement of comparator risks political or other sensitivities
Pre-implementation comparators	• Suited to interventions with well-defined phased roll-out with sufficient outcome lead time between start-waves	• Not suitable if outcome lead time durations are longer than wave phases • Unsuitable with inter-phased changes or improvements • Requires consistent eligibility and delivery between waves
Intermittent comparators	• May be only QED choice for intermittent activity interventions	• Not suitable with changes between intervention intervals • Requires separation of effect between interval waves
Opt-in–opt-out comparator	• Common possibility with open invited participation to intervention • Sampling within 'in'/'out' groups can improve comparison quality	• Likely to need large opt-out sample sizes to ensure adequate matches • Opt-out population may be reluctant to cooperate • Subject to comparator bias from reasons for opt-out (limited internal validity where these cannot be controlled for)
Parallel modalities	• Comparators will be engaged in current/recent actions so likely to be motivated to engage • Some outcome/situation data for comparators may be available from monitoring or past evaluation	• Needs close fit of modality for comparability • Subject to unobserved situational and behavioural contrasts from comparators • May lack intrinsic comparability for users (not comparing like with like actions)
Close match eligibility	• Close match possibilities are likely, since most interventions will have defined eligibility	• Close match will lack coherence with eligible participants, so weak potential for internal validity • Greater challenges for user credibility in comparator

Quasi-experimental impact evaluation

method works by contrasting the before-and-after difference for an intervention group with the same before-and-after difference for a comparator group (not in the intervention) over two or more specific and concurrent time periods. Its strength comes from how it counters the limitations of a single spatial or a before and after comparison if they were to be used separately.

As an illustration of the respective limitations of using either method on its own, a matched comparator QED for a new welfare programme being piloted in one place would set outcomes there against those from a comparable area (that is, one which had elected not to take part). This would provide a counterfactual estimate from that difference, but could not allow for unobserved influences, such as reasons why the comparator chose not to take part. If the evaluator chose instead to use as an alternative, a 'before-and-after' approach, this would use 'start to end' outcome contrasts within the pilot area alone. This would have larger bias, since this 'distance travelled' contrast could not account for non-intervention influences occurring over that time. Both methods provide an estimate of the counterfactual, but both, used on their own, have limitations.

DID addresses those limitations by combining the two methods at the same time. By looking at the 'before-and-after' change in the intervention group, this controls for outcome influences over time in that group, because it is comparing itself with itself. However, that cannot allow for time-varying influences. To tackle those, DID brings in the comparator area to assess changes for the same outcome variable over the same time period. Merging the two assessments controls for both comparator and time distortion – hence 'difference-in-difference'. Example 13 illustrates how this works from an early use in the US (Card and Krueger, 1994).

Example 13: HARNESSING 'DIFFERENCE-IN-DIFFERENCE' – AN EVALUATION OF THE IMPACT OF THE ENHANCED MINIMUM WAGE IN NEW JERSEY, 1992

Minimum wage legislation in the US has more complex arrangements than for other major economies, with the baseline wage levels prescribed by a combination of federal, state, and local laws. In April 1992, New Jersey's minimum wage rose from $4.25 to $5.05 an hour. Card and Krueger evaluated the possible negative employment impacts of the higher minimum wage on lower paid sectors using DID, then a novel technique.

Card and Krueger compared employment in the retail fast food sector in New Jersey between February and November 1992 with that in Eastern Pennsylvania, where the minimum wage level remained constant. Data from 410 fast food retail outlets across the two areas showed changes in employment levels over the period for employers previously paying near the higher wage level (at $5) and those under.

Their DID method recognised that observing before-and-after changes in establishment level (aggregate) employment in New Jersey outlets would not control for other factors, such as macroeconomic (and weather) conditions of the region. By retaining the over-time outcome change in New Jersey and contrasting it to Eastern Pennsylvania as a comparator (over the same sector and period), bias caused by job-level influences common to both areas would be allowed for. This recognised that New Jersey and Pennsylvania would have parallel influence trends over the same time period – the parallel trend assumption.

The Card and Krueger DID analysis showed that the New Jersey increased minimum wage did not lead to a fall in full-time equivalent (FTE) employment in its fast food outlets. In fact, contrary to some economic theorists, they estimated that the 19 per cent rise in the minimum wage increase led to a modest increase in employment.

Note: This summary is drawn from the published account by Card and Krueger (1994).

This is not to say DID is universally applicable or always the best QED choice. It requires the comparator to closely reflect the intervention situation and a 'parallel time assumption' that time variations will be consistent between the two areas. The approach, however, can be adapted to various circumstances, with appropriate time-paralleled comparators and time-based data on outcome(s). In 2021, David Card (who had used modified forms of DID ahead of the famous instance shown in Example 13) shared the Nobel Memorial Prize in Economic Science for his contribution to labour economics.[1]

Regression discontinuity

Regression discontinuity design (RDD) is an econometric method which can be used in situations where entitlement for taking part in an intervention (for example, as a beneficiary or service user) is subject to an eligibility cut-off. RDD then contrasts the effects from units close to either side of the cut-off threshold – that is, those taking part but close to being ineligible, and those not taking part because they are (only just) outside the eligibility criteria.

As an illustration, owners of small farms might be offered advisory and technical support to encourage eco-friendly, sustainable approaches to improved profitability. Funds and advisory capacity would not be available to all interested small farms so those applying might be filtered by a multi-variable needs assessment diagnostic; those scoring above 50 per cent would be deferred to a planned phase 2 for support; those at or under 50 per cent would receive immediate support. RDD would take units from near to either side of the diagnostic cut-off, on the assumptions small farms 'close to eligible' will be similar in profitability characteristics. This might then evaluate profitability changes over time between those scoring 45–50 per cent and immediately receiving support, with the comparator for those scoring 51–55 per cent who were deferred to a second phase.

An RDD example for a school retention programme in a low-income country (Filmer and Schady, 2009) is set out in Example 14.

Example 14: RDD AND ELIGIBILITY CUT OFFS – EVALUATING EDUCATION AND HEALTH AWARENESS OUTCOMES FROM A MULTI-DONOR PROGRAMME IN CAMBODIA

In 2005, the Cambodian government started an Education Sector Support Project (ESSP) as part of a wider policy goal to expand access to educational services by addressing constraints in supply, demand, quality and efficiency. The ESSP had a special focus on poor and under-served communities with high student drop-out (as children were often required to support family incomes) and under-developed facilities and high average student–teacher ratios (49:1).

The multi-donor funded programme expanded educational facilities in poor areas, also delivering a programme of $45 scholarships to over 27,500 local children (grades 7–9). Over 6,300 primary school teachers (grades 1–6) were trained to become basic education teachers (up to grade 9) and some 900 school directors were trained. A World Bank team used a regression discontinuity design (RDD) with programme data to assess scholarship outcomes for enrolment, selection, and test achievements. Eligibility for the scholarship was based on a drop-out risk index, with the score based on household characteristics: 50 pupils with the lowest ranked scores received scholarships in larger schools and 30 in smaller schools (under 200 students).

The RDD analysis took children within a ten-point range either side of the indexed cut-off score. This showed scholarships raised school enrolment and attendance by nearly +25 per cent, with small positive effects on other outcomes, such as overall years of schooling, knowledge of health practices, future expectations, and adolescent mental health.

Note: The author has drawn on programme reports and the RDD analysis by Filmer and Schady (2009) of the World Bank Development Research Team. Any errors are the author's.

In addition to a clearly defined cut-off point, RDD needs suitable 'bandwidth' around the cut-off. A narrow bandwidth will mean the two groups are more likely to be similar, minimising non-intervention disruptions to the counterfactual, but the numbers captured (bandwidth) might be too small for validity. Although it lacks randomisation and cannot account for causal factors (without additional study or qualitative work), RDD studies have been compared favourably to the internal validity of RCTs (Chaplin et al, 2018). RDD refinements have seen a distinction between what are called 'sharp' or 'fuzzy' RDDs.

- 'Sharp RDD' will be in situations where there was universal engagement of those eligible below the cut-off point for the analysis, as was the case in the Cambodian example where all lowest ranked pupils (that is, below cut-off) received the scholarship.
- 'Fuzzy RDD' applies where not all units below the eligibility cut-off would necessarily be engaged in the intervention. If participation was voluntary, some of those eligible might not be motivated to take part. This would be the case in the (hypothetical) small farm advisory support situation where some farmers eligible for phase 1 support might opt not to take up the offer.

Neither sharp or fuzzy RDD can be used where programmes do not have a uniform and well-defined cut-off point for engagement. They also have limited external validity, unless looking at very similar interventions with much the same eligibility and cut-off arrangements. There are also some practical considerations which may limit RDD use, such as for how an appropriate bandwidth is set (Ludwig and Miller, 2007), the sufficiency of data and consistency of units on both sides of the cut-off. Where it is appropriate, RDD is nonetheless a powerful and highly credible QED option for purposeful impact evaluation.

Synthetic control designs

Despite the label, synthetic control designs do not use control methods. They are quasi-experimental 'comparator' approaches, but with one big difference over natural comparators: the comparator is artificially constructed or 'synthetic'. More common in the data-rich environments of health and medical interventions, these also have scope for use in some social settings if a quality natural comparator is not possible.

Although various approaches are open to synthetic 'control', they are commonly based on finding, manipulating and using available 'external' data to create a simulated comparator, hence 'synthetic'. In data-rich environments, they may provide an option where natural comparators are not viable. For example, a community engagement initiative might be being piloted by a regional authority to reduce anti-social behaviour in one of its ten constituent metropolitan areas. The other nine areas all have very different characteristics (for example, levels and causes of anti-social behaviour), so none would be a suitable natural comparator. However, by aggregating suitable data from the other nine and weighting this for key variables and indicators for the same or a recent period, it would be possible to produce a cross-area weighted average as a synthetic comparator.

In medical trials, synthetic controls have sometime been constructed from manipulating past RCT data of an outcome for 'near-fit' populations where participant situations are also similar. Past large-scale survey data could also be used (where data records can be selected to isolate specific 'near-fit' units) and aggregated into a new (artificial) sample set, to act as a comparator. Whatever the pathway, the suitability of a synthetic control hinges on the relevance of its selection, the suitability of source data and the potential for data manipulation to produce the necessary close-fit simulation. This depends, in particular, on:

- the quality of the original data collection underpinning its suitability as a comparator source;
- similarity between the populations of the intervention group and the synthetic choice, and sufficient coherence of characteristics;
- the comparability, reliability and comprehensiveness of the external dataset and the quality of its matching to the intervention data.

A high-quality synthetic control will need to use concurrent (or near concurrent) comparator data from similar subject characteristics, situations and practice settings, with no significant biases and where data are of an adequate sample size (for manipulation) and capable of adjustment. It will also require consistent classifications and definitions in the source data (for example, eligibility or outcomes) with the data with which it is to be compared for the intervention (as in Example 15).

Example 15: APPLYING SYNTHETIC CONTROLS – AN IMPACT EVALUATION OF POLICE OFFICER LAY-OFFS IN OREGON, US, ON FATAL ROAD TRAFFIC ACCIDENTS

In February 2003 following a cut in the Oregon state budget, a third of the state police force was laid off, mostly among traffic police (roadway troopers whose numbers reduced by 35 per cent). Two evaluators, DeAngelo and Hansen constructed a synthetic 'control' of the impact on road traffic fatalities. A natural comparator was not viable because numerous factors, other than police levels, were expected to affect fatal accidents in different states, making close-fit QED comparators impractical.

The authors, instead, used multiple data sources at national level, and for two neighbouring states (Washington and Idaho) where there were specific police and survey records for key data sets, to construct a data-driven comparator for the Oregon data. These provided 'counterfactual' estimates from Washington and Idaho for the causal effect of the Oregon police lay-offs on traffic fatalities and injuries. The decrease in enforcement following lay-offs was associated, among other effects, with a 12–14 per cent increase in fatalities per mile travelled, with the effects strongest outside city-limits where state police employment levels were most relevant.

The DeAngelo and Hansen analysis demonstrated what could be achieved from a well-constructed, data-driven synthetic comparator. In a subsequent difference-in-difference

> analysis, they came up with very similar measures for the lay-off effects.
>
> Note: This summary is drawn from the DeAngelo and Hansen (2014) paper in the *American Economic Journal: Economic Policy*. Any errors of summary are from the current author.

Synthetic controls are challenging to construct and are unlikely to be a common fall-back option for evaluators also facing political as well as technical constraints in their utility. Where they are possible, purposeful evaluators may need to put time and effort into explaining their utility to any doubtful commissioners and users, who may be hesitant to rely on what is seen as a fictitious comparator.

Using fall-back designs

This chapter has sketched out the range of QED options, but evaluation situations may arise where neither a natural nor synthetic comparator is possible. This is most commonly where a need for very fast starts or small budgets leave too little time or resource for designing something more robust. Where this happens, there are fast-track and less resource-intensive options which can go some way towards bringing some quantification to attribution when nothing else is viable.

These are not quasi-experimental methods, but in this chapter are placed alongside QEDs as constrained designs or 'fall-back' options. There are two common pathways:

- a 'before-and-after' analysis within the intervention;
- a 'trajectory' analysis, projecting pre-start data to estimate probable outcome effects.

Before-and-after designs

The discussion of difference-in-difference (see earlier sections) has introduced what is probably the most common constrained design – 'before-and-after'. When used as a stand-alone method, it looks only at the intervention (there is no external comparator) to consider the 'distance travelled' by participants for specific outcomes, between the start and end of the intervention. In an alternative universe, Card and Krueger's assessment of the effects of the raised minimum wage in New Jersey (Example 12) might have relied on a before-and-after analysis, by using only the data on fast food outlets in New Jersey. There would have been no matched comparator in Eastern Pennsylvania, and no DID.

'Before-and-after' is a simple design which can be used in almost any situation where there is start data on participation (perhaps for monitoring or for enrolment), but it has one chronic flaw for assessing attribution. It assumes that the pre-start situation of participants would have been unchanged over the observation period if the intervention had not taken place, making no allowance for other (non-intervention) influences or changes over time. So, in the New Jersey example, it would have assumed demand for fast food would be constant, the weather would not change, there were no competing new employers or any number of other non-intervention effects on fast food outlet job levels. This is a major limitation, so for purposeful evaluation, 'before-and-after' must be recognised as only a low-level estimate of attribution.

Trajectory analysis

This takes a different approach, although still relying on comparative data from within the intervention by using legacy time series data to estimate attribution. Staying with the New Jersey alternative reality, a trajectory analysis would have taken annual data from several past years, to set a trend line for fast food outlet employment levels in New Jersey (averaged per outlet); it would then have projected out a 'smoothed' trend line for changes over that period, to the end of the review period, for assessing the effect of the raised minimum wage. The legacy data for the 'trajectory' would have to be limited to that where the pre-existing minimum wage level was applied. The projected 'end' level could be set against the job level observed at the end of the actual evaluation, to estimate attribution.

Trajectory analysis has the benefit that it smooths out non-intervention influences (assuming weather changes and other disturbances varied in more or less the same way each year). However, it remains a constrained design, in particular because it cannot allow for over-time changes such as the New Jersey labour market tightening over the legacy period due to demographic or labour supply changes. Trajectory analysis also demands legacy data are available over a sufficient time period and for several pre-intervention data points to ensure a useful smoothed projection of effect. In the real world, necessary data collection or classification of key variables might change, thereby invalidating a trajectory approach.

For both 'before-and-after' and 'trajectory' analysis, it may be possible to make some allowance for extraneous influences, through supplementary surveys, data analysis or participant interviews which might explore other effect influences. These may go some way to allowing for non-intervention influences, but they will be constrained by knowledge of what other influences to allow for, how they are analysed and the resources available.

Purposeful evaluation relies on use and utility of evidence as a primary consideration in method choice. These fall-back options will always lack credibility among some users; they are not only constrained in the approach to assessing 'net' impacts, they will inevitably also constrain confidence, and, by implication, the likely use of findings. If evaluators have no other choices open to them, they will need to put a lot of effort into explaining the choice and managing users' expectations of them.

Threats to validity and unintended consequences

QEDs cannot offer the internal validity of a well-placed RCT, so evaluators using QEDs will need to pay very close attention to any validity weaknesses. Some of the validity threats are common to RCTs and QEDs, such as attrition and heterogenous intervention effects (see Chapter 8). Managing them will be largely about attention to detail, but two threats more specific to QEDs deserve special attention:

- selection biases from the quality of matching, in selecting (and using) comparators;

- effects of unintended consequences on outcomes and the quality of attribution.

Matching bias

No QED approach will be able to choose a natural (or synthetic) comparator which is a perfect match for the intervention. Lack of randomisation means that the use of comparators, not controls, requires the evaluation to optimise the quality of the 'match', by smoothing out risks from selection biases. All comparators will involve some compromises in the quality of matching so, for purposeful evaluation, it is vital those compromises are made consciously and shared with stakeholders.

Fortunately, there are some solid statistical tests which avoid relying on judgement alone to assess selection bias:

- 'Propensity score matching' (PSM) can be used to contrast distribution bias, between the intervention and the proposed comparator;[2]
- 'Inverse probability treatment weighting' (IPTW) methods have also been used in health and medical evaluations and may be preferable when working with small samples (Pirracchio et al, 2012).

Using these, or similar, tests also provides an ability to demonstrate to stakeholders the quality of match.

Unintended consequences

Unintended consequences are an almost inevitable effect of interventions carried out in social settings, leading to unanticipated outcome effects. These may be discounted in RCTs because of their fixed design and robust trial management but are an inherent validity risk for QEDs and typically for the risks of leakage, substitution, spillover effects, additionality and deadweight effects. These terms have their roots in econometric analysis and can be easily confused by non-economists. Table 9.2 present a simplified description for each, with some illustrations (from a hypothetical, place-based, skills training pilot programme for 16–17-year-olds).

Table 9.2: Understanding unintended consequences

Unintended consequence	Validity/integrity effect	Example (from a 16–17-year-olds youth skills training programme)
Leakage	Loss of opportunity to the intervention or participants from ineligible participation occurring	Unintentional recruitment to the pilot programme of 18-year-olds (that is, outside eligibility)
Substitution	Observed participation effects or benefits on individuals, group or area, from the intervention actions realised at the loss of opportunity (potential benefits) elsewhere	Skills trainers recruited from outside the intervention pilot area to support the pilot programme, causing reduced skills training capacity in the area drawn from
Spillover	Where an intervention affects a non-participant (either positively or negatively)	16–17-year-olds receiving skills training who were resident outside the pilot area. (Note: This would also be leakage)
Additionality	Observable intervention gains/changes beyond that which would have 'naturally' occurred	Skills trainers in the programme who secure higher-level professional qualifications as a result of their participation
Deadweight	Observed intervention gains which would occur if the intervention had not taken place	16–17-year-olds joining the pilot who already had course place offers from existing skills training providers in the pilot area

Unintended consequences can occur as a result of mismanagement of the intervention by service agents or providers, or from naturally occurring (but unintended) effects. They are unlikely to be eliminated by the way a quasi-experimental evaluation is designed, but anticipating these risks means they can often be adjusted for in subsequent analyses. This often involves additional evidence-gathering to assess any of these effects and to set them against whatever intended outcomes and impacts occur.

Some purposeful tips

Quasi-experimental approaches can offer greater flexibility to meet challenging evaluation circumstances, but with this flexibility come responsibilities for due diligence in making the 'best' choice of method and ensuring optimal rigour. This chapter has set out some of the many QED options, where choosing well from among them can be helped by attention a few practical issues:

- Different methods offer different levels of likely rigour and internal validity. Have key stakeholders been brought into the justification of method choice? Do they recognise the known limitations of that choice and do their expectations align with these?
- Some QED approaches have more scope for external validity than others. Does the choice being made have an appropriate balance between informing decision-making about the intervention itself, set against evidence generalisability to other situations?
- Synthetic designs are a possibility where the quality for matching a natural comparator is challenging but should be cautiously applied and very carefully positioned to avoid higher risks of internal validity flaws and questionable credibility.
- Much of the flexibility in QEDs comes from not randomising assignment, but this, in turn demands confidence that comparator choices have minimised selection biases. Is the evaluation able to demonstrate the quality of matching and attention to detail for adjusting for any selection bias?
- QEDs can readily look at different outcomes and effects across an intervention but are the 'right' outcomes being targeted by the design? Are they viable, realistic for lead-times and recognised as most relevant to decision-makers?
- The intervention will have effects beyond those intended – positive and negative. Can the approach taken provide sufficient account of unintended consequences?
- Managed expectations are crucial where a 'fall-back' constrained design is to be used. Have the attribution limitations been rehearsed with stakeholders, and is supplementary evidence being built-in to explore other influences on attribution?

Many of these 'choice' risks can – and need to be – anticipated before the design is put into practice. Potential flaws can be identified by stakeholder engagement and probing for selection or situational consequences. There is also greater scope to use external frameworks to guide the making of sound method choices, perhaps harnessing the easy to use 'Maryland Scale'[3] which has gained some currency for both pre-testing QED designs and demonstrating likely choice quality.

10

Theory-based impact evaluation

Introduction

Although others are cautious, many in the evaluation community see 'theory-based evaluation' (TBE) as an attractive new set of approaches for tackling complexity evaluations. In fact, this 'new' idea has been around a long time, with its roots in the early 20th century in analytic philosophy[1] which helped shape design and delivery in engineering and technology through 'conceptual design'. This later contributed to ideas about 'programme theory' in social and behavioural sciences, going on to influence evaluation thinking from the 1970s (Carol Weiss, 1972; Huey Chen and Peter Rossi, 1980).

As a cohesive evaluation approach, TBE came to prominence with Chen's *Theory-driven Evaluations* (1990)[2] and 20 years later its use could be cited in nearly 50 evaluations,[3] mainly from the US (Coryn et al, 2010). Despite an important formative contribution in Europe from Ray Pawson and Nick Tilley in *Realistic Evaluation* (1997) the practice outside the US was slower to take off. Much evaluation activity in Europe was directly funded or co-funded by governmental and other public bodies which, until recently, often discouraged use of these approaches.[4]

Opportunities for the use of TBE are rising. In the UK, for example, government has since 2020[5] encouraged the use of such approaches for some of the complex evaluation circumstances which characterise many public policy and programme interventions. Yet cautions continue in many parts of government and for many other funders, with TBE use remaining embryonic, especially for public bodies. It seems that while the methodological foundations are in place, their expression remains under-utilised and under-developed. This chapter looks at their considerable potential for purposeful impact evaluation.

TBE, theory and 'wicked problems'

The 'theory' in theory-based evaluation (TBE) is not theoretical. It is a uniquely constructed, well-honed tool which sets out an anticipated model for how a particular intervention is expected to work, to achieve what is expected of it, in particular diagnosed circumstances. For impact evaluation, this provides a conceptual reference framework around which the inquiry focus, design, evidence-gathering and analysis for an evaluation can subsequently be set.

All interventions will involve thinking and assumptions about how they are meant to work to secure their end gains. Some of that thinking may be little more than well-intentioned guesswork by those making a case for, or developing, the intervention; some of the assumptions underpinning the ideas may be loosely framed or only implicit. For TBE, that thinking (theory) needs to be made explicit, usually in the form of an intervention-specific 'theory of change' (ToC), on which more later. Of course, the use of theory about intervention formation is not the sole prerogative of TBE; it can influence just about any evaluation methodology. For TBE, however, it is central to its exploratory focus.

This may make TBE sound rather conceptual and not very relevant to purposeful evaluation. In fact, the 'theory' on which it draws is practically centred, unpicking and plotting the situation and assumptions behind how the intervention to be evaluated is to achieve its aspirations. Through the ToC, it draws out the layers of thinking behind an intervention and its context, to set out a 'testable', anticipated working model of the intervention processes and situation. TBE is the agent for testing that model to see what is and what is not working in the ways expected, why and how against the formative thinking, and what can be learnt from it for improvements. This will involve some (and possibly extensive) measurement of intervention processes and results, but it is fundamentally about exploring how those results do or don't come about against assumptions.

TBE is obviously not the only impact evaluation method to find out what is working, but it goes much further to set results against the original intervention 'theory' to find what assumptions are confirmed by practice, or where they may have been misplaced (or not sufficiently well-conditioned) causing necessary performance to be held back. This involves a structured, investigative approach, to unpick the impact journey and causation rather than measuring causation through a counterfactual. The approach is essentially exploratory and explanatory, not 'experimental'. These aspects of TBE can benefit many evaluation circumstances, but they have special relevance where the journey from intervention actions (and their interplay) to effects is complex and beset by many contributory and confounding influences.

There are various approaches to TBE (of which more later), but these can be referred to collectively as 'complexity evaluations'. That complexity is about complex causal situations – and not the relative complexity of an evaluation design – where Rittel and Webber famously referred to complex causal situations as 'wicked problems', contrasting those to: '… problems with relatively "tame", solvable problems in mathematics, chess, or puzzle solving' (Rittel and Webber, 1973). In evaluation, 'wicked problems' reflect situations where what's evaluated takes place in a complex (generative) system, where there is no simple route to 'puzzle solving' because there will be no likely clear demonstrable (causal) pathway between cause and effect.

Complex causal situations for interventions are widespread, especially in social settings. For example, the ban on credit card payment for any form of gambling (Example 4 in Chapter 2) might have assumed a simple and direct causal pathway between bringing in the ban and 'problem gamblers' not subsequently being able to build up unsustainable levels of credit-based personal debt. In reality, that causal pathway was never going to be quite that straightforward. Gambling premises might find other ways of circumventing the regulation (for example, other forms of credit); credit card processing bodies might not be able to classify all forms of card payments on gambling, leaving some such activities where debt might build up. Added to these, there was always the likelihood of 'work arounds' being found by gamblers to find other ways of accessing credit. Many interventions face similarly 'wicked' causal situations, where TBE has particular value by:

> ... regarding the programme [intervention] as a 'conjunction' of causes, which follows a sequence ... from initiation through various causal links in a chain of implementation, until intended outcomes are reached. The [TBE] exploration is built around a 'theory' – a set of assumptions about how an intervention achieves its goals and under what conditions. (Stern et al, 2012)

Looked at in this way, TBE is not just a fall-back alternative to where experimental or quasi-experimental approaches are not best placed. In 'complexity' circumstances, they may be a first choice for a purposeful approach, where the novelty of an intervention and uncertainties about how it will work call for an approach which is exploratory and explanatory. However, many commissioners and users will have little (or no) experience of TBE, so its use will need very careful positioning, reasoning and explanation if it is to be harnessed.

Where does TBE fit?

Although recent years have seen more commissioners becoming receptive to the potential for TBE, some of those they will be working with may remain more sceptical. To be able to use TBE in appropriate circumstances, evaluators may need to rationalise their utility; here, they can exploit both 'push' and 'pull' factors in making that case.

TBE 'push' factors

'Push' factors are largely situational influences reflecting where the particular characteristics of an intervention may be better suited to TBE. Proponents make much of TBE's ability to be applied to intervention situations where experimentation was likely to take insufficient account of non-intervention influences or of the complexity in the interplay between those influences. The capabilities for TBE to probe causal complexity through 'theory' exploration is consequently an important 'push' factor in explaining to funders TBE's value in such situations over 'experimental' approaches. Other 'push' factors can also help to embellish the case for TBE use in appropriate settings (Table 10.1).

Not all of these are likely to feature in any one 'complexity' intervention, but some will. Their combination will further compound difficulties in using experimental approaches, and 'push' towards use of TBE.

TBE 'pull' factors

Pull factors are largely about the added-value of using TBE over experimentation in some circumstances. These can be persuasive

Table 10.1: Other complexity 'push' factors to justify TBE preference

	Likely intervention circumstances where (with) ...
Variation in delivery of intervention	• Eligibility or actions are due to be applied in different ways to different participants, circumstances, situations (for example, geographical areas). • Implementation likely to change over time (different cause–effect pathways)
Unclear outcome effects/successes	• Novelty of the initiative (or actions) mean there is uncertainty over the likely characteristics of desired outcomes • Stakeholders holding inconsistent or conflicting expectations of 'necessary' outcomes
Uncertain efficacy or integration of intervention mechanisms	• Innovative mechanisms subject to high levels of uncertainty on likely efficacy • Uncertain quality of integration with non-intervention services relevant to outcomes (for example, external referrals)
Likely volatility in context or actions over course of intervention	• Volatility in environment in which intervention takes place (for example, changing labour market) • Likelihood of changed intervention priorities or focus modifying or causing risks to delivery
Transitional outcomes effects	• Anticipated end-gains (impacts) involve intermediate outcomes as 'tipping' points for intervention success
Dynamic and adaptive participant responses	• Risk of unintended/adaptive changes to participant behaviour compromising efficacy of actions/outcomes • Practitioners/providers delivering actions responding unevenly to intervention

Source: Adapted from author's teaching materials

where funders are cautious about TBE but where the evaluator can explain how TBE's exploratory focus can optimise gains from the evaluation, especially for intervention improvement and learning for:

- Exploring novel interventions where the ambition for innovation means funders accept that they are unlikely to get it 'right first time' or without ongoing adaptation;
- Clarifying the operation and interactions of an intervention where stakeholders have uncertainties or limited confidence on what might work and how;
- Clarifying also how what the intervention does needs to effectively join up, and integrate, with existing services or activities conducted to optimise effects;
- Testing the interventions start-up 'theory' to provide early (formative) evidence of what needs to change to provide more solid foundations for how, when, and why;
- Evidencing 'theory gaps' or flaws in intervention assumptions to inform adaptations and progressive improvement.

Pull factors provide an opportunity to motivate take-up of TBE as an evidence-based 'action evaluation' approach which can help interventions develop an understanding about what works to give it a better chance of eventual success.

Harnessing a theory platform

A solid theory platform helps shape any evaluation, but for TBE it is an essential starting point. The theory is a causal model, setting out how an intervention is expected to produce results by mapping the steps between intended actions and expected effects, alongside the assumptions needed for those steps to be effective. How well a TBE delivers its potential for a purposeful evaluation hinges on the sufficiency of this theory platform.

Evaluators may find themselves in control of that sufficiency if they are asked to construct, or contribute to, that theory as a precursor to the evaluation. Elsewhere, they may start with a theory platform previously put together by others, perhaps as a development tool for the design of the intervention. Such inherited theory platforms may be found lacking in clarity or sufficient detail, requiring early effort by the evaluator to enhance content. Whatever the starting point, TBE demands that evaluators are comfortable that the platform covers what is needed to guide decisions on evidence priorities, methods and as a 'theory' reference frame for probing the evidence to be gathered.

This is not the place to demystify the different ideas about what constitutes a 'good' theory platform.[6] However, some idea of the necessary content will help those putting together a TBE to have confidence in its sufficiency. A simple theory platform will set out an anticipated sequence of events (intervention inputs, activities, outputs) and results from them (outcomes and longer-term impacts). This will be a 'logic model'[7] setting out a results pipeline for the intervention. Although this may go some way towards a reference frame for TBE, it will likely leave critical considerations

Figure 10.1: Essential content for a theory of change (ToC)

Source: Author's teaching materials

such as assumptions and risks unexplored. Something more refined is needed (Figure 10.1), usually set out as a theory of change (ToC). The ToC goes further than a description of an intervention's component parts and sequence, as in a logic model, by adding:

- 'Context': This synthesises the context within which the intervention takes place. It sets out the origins in whatever issue, problem or challenge it is to address, the policy eco-system within which it takes place, and any parallel actions by other stakeholders. It is also likely to include a summary description of what is known from data or past research to scope the target population: its scale, characteristics and willingness to engage. These contextual factors are important for a TBE, because they help position influencing factors which may need to be taken into account, perhaps as independent variables in its design and analysis of causal mechanisms.
- 'Expectations': A logic model will set out expected end-gains, but the ToC goes further to set out a ladder of expectations differentiating between:
  - early anticipated consequential changes or outcomes from the intervention;
  - intermediate outcomes which may be transitional or trigger points to eventual end-gains;
  - end impacts which will likely involve longer lead times and build on early and transitional outcomes.

  Expectations may also touch on any likely indirect effects and achievements and issues such as sustainability of outcomes.
- 'Assumptions and mechanisms': This will set out the mechanisms for delivery and intended sequence (as in a logic model) but dig much deeper to set out the thinking behind them, and what is needed for them to work effectively. The depth and quality of these assumptions are often the difference between a sufficient ToC and one that is poorly defined and lacks content or granularity. The sufficiency of this detail is critical to what is to be tested in the TBE; it is the backbone behind the causal 'thinking' which the evaluation will be exploring. For example, a logic model might set out that one mechanism is the development of a web-based self-enrolment portal for participants; a ToC will add assumptions behind

how that website will be built, delivered, tested, its user-functionality, as well as for its accessibility and use.
- 'Risks': The fourth essential component for the ToC is the 'negative theory' anticipating disruptions that might counter the intervention, its mechanisms and assumptions from working as expected. This is also important to the TBE, in setting out the likely focus needed for evidence on potential barriers and to probe for any improvement messages from what was done to anticipate or counter them.

Put together, this makes up what the author has elsewhere described as 'the elements of a *Context, Expectations, Assumptions, Risks (CEAsR) profile*'[8] for building and scrutinising of the necessary ToC content. ToC content can be put together in other ways but, one way or another, will need to embrace these elements to provide the necessary theory granularity and nuance on which the TBE acts.

Theory-based evaluation harnesses a necessary theory platform but is not method prescriptive in how it does this. It may focus wholly on the processes through which the intervention is operating but more commonly will explore how it has, or is working towards, securing the outcome and impacts expected. Both nonetheless use what Stern and others (Stern et al, 2012) have referred to succinctly as 'process-orientated' methods; these can be loosely grouped into three different sets of methods:

- 'inclusive theory-based methods', drawing on scientific realism and including 'realistic evaluation' and 'contribution analysis' to look across interventions;
- 'adaptive methods', such as 'most significant change'*,* using highly participatory methods, usually based on small data sets;
- 'configurational methods', including set theoretic methods, for example, process tracing and qualitative comparative analysis (QCA).

This chapter has referred to these three groups collectively as 'theory-based evaluation'. Each of the three has different specific method options with distinct benefits and limitations, which are introduced in the rest of this chapter.

Inclusive theory-based methods

Following earlier foundations in the US, theory-based evaluation took a significant step forward in Europe with Pawson and Tilley's *Realistic Evaluation* in 1997. Their contribution acknowledged earlier conceptual roots but drew specifically on longer established ideas of 'scientific realism'. At its heart, *Realist Evaluation* assumes an inquiry into an intervention can test selected unobservable influences and their effects, through an evidence focus on context-influenced behavioural responses to intervention mechanisms. Others have since adapted realist principles within evaluation, notably the Canadian evaluator John Mayne in *Contribution Analysis* (CA) (Mayne, 2008). Both methods represent 'inclusive theory-based methods' which can be used at scale to evaluate causality across a whole intervention.

Realist evaluation

Theory in realist approaches may start with an overarching programme theory, usually a theory of change, to set out specific 'context-mechanism-outcome' (CMO) configurations for the evaluation to test. These are the specific causal threads for what works, for whom, and in which circumstances which lie at the core of realist methods, although others have suggested modified CMO configurations to widen scope.[9] The three CMO elements are drawn together on the assumptions that:

- Participants will be unique in their circumstances and potential for engagement, and *context* shapes their conscious and sub-conscious reasoning and responses to intervention actions.
- Those intervention 'actions' are its *mechanisms* of implementation and participants choose and engage with them in response to their context.
- Those choices and processes of engagement in turn shape what does (or does not) change (for individuals) – the *outcomes* of the intervention.

The CMO configurations are integrative in specifying what mechanisms will lead to what outcomes and what features of the context will affect whether or not those mechanisms operate to deliver those outcomes.

Realist approaches are not prescriptive on what evidence is needed and can work across different scales and kinds of theory, typically by combining several CMOs to test particular mechanisms. They commonly use mixed mode methods with quantitative data being the usual focus for both context and outcomes and a mix of quantitative and qualitative data on generative mechanisms.

Contribution analysis

Recognising the challenges of applying experimental approaches to policy and programme evaluation needs, John Mayne (as a senior analyst with the Canadian Federal Auditor-General) developed 'contribution analysis' (CA) as a flexible way of reviewing programme performance and attribution. Strongly influenced by realist principles, CA has been refined in a series of publications by Mayne (Mayne, 2001; 2008; 2011). In collaboration with others (Stern et al, 2012), this has been refined as an adaptable, six-step TBE process (Figure 10.2).

CA has consequently developed by application, initially largely in international development and aid programmes. This has included refinements to combine CA with specific techniques for causal inference including, for example, process tracing (Befani and Mayne, 2014). Some CA guides refer to a 'seven step' process (Apgar et al, 2020), but the principles behind its staged practice remain much the same. Robustly applied, CA provides a flexible framework for integrative TBE which has gained widening appeal to set and test an intervention-specific theory of change (referred to by Mayne as a 'contribution story') using multiple evidence sources. Its six steps involve two phases:

- Phase 1 (stages 1–3) positions and constructs a theory of change and collects necessary evidence of its implementation and performance. Where an existing ToC is the starting point, it may use stages 1 and 2 (Figure 10.2) to test its efficacy for the evaluation and refine it.
- Phase 2 (stages 4–6) takes the stage 3 data set and uses it to explore the ToC, or particular parts of it, for coherence, discontinuities or theory gaps (stage 4), going onto a second phase of evidence collection (stage 5) and assessment centred on a probative, evidence-led exploration of the theory gaps and causal 'alternative explanations' for them.

Figure 10.2: Key inquiry stages for contribution analysis

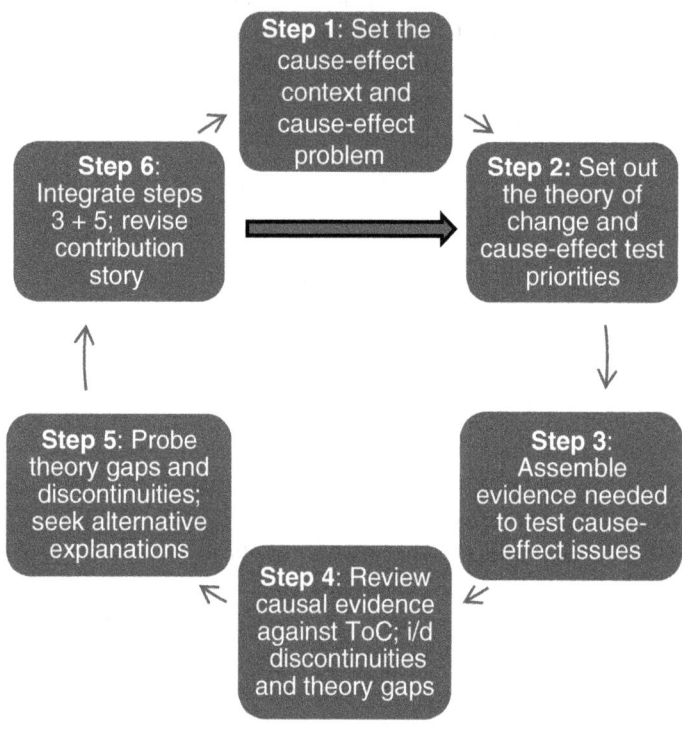

Source: Author's teaching material; adapted from Mayne, 2011; Ton et al, 2019

The two phases combine for the final evaluation, although CA can be used, where resources allow, for an iterative approach, testing for theory gaps as they emerge and proposing intervention improvement as responses.

As with realist evaluation, CA is not prescriptive about methods. For its stage 5 exploration of theory gaps, it is likely to use more than one explanatory method perhaps combining deconstruction analyses of earlier data sets (stage 3), case-base causal testing using process tracing or qualitative comparative analysis (of which more later) or deliberative review with 'knowledgeable others'. It can also use specific behaviour change models to explore explanations for the theory gaps.[10] CA does not aim to measure attribution of effects, but to unpick how they come about by exploring causal influences within the ToC framework. However, more ambitious evaluators will find its flexibility provides an opportunity for assessing, and perhaps estimating, likely attribution (Ton et al, 2019).

Realist evaluation and CA offer different approaches to deep process review within an intervention for causal explanation of how effects come about against what was anticipated (in the ToC). Both offer an adaptable approach to capturing and harnessing evidence. With different pros and cons (Table 10.2), CA is perhaps the more intuitive and flexible, and can combine well with other theory-based causal explanation (as later). Realist evaluation offers sharper precision, testing at a more granular level, and has established currency for some commissioning bodies.

Table 10.2: Some pros and cons of integrated theory-based methods

Contribution analysis	
Pros	Cons
• Use does not require prior skills training • Well-placed to review cause–effect relationships across an intervention • Highly flexible; can be applied in widely different intervention contexts and evidence mixes • Iterative process well-suited to active stakeholder engagement and/or where they hold varied of conflicting views on outcome cause–effects • Potential to integrate deep exploration methods, for example, process/contribution tracing	• CA quality dependent on well-defined ToC causal chain • Causal assessment stage is essentially subjective; lack of quantification may not give users confidence in 'assessed' attribution • Not well-suited to evaluation contexts where there is a lot of variation in implementation, or changes over time
Realist evaluation	
• Long-established theory-based method with credibility among (some) users • Extensive past practice examples to guide practice • Well-placed to review targeted cause–effect relationships in whole intervention	• Quality depends on reduction of ToC to appropriate and well-articulated CMOs • Can over-emphasise internal coherence of cause–effects (over external)

Source: Author's teaching materials

Adaptive approaches to TBE

Realist evaluation and contribution analysis both value participant and stakeholder engagement, but 'adaptive' methods offer greater participation opportunity. This may be of special value where evaluations require a more iterative approach to how an intervention is developed, or where its credibility places a particular emphasis on deep stakeholder engagement. Two rather different groupings of 'adaptive' methods are useful in these situations:

- 'developmental evaluation' approaches, involving an action research type model and progressive development;
- 'peer challenge' approaches, using a modified form of deliberative review through methods such as 'most significant change' or 'outcomes harvesting'.

Both involve deep 'process' interrogation and are usually based on intensive but smaller-scale evidence.

Developmental 'theory-based' evaluation

Chapter 6 has introduced 'developmental evaluation' (DE) as a largely process-orientated evaluation method. It is relevant to other circumstances, including non-experimental assessment of impacts in interventions with cause–effect uncertainties in dynamic or volatile operational circumstances. Using DE in those circumstances needs those funding and operating the intervention to be genuinely open to using evidence to change logistics, and adapt it, as it progresses.

As with process-orientated DE, using these approaches within TBE involves an open and interactive collaboration, using near real-time evidence to nurture adaptive learning, for those delivering an intervention. This demands an inherently participative approach to shaping and collecting evidence within the framework of a ToC to progressively understand cause–effect chains and implications for adapted practices. This shares some similarities to CA (notably in stages 4 and 5), but it is applied more iteratively and involves evaluators in a closer relationship with adaptive learning.

Chapter 6 warned that commissioners may be cautious about using DE, but in the author's experience they may be more open to its use when it is a part of a wider theory-based approach, as in Example 16.

Example 16: DEVELOPMENTAL 'THEORY-BASED' EVALUATION – EVALUATING CAPABILITY-BUILDING IMPACTS FOR SCHOOL BUSINESS MANAGERS

The author led a consulting team evaluating a new strand of an established programme, aimed at increasing school business management capability among non-teaching staff (see Example 2). The focus was on the impact of a one-year blended learning programme for higher-level non-teaching staff, to develop 'School Business Directors'; the lead government agency was concerned to better understand uncertainties about motivation to engage, both from individuals and their schools.

Using a programme-level enhanced logic model, a subset of the wider evaluation applied DE to constructing and following a longitudinal, staged series of 18 'process tracking' participant case studies with an open brief to explore implications for selection, support and utility. Each case was prepared as a situation and motivation multi-source baseline analysis from selection for the programme (but ahead of start), and updated at 4–6-month intervals to take account of emerging experiences.

Each review stage involved an open, evaluator-led 'triangulated' set of interviews for each case, with the participant, in-programme personal tutor, in school-mentor, and a link-school senior manager. Case reports assessed change against the assumptions of the logic model, individually modified and subject to further written commentary and staged reports. An aggregated assessment of improvement implications was then developed after each stage with 'ripple effect mapping' workshops with the provider and funding body. The review process continued over 30 months, concluding with a post-six month and post-12-month triangulated review after the first cohort of entrants had completed the programme.

Peer challenge

Another 'adaptive' method, this has particular value for purposeful evaluation by optimising stakeholder engagement in disentangling cause–effect influences on outcomes. This is not an iterative process, and is also a less open and dynamic arrangement than for DE. Two methods are of particular value:

- '*Most significant change*' (MSC): This is a highly participatory method, with stakeholders embedded in the process of determining effect determinants. MSC uses 'stakeholder panels' to critically review, for selected participants and usually through case studies, the 'most significant change' influences of the intervention mechanisms on emerging outcomes. Panels can be constituted in different ways but often involve cross-stakeholder workshops, to critically appraise common cause–effect features across participants' situations and context. Most commonly applied in a monitoring situation, MSC can be extended to TBE in complex intervention settings or where outcomes vary widely across participants.
- '*Outcome harvesting*': Outcome harvesting collects evidence of change, often through case-study based collation of multi-influence change situations. Multiple source evidence will set out verifiable positive and negative effects, for target units, against a pre-determined 'outcome map', usually as part of a theory of change. It then uses deliberative review methods to encourage retrospective or real time participation of key stakeholders in a structured process of reverse (critical) review of the evidence, to assess emerging (for formative) or emergent (for summative) cause–effect processes and contribution to the change.

Both methods involve structure in the critical review aspects and require active, collaborative and constructive engagement of those to be involved. Table 10.3 summarises some of the respective pros

Table 10.3: Some pros and cons of selected adaptive theory-based methods

Most significant change	
Pros	Cons
• Useful in multi-stakeholder contexts with diverse views on which outcomes are important • Participatory depth helps build 'theory' understanding across stakeholders	• May not be credible to stakeholders used to quantifying impact • Needs a constructive participatory context and well-engaged stakeholders • Time consuming for stakeholders • Effective only with commitment to strong and capable moderation
Outcome harvesting	
• Highly flexible; can contribute to many evidence and evaluation circumstances • Harnesses stakeholder insights which may not be otherwise accessible • Cohesive approach where stakeholders offer differing (contrasting) views • Embeds 'theory' consideration of diverse situational effects	• Requires well-placed and situated evidence accessible for constructive critical review • Set up and management can be time and resource intensive for evaluator

Source: Author's teaching materials

and cons. Well-chosen and applied, they can be a valuable aid to purposeful evaluation in boosting stakeholder confidence in findings and implications.

Configurational and case-based TBE

Not all uses of non-experimental methods will need to look across a whole intervention. For early-stage intervention development or small-scale piloting, there may be value in exploring particular areas of uncertainty or significance for scale-up or roll-out. Staying with the credit card ban on gambling payments as an example, an uncertainty for launching the new regulation was how gamblers might substitute card-based credit in ways which risked circumventing the policy aim to reduce their propensity to build up unsustainable debt levels. This was recognised to be a critical work-around risk to the effectiveness of the ban, but there was only speculation about if, how and in what circumstances, 'at-risk' gamblers might draw on substitute behaviour.

In situations like this, policy bodies might opt to commission theory-based evaluation to explore not the whole chain of implementation but specific cause–effect issues or combinations for key areas of uncertainty. Two 'configurational' methods[11] are of particular value for testing selected cause–effect associations (configurations):

- Process tracing
- Qualitative comparative analysis (QCA)

Process tracing

This is a high intensity, systematic method of theory-testing to assess a level of inference for a specific cause and an observed effect. Process tracing centres on one or more pre-defined 'testable' cause–effect hypotheses, using a formulaic assessment of cause–effect strengths. Evidence to be reviewed is often case-based, where each evidence-set relates to a specific point of time and is sufficiently fine-grained to support the review.

The method focuses on applying four tests to see if they are passed or failed, with each assessing if what is being tested is necessary and/or sufficient to justify the causal claim of the hypothesis. The test 'levels' are referred to under the defined labels of:

- 'Straw in the wind' shows only a weak causal association but does not rule out some influence. Passing this may help identify cause–effect associations worthy of further exploration.
- 'Hoop' indicates this is a contributory precondition for an outcome to be met but is not of itself a sufficient causal explanation. Failing a hoop test eliminates this as a possible causal explanation.
- 'Smoking gun' provides strong support for a causal explanation; it weakens other explanations but does not eliminate them altogether. Failing a smoking gun test will not eliminate a possible causal explanation but weakens its likely outcome influence.
- 'Doubly decisive', if passed, is the strongest cause–effect association, confirming the hypothesis being tested and eliminating other causal possibilities.

Theory-based impact evaluation

This description only touches on what is involved.[12] Process tracing has strong theoretical roots, but it is not for the incautious and needs solid evidence for its diagnosis, robustly defined hypotheses for testing, and skills (and confidence) to apply and demonstrate results from the tests. Where robustly used, it offers purposeful evaluation a targeted causal assessment, which adds inferential leverage lacking in less systematic approaches.

Qualitative comparative analysis (QCA)

QCA is also an established evaluation method with roots in research. It provides for systematic comparisons of outcome influences, based on a 'set-theoretic' assessment of conditions affecting outcomes. As with process tracing, QCA usually works across small sets of comparable case studies often selected to provide high and low outcome contrasts. It is challenging to use with larger data sets (Schneider and Wagemann, 2012); an analysis of multiple QCA inquiries suggested an average of 22 cases across those studies (Mello, 2012).

QCA starts with a choice of significant cause–effect conditions to be examined, often selected from a theory of change. Selected conditions are precisely defined, including for the circumstances of when and where they are likely to be present to allow for consistent and accurate coding of the presence/absence of the condition in different cases. Example 17 highlights how QCA was used in the late 1980s by Charles Ragin, a QCA originator, for assessing causal conditions affecting social disturbance in countries supported by the International Monetary Fund (IMF), with debt renegotiation conditionality.

Example 17: APPLYING QCA – ASSESSING AUSTERITY-RELATED SOCIAL DISTURBANCE IN COUNTRIES SUPPORTED BY IMF DEBT RENEGOTIATION FUNDS

Ragin's classic example of QCA assessed the conditions under which specific defined social disturbances affected countries in receipt of IMF funds mandating fiscal and other austerity measures. Ragin used a three-stage process:

1. Identifying comparative countries in receipt of austerity-mandated IMF funds to contrast those which had seen mass protest outcomes (Peru, Argentina, Tunisia, and others) and others which did not (Mexico, Costa Rica, and others).

2. Developing (from a theory stance) a series of causal conditions and indicators which, in different combinations, might influence the tested outcome (social disturbance), including: austerity severity, degree of debt, living conditions, consumer prices, prior levels of political mobilisation, government corruption, union strength, trade dependence, investment dependence, urbanisation, and other structural conditions relevant to mobilising protest.

3. Constructed a series of QCA 'recipes' (causal combinations) across the conditions to test (for example, severe austerity measures combined with government corruption, rapid consumer price increases and high levels of prior political mobilisation) with data on the combined conditions and outcomes represented in 'truth tables' for each causal combination-outcome condition.

4. Matrices were subsequently minimised to provide valid comparisons.

Further assembly and analysis drew together the conclusion that IMF-austerity mandated protests erupted where there is severe austerity, but not on its own. Severe austerity needed to be combined either with rapid price increases or with the combination of prior mobilisation, government corruption, and a non-repressive regime, to stimulate mass protest.

Source: Adapted from Ragin, C. and Rihoux, B. (2009), *Configurational Comparative Methods: Qualitative Comparative Analysis (QCA) and Related Techniques*

Space is too limited to describe QCA in more detail, but it can be seen to rely on a theory-based, case-by-case assessment of the target condition(s) and outcomes. These are set out in an analytical matrix ('truth table') to state (often numerically by binary code or coded values) whether each individual condition and outcome is present or not and assessing if it is either:

- 'necessary' – where that condition must be present for the tested outcome to occur;
- 'sufficient' – if its presence ensures the outcome is achieved; and where a condition can be both necessary and sufficient, if it is required and ensures the outcome;
- 'insufficient but necessary' (INUS) – where a condition must be combined with other conditions to produce the outcome.

Taken across the cases, QCA can be a powerful tool for complexity evaluations, but its strength relies on solid data and how well the ToC is used to define key causal conditions to test. It has particular value in identifying causal combinations for outcome achievement.

Process tracing and QCA offer a greater level of demonstrable robustness in the causal assessment, but this requires skilled use and is confined to more selective and smaller-scale approaches than some other methods. Some of their respective pros and cons are summarised in Table 10.4.

Hybridisation for non-experimental evaluation

There is no lack of method possibilities for using TBE in complex causal circumstances, if their use, and suitability, can be rationalised to funders and stakeholders. What they lack in quantifiable proof of effect is counterbalanced with their exploratory and explanatory value to provide rich insights on causality in the impact journey. They commonly lack a structured counterfactual to measure or estimate attribution, but this need not be the case. If plural (hybridised) mixed methods are used, these can complement TBE methods with, or within, a separately constructed counterfactual either by:

- Adding an adaptive method, such as outcome harvesting, to a QED, where that has adopted a mixed-methods evidence

Table 10.4: Some pros and cons of selected configurational methods

Process tracing

Pros	Cons
• Uses a tried and tested rigorous causal analysis framework • Well-suited to post-hoc assessment of robust case-based evidence • Integrates use of ToC to define key (likely) causal conditions • Goes beyond cause–effect testing to identify causal combinations • Provides potential for inferential leverage with evaluation users and stakeholders	• Small-scale focus on usually narrow range of tested cause–effect relationships • Requires prior skills training for robust use • Quality needs well-articulated test hypotheses, avoiding the risk of inferential errors • Needs nuanced, time-specific and comparable data • Not well-suited to most formative assessment

Qualitative comparative analysis

Pros	Cons
• Testing process uses a long-established causal analysis framework • Allows for both complex causation (combinations of factors) and multiple causes of an outcome to be accounted for (equifinality) • Works best when consistent and comparative data on all the cases of interest are available • Can work at an intermediate level of scale (as well as small-scale)	• Requires prior skills training for robust use • Not well-suited where involving large numbers of cases (<50 cases) • Risks from weak differentiation (for example, which cases represent more 'success' or 'failure' than others) • Quality dependent on judgements in minimisation stage; risks from exclusion judgements • Not well-placed to allow for unobserved influences

Source: Author's teaching materials

approach, which includes well-structured ex-post case studies of impact. Both MSC and outcome harvesting could add value and deeper theory-based causal insights to such an inquiry.
- Making provision, also within a QED design, for streamlining broader evidence from the intervention and comparator design, into selected case sets, where emerging causal questions or conditions could be reviewed through, for example, process tracing or QCA.
- Adding to an integrative theory-based evaluation such as CA, a smaller scale comparator QED to provide a conditional estimate of a quantified counterfactual. In some TBE circumstances, the

source data being drawn on will also usually provide for at least a 'before-and-after' analysis as a simple proxy for a counterfactual.

For purposeful evaluation, any hybridisation will need to clarify the balance of inquiry between the two separate approaches – experimental and non-experimental. There are also some limitations to what can be done. Theory-based supplementary investigation is also not readily applied to RCT-based inquiry; elsewhere, hybridised approaches may be desirable but difficult to justify if extended timeframes or more budget are needed.

Some purposeful tips

Despite the strength of research and evaluative theory that has gone into TBE methods, and their rising currency for some users, they continue to face resistance among many others. They offer inquiry approaches to which many users are not accustomed and, where this is the case, to effectively apply TBE it may help to:

- Take time to build a case for the use of theory-based methods and to bring users and any reluctant stakeholders with you. TBE cannot be a forced fit and needs to recognise that many commissioners and users will have little (or no) experience of it and may be sceptical.
- Rationalising TBE use, and a choice of a specific method, starts and ends with close attention to the intended purpose of evaluation which determines what 'push and pull' factors may have particular leverage for educating and informing their use.
- Any TBE method is only as good as the theory platform drawn on. If limited to a logic model, user expectations of what can be achieved need to be substantially reduced.
- Where a ToC is available, evaluators need to be confident this has sufficient and nuanced content with the necessary granularity in description.
- A good ToC is only a starting point; most TBE methods need a reductive stage to assess what aspects from the overarching theory are the most significant for testing. TBE quality depends on both appropriate and precise articulation of what

is being tested and stakeholders' engagement in making those reductive choices.
- Some TBE methods can be chosen intuitively and harnessed by those with relevant research skills. Others, including process tracing and QCA, need specific skill sets to use them robustly.
- The utility of a TBE can be greatly enhanced by building in some consideration of a quantified counterfactual, often by harnessing data that are already available for the intervention or using combined methods.

A final consideration for the practical use – and choice – of a TBE method is for stakeholder engagement. This is important in any purposeful evaluation but often vital in in making TBE choices.

11

Meta-evaluation

Introduction

Meta-evaluation has been introduced (Chapter 5) as a distinctive evaluation 'type', but one which, unusually, does not collect its own evidence. It remains an evidence-based set of methods, employing structured and systematic 'legacy' inquiry and based wholly on harnessing evidence from other research-based (and/or evaluation) studies. The methods have a useful role to play in purposeful evaluation, especially in resource- and time-constrained situations.

Meta-evaluation can be an evaluative focus of itself or an 'ex-ante' aid to setting a sharp focus for a subsequent process, economic, or impact evaluation. Whatever the starting point, simply because a meta-evaluation uses existing evidence does not mean this is more informal than evidence-generating evaluations. To be effective, meta-evaluation shares with other types of evaluation the need for a clear and realistic purpose, acquisition of systematic evidence, and structured, comparative inquiry. There are also choices to be made about what synthesis approach is most appropriate to circumstances and purpose.

What is meta-evaluation?

Most evidence-generating evaluations draw on some aspect of 'legacy' information, perhaps for informing scope and design. Any of these will look to make best use of preceding research (or evaluation) or intervention data that is already available for profiling target populations or needs groups, past trends, or from ongoing monitoring or other sources. We might ask, how is meta-evaluation different in also doing so? The answer lies in the simple distinction that this is the only set of approaches which relies exclusively on pre-intervention legacy data.

A further question is how that exclusive focus is different from mainstream methods looking across similar situational evidence, for example with pre-research literature reviews. The distinction is subtle, but lies within how bias is minimised in making inferences from past evidence, together with the specific evaluative intent of meta-evaluation, where:

- Meta-evaluation needs to apply appropriate rigour for describing and minimising the sorts of bias that can, inevitably, result from less formalised approaches such as narrative literature reviews. The rigour comes from developing an evidence *protocol* (of which more later) to set criteria for evidence identification and sampling.
- Meta-evaluation shares, with other types of evaluation, a focus on using structured and comparative analysis to interpret evidence (albeit legacy evidence) to make inferences to inform decision-making processes.

At the heart of its practice is a process of evidence synthesis based on clarity of focus and discipline to select, reduce, critically assess and contrast selected legacy evidence to put together an analysis for whatever is being targeted by that evaluation. As an illustration, a meta-evaluation of a proposed pilot for feminisation of rural water supply in a low-income country might identify data-based studies of similar initiatives to aid women's access and management of clean water in rural settings in other similar countries. Such a meta-evaluation might be used 'ex ante' to draw together messages to guide the design of the pilot or plan its evaluation.

What is 'systematic' in the synthesising process draws on well-defined 'cumulation' principles progressively refined over the last three decades. Much of this stems from practices developed by, and from, 'Cochrane'[1] principles and the subsequent Cochrane Collaboration ('Cochrane' is now set up as a charitable organisation). These have been applied (mainly) across medical RCTs and more recently in other areas such as environmental science.

Well-placed meta-evaluation is now widely recognised as part of the evaluator's toolkit. There are several different pathways, each of which has some inheritance from the early Cochrane principles, in particular:

- systematic reviews
- rapid evidence reviews
- meta-analysis

All have value for different circumstances, and each is considered separately in this chapter, with a concluding brief look at some other possibilities.

Systematic review

Systematic reviews are not exclusive to evaluation. They are widely used within research studies (especially in medicine) to draw together past evidence-based learning, but the methods used in research and evaluation settings are nonetheless much the same. Well-organised 'systematic reviews' in evaluation echo RCTs' status as a 'gold standard', and, as with RCTs, those technical demands often limit their use in many practical evaluation circumstances. Those constraints include the quality of the source studies to be synthesised, the application's (considerable) time needed, and the skilled resources required.

Where sources and resources allow, systematic review involves a high integrity, targeted approach usually focused on a specific, clearly defined research question(s). For simplicity, the approach can be reduced to six sequential stages[2] (Table 11.1).

For purposeful evaluation, the first stage is critical to defining a utility-centred focus for the issue for inquiry, refining this through closely engaging users and key stakeholders to sharpen its ambition.

Robustly applied, this staged process aims to minimise bias in the selection and synthesis of evidence and, to be credible, the process will need expertise, rigour and care (O'Leary et al, 2016).

Table 11.1: Key stages in systematic review

Stage and sequence	Description of essential tasks
1. Defining the review	• Developing and refining a researchable 'question' • Ensure consistency with inquiry purpose, realisable 'data' and available resources
2. Setting search focus	• Translating the review question into key words (for search) which encompass the field of inquiry
3. Inclusion criteria	• Setting appropriate inquiry boundaries • Define the parameters for evidence eligibility and what will be ineligible
4. Search and selection	• Using key words within the set criteria to identify in-scope evidence • Validating eligibility to ensure appropriate selections • Establishing the eligible source data; ensuring transparency of inclusion and ethical coherence
5. Synthesis	• Systematic review and reduction of eligible content against research question • Shared synthesis
6. Assessment	• Impartial review of source data to identify utility, quality, and findings against inquiry question • Reductive presentation (usually to subsidiary elements for knowledge exchange and assessed implications)

It also requires judgement in application and how it translates the 'question' into the agreed inquiry focus (stages 2 and 3) and in reflecting this in the selection of review data (stage 4). The journey across these stages is amplified elsewhere, with a wide literature, which is helpfully brought together in some useful practical guides (Pettigrew and Roberts, 2006; Higgins et al, 2019).

Following this sequence and applying well-set principles for practice, systematic review brings a high level of rigour – and confidence – to the assessment. However, some caution is necessary. Evaluators need confidence to apply the rigour and to demonstrate compliance through the iterative process. They also need appropriate source material to draw on which has sufficient scope, range and evidential quality. This may not be met in many settings, where necessary legacy evidence is too limited for sufficient synthesis or where what is available may be of inconsistent quality, inadequate scale or comparability.

Rapid evidence review

Rapid evidence reviews (RERs) share much of the structure of systematic review but offer a more streamlined and intensive approach. Unfortunately, unlike systematic review, there is less consensus or practical guidance on how to go about them or get this accepted as appropriate. As in many aspects of evaluation methodology, the terminology is often used loosely, with a 'rapid evidence review' sometimes used to label less structured and systematic approaches such as broad scoping studies or literature review. Those methods have value for the preparatory stages for evidence-based evaluation, but they lack the structure and systematic approach needed for meta-evaluation: they are not RERs.

The main differences between evaluative RERs and systematic review are in the intensity of the former and in condensing the approach to defining what past evidence is relevant. This condensing can be loosely described as a three-stage sequential process (Table 11.2).

Different RERs may describe these component parts in different ways, but the reductive sequence is at the heart of structuring the inquiry by differentiating:

- a preliminary defining stage to set the inquiry focus (Phase 1);
- a (usually) two-stage approach (Phase 2) to identify and collate potential sources and then reduce that initial long list to a more focused and manageable second stage;
- a concluding comparative synthesis from the stage 2 focus sources (Phase 3).

This more streamlined approach means the RER can be conducted more intensively. Set against this, however, the selection and reduction arrangements (Phase 2) involve more judgement by the evaluator, so they are open to greater risk of bias.

RERs also bring challenges in how to synthesise stage 2 evidence and then present it. A useful, practical approach is to put together comparative templates or synthesis matrices for summarising (reduced) evidence. A single RER might typically involve three or four such matrices, each presenting highlighted data or evidence for a small number of key variables, as evidence

Table 11.2: A three-phase approach to rapid evidence review in evaluation

RER key phase	Description
Phase 1: Definition	• What is the question? • What review evidence strings and boundaries can be defined to ensure the review remains relevant and researchable?
Phase 2: Sourcing and reduction	• 1st stage search for sources using search strings to identify in-scope evidence within inquiry boundaries (Note: Where evidence is limited, modify (expand) the search criteria) • Reduce preliminary source selections by 'quality' screening • Identify and confirm 2nd stage focus for sources of most value, accessibility and relevance
Phase 3: Synthesis and reporting	• Synthesise 2nd stage sources by key evidence (comparative) mapping for evidence consistency and inconsistency. • Define transferability implications

'strings' addressing specific parts of the inquiry or research question. The matrices will mix some descriptive information, with findings from each source (reduced to key/bullet points). Returning to the earlier example of a scheme for feminisation of rural water supply in a low-income country, this might set four matrices, each with three of four constituent variables, representing selected evidence strings for:

- Matrix 1: Source description (what source; eligibility and scope of that inquiry; method of inquiry and scale);
- Matrix 2: Evidence from process assessment of parallel feminisation initiatives in (any) low-income countries (which, what focus, where and what comparability; what actors/mechanisms and how applied; key findings for effective delivery and outcomes; key findings for constraints and successful adaptations);
- Matrix 3: Evidence from summative assessment of engaging communities (what done by whom; outcomes and quality of feminisation for enhanced access; outcomes and quality of feminisation for clean water supply and management; outcomes and sustainability for communities);

- Matrix 4: Lessons and transferability (lessons for responsive delivery; lessons for efficiencies, outcomes and equitability; policy implications for transfer to proposed pilot).

As with systematic reviews, RER quality depends on the precision with which the terms of the inquiry are set, both for the review question being addressed and the inclusion criteria for source material. Example 18 provides an illustration of the use of an RER for a children's reading and early years learning programme.

Example 18: STRUCTURING AN RER EVALUATION – APPLYING AN RER TO A META-EVALUATION FOR AN EARLY YEARS LEARNING PROGRAMME

The author and a colleague undertook a meta-evaluation of past evidence-based studies of former charity-based programmes to enhance young children's reading. The funding charity had delivered a national programme of changing activities over the previous four decades, funded by government and philanthropic sources, which included various summative assessments although not following any set scope, focus or method.

Source material and the funder's timelines contraindicated a systematic evidence review and an RER was developed to look across past programme reviews and methods to shape a future evaluation strategy. The funder asked for the RER to: 'look at what can be learnt from what we have done in the past'; this was refined to: 'What are the transferable lessons for the choice, resourcing and effective practice of proportional evaluation of our funded programmes?' Eligibility criteria were also agreed (studies with some quantification post-1990; national, home country, or regional), together with an objective-set requirement for evaluation or review; and accessible summative reports.

The RER's next (second) phase identified 43 eligible studies. Screening of each reviewed their evidence, scale and quality of reported method description, geographical coverage, year of reporting, and whether conducted internally or externally, to inform a reduction to 24 (of the 43) studies for the next (synthesis) stage. It also set out a four-matrix proposed synthesis protocol, with 13 variable-based rubrics across these (one with four rubrics; three with three). This was discussed and, following some clarifications, 21 of the 24 studies were agreed.

The third and final phase of the RER, synthesised each study into the comparative 'mapping' matrices. Matrix 1 set out: study/review title; focus and programme scale; and, review/evaluation resourcing/lead. Matrices 2 and 3 had three variables, each to set out targeted aspects of what was done in review/evaluation for each study. Matrix 4 had summative analysis for: what worked well; what worked less well; transferable lessons for practice; and, transferable lessons for an evaluation strategy. After a total of 13 weeks, the final meta-evaluation report drew together a method description of the RER, a narrative synthesis (one chapter for each matrix) and a concluding 'authors' assessment' chapter on 'issues and implications' for the proposed cross-charity evaluation strategy. Matrices were added as an annex.

Both systematic review and RERs are highly structured approaches to evidence synthesis, which fit different needs and intensity circumstances, and have different 'pros and cons' (Table 11.3).

RERs have the advantage over systematic review, in being easily comprehensible to users, intuitive and in providing for much greater intensity. A solid RER may take perhaps three to six months to complete in contrast to at least nine to twelve months (or much longer) for systematic review. However, these benefits for an RER need to be traded against the risks of greater bias in the synthesis. Systematic reviews may take longer and require familiarity with the highly structured process and disciplines involved, but they do offer a more substantial, and time proven, level of rigour and validity, which users may value highly.

Table 11.3: Systematic review and rapid evidence review

Descriptions	Pros	Cons
Systematic review		
Systematic method of identifying, assessing, extracting and integrating evidence from multiple studies to assess one (or more) specific inquiry questions	• Widely credible approach to evidence synthesis • Minimised bias in selection and synthesis • Provides a comprehensive assessment of available evidence • Has a rigorous approach to assessing and referencing studies	• Not well-suited to broad inquiry: difficult to reduce to a specific review question • Substantial body of 'quality' evidence needed • Likely to be resource intensive; requires evaluator knowledge and skills of 'Cochrane' compliant approaches • Needs a considerable timeframe, typically of at least 9–12 months
Rapid evidence review		
More intensive synthesis approach which continues to use systematic principles for selection and reduction of evidence. May be more appropriate where timeframe or available skills do not lend themselves to systematic review	• Useful for more intensive synthesis requirements with limited timeframes • Credible approach to synthesis, based on coherent search and selection criteria • Better suited to inquiry, drawing on variable evidence quality • More flexible approach to selection and synthesis	• Subject to greater selection and synthesis bias than a systematic review • May be less credible to users and stakeholders

Realist synthesis

Systematic review and RERs have served evidence synthesis very well in their different ways, but they do not fit evaluators' requirements in all situations. In particular, there have been concerns (Pawson et al, 2004) that such approaches are not well-suited for evidence synthesis in complex causal situations.

Realist synthesis has been proposed as an alternative meta-analytic approach for theory testing. An emerging approach, which continues to develop by application, it also uses a more iterative approach to collating and assessing available studies framed around an intervention theory. It can be applied ex ante when the intervention is being planned or while it is ongoing. The approach draws on realist perspectives (Chapter 10) in addressing complex, multi-faceted cause–effect circumstances, with a more adaptive potential for evidence synthesis. It anticipates an embedded approach to engaging users and stakeholders, and as such is well-aligned to purposeful evaluation needs.

Realist synthesis is a structured approach which involves four overlapping stages (Table 11.4). This description leans heavily on a seminal description[3] by Ray Pawson and colleagues (Pawson et al, 2004), supplemented by the author's own experience.

The approach is different from systematic review and RERs in how it iteratively searches for and harnesses legacy evidence geared to testing a specific theory framework, and in its highly collaborative approach. Here, evidence search continues to be disciplined by specific research questions but with the process described as 'purposive' (Pawson et al, 2004), evolving progressively as the search matures. Unlike other synthesis approaches, it does not seek a 'census' review of eligible sources but uses a principle of 'saturation': when evidence for a particular review string shows much the same issues starting to emerge (that is, nothing distinctively new), then the search moves onto another string.

Realist synthesis has value for meta-evaluation where circumstances align with its theory-based focus, although its distinctive iterative process can provide uncertainties which are difficult to accommodate in intensive or fixed timeframes. It may not be as intuitive to commissioners and users as the sharp structure of systematic review and RERs, so close engagement of stakeholders is important in building credibility.

Other options for meta-evaluation

Systematic reviews or RERs are the most common synthesis approaches for policy and programme evaluation, but other approaches are possible, including:

- **Meta-analysis** works with selected and combinable quantitative studies to provide an estimate of an effect size across them. It

Table 11.4: A four-step approach to realist synthesis

Stage and sequence	Description of essential tasks
Stage 1: Define the scope of the review	
Establish review scope with key stakeholders to clarify purpose and utility; set theory framework (underpinnings) of the intervention	• Establish review purpose, use and context • Set and agree review question(s) to be addressed, informed by exploratory evidence searches • Find and articulate relevant programme theories (from literature); clarify theory integrity with stakeholders and others • Design and agree a theory-geared review protocol
Stage 2: Search for and appraise evidence	
Stage 1 theory framework used to identify and integrate relevant empirical evidence. Evidence search is purposive and iterative to indicate emerging themes	• Define search sources, terms and methods • Develop data extraction matrices or templates • Set 'saturation' thresholds for when no new evidenced observations are emerging • Search/scrutinise quality sources for relevance to 'theory' (confirming and contradictory evidence) • Develop (and agree) data extraction matrices/templates
Stage 3: Extract and synthesise findings	
Findings are synthesised progressively; new evidence from one theory area might impact on added evidence in another	• Extract source evidence; include only evidence-based sources (quantitative and qualitative) • Map on data extraction matrices/templates, to compare/contrast findings from different studies • Link study findings to relevant theory areas using theory-confirmatory and contradictory findings • Evidence is synthesised within and between stages to refine theory framework (and evidence search) in the light of emerging evidence
Stage 4: Draw conclusions and make recommendations	
Collate and interpret review results, focusing on users' needs for both theory testing and explanatory evidence for how the intervention works (or is intended to work)	• Draw together findings with preliminary assessment of implications (pre-recommendations) • Closely involve commissioners, users and key stakeholders in review of findings and implications • Refine analysis; report findings with conclusions and recommendations (and matrices/templates as annex)

Source: Author's teaching materials; after Pawson et al, 2004

can be conducted with well-forged and comparable RCTs (and, with less reliability, with quasi-experimental designs) to provide either a stand-alone or supplementary assessment to a conventional systematic review. It is best suited to assessing across small numbers of studies, to statistically assess weight 'average' effect across them; this requires strongly comparable source data.

- **Meta-ethnography** is a legacy approach designed for qualitative evidence (Britten et al, 2002), combining data to translating evidenced concepts across studies into a synthesis assessment. There are no standard procedures for meta-ethnography, but it follows some of the design disciplines of other meta-evaluation approaches to agree a specific focus for the inquiry, inclusion and selection requirements. It is likely to use (as with realist synthesis) a grid or template approach to map and translate the studies into each other, followed by some appropriate use of deliberative review to critique the synthesis.

Both have distinctive uses in meta-evaluation and some of their respective pros and cons are summarised in Table 11.5.

Some purposeful tips

Meta-evaluation methods are a natural extension into the evaluation domain of often long-established research procedures. The methods offer choices across different synthesis circumstances, levels of validity and some flexibility in application. Making those choices and applying the necessary discipline for effective use can be guided by some cross-cutting tips:

- These methods are not a substitute for evidence-generating evaluation.
- As with any evaluation method, effort and time needs to go into solid 'intent' foundations. For any of these synthesis methods, this calls for robust groundwork to set research question(s) and a well-defined review protocol to mobilise the inquiry.
- Time constraints loom large, in choosing what synthesis method is most appropriate. These need to be placed 'up

Table 11.5: Other options for meta-evaluation

Description	Pros	Cons
Meta-analysis		
A recognised statistical procedure to integrate results of a small number of quantified studies to dimension an average effect size	• Applicable to RCT and QED primary studies • Offer precision and demonstration of cross-study effects • Small study differences can be 'weighted' in analysis • Can explain heterogeneity between studies of similar interventions	• Quality requirements for consistent, coherent and equivalent source data often not possible in practice • Where used for QEDs may not account for bias and confounding factors
Meta-ethnography		
Selects, analyses and interprets qualitative evidence from selected studies to identify new concepts and cross-cutting insights from them	• Works to synthesise across qualitative-method studies • Draws on well-profiled, lived experience evidence (often important to user credibility) • Strong focus unpicking and explaining heterogeneity	• Inappropriate for more structured synthesis approaches • Quality depends on that of original studies, which may be variable in practice

front' in managing user expectations and ambition for what can be achieved.

- Evidence synthesis is inherently comparative and, in all meta-evaluation methods, this puts particular demands on the scrutiny stages to confidently critically assess the quality of cumulation from source evidence.
- Applying the different meta-evaluation methods has one common theme: the necessary discipline of working within the inquiry focus and evidence boundaries. This places a responsibility on the evaluator, not only in following their own rules, but in demonstrating they are doing so, to users and stakeholders.

Synthesis approaches offer considerable potential value, but for purposeful evaluation their structure and specificity raises particular challenges for necessary stakeholder engagement. Realist synthesis has an inherent focus on engaging key stakeholders, but other methods need close attention to finding and prioritising early opportunities for involving key stakeholders, focusing the inquiry, and in quality assuring for pre-summative assessment of evidence and implications. Translating evidence synthesis into policy and practice actions may depend on how well and creatively evaluators embrace and integrate those opportunities.

PART IV

Putting it in place: preparation into delivery

> Before anything else, preparation is the key to success.
> Alexander Graham Bell

12

Preparation and groundwork

Introduction

A well-placed and purposeful judgement on method is the starting point for choices to be made about how best to apply it. The four chapters making up the concluding parts of *Purposeful Evaluation* are concerned with those choices and where the groundwork for optimising how a chosen method is put in place can boost or impair the integrity and influence of the evidence it is to provide. The focus of this chapter is on the initial preparation and planning for delivery; those that follow look at managing the evaluation when it is underway, delivering the evidence and maximising the opportunity for its influence.

Planning for the evaluation falls into two parts: before and after the choice of method. The first part is concerned with scoping intent, setting objectives and managing expectations, and embedding the ethical dimension, as covered previously (Chapters 2 to 4). This chapter focuses on the second part which follows the choice of method from the wealth of possibilities set out in Chapters 5 to 11. Time pressures can mean this groundwork receives less thorough attention than it merits or needs, risking insubstantial foundations. This can leave delivery vulnerable to implementation gaps, and in a poor position to adapt to challenges as and when they arise. It will be difficult to push back on such pressures, so well-focused actions and energy for preparations need to be guided by anticipating what is needed, and addressing this with intensity, agility and confidence.

When to evaluate

The likely first planning judgement will be on when to evaluate. If the evaluation is to be externally commissioned, this may be pre-determined and effectively out of the evaluator's hands (and non-negotiable). Those developing an evaluation for internal design and delivery, or specifying it for commissioning, have more choice; here, decisions will depend largely on the state of play for what is to be evaluated. There will be three broad situations:

- 'ex-ante evaluation', conducted before an intervention starts, perhaps as an aid to its resourcing or design;
- 'in-parallel evaluation', taking place alongside the intervention, either from its outset or commencing part way through;
- 'ex-post evaluation', carried out after an intervention has concluded.

Yet again, terminology can be confusing about timing. In-parallel evaluations have been referred to commonly as 'ex-post', presumably to reflect that they commence at, or after, an intervention is designed. 'Ex-post' is used through this book to describe those evaluations which commence after the intervention concludes. Choosing between these three categories is not just a matter of when the evaluation needs to start (Table 12.1).

Different start timings consequently depend on what evidence is needed to inform decisions at different points in an intervention's life-cycle. Decision-makers could in principle tap all three in sequence for the same intervention, although in a resource-constrained environment this is unlikely. Planning lead-times vary considerably across these timings:

- Ex-ante evaluations require sufficient lead-in time to generate the insights and analysis needed, and for that to be taken into account in setting critical decision points such as for the design or budgeting of the intervention it is to inform . In a recent ex-ante evaluation of a community-based anti-addiction programme for a public body, the author and colleagues concluded the (intensive) evaluation (and final report) in seven months, but it took a further eight months for the commissioning body, with stakeholders,

Table 12.1: Evaluation timing and the consequences for planning

	Context and circumstances	Likely issues include ...
Ex-ante	• Conducted before an intended intervention • Reviewing context/circumstances to inform subsequent intervention scope or focus • Providing empirical baseline to assess later achievements	• What is needed to inform an intervention rationale/business case? • Who should be the beneficiaries; are there participant priorities? • What past practice implications for a ToC/ intervention mechanisms/design? • What might success look like: what targets, success conditions and risks? • What is needed for resourcing (budget, delivery and time)?
In-parallel	• Conducted during the intervention • Evaluation commences in parallel with intervention start; or • Commences at some interim point in delivery (deferred start)	• What is the achieved process, performance or impact (so far)? • Is it working as intended; why? • What output/outcome determinants? Any unintended effects/consequences? • How effective? What improvements? • What findings and implications (at intervention end or at critical points)?
Ex-post	• Conducted after a targeted intervention has concluded • Retrospective review of process, performance or transferable potential • Fills evidence or review gap (no parallel evaluation conducted) or to be supplementary to it	• What worked? (post intervention reflection on what, how and why) • What 'long run' difference was made? • Were the changes sustained? • What lessons can be learnt after the event for enablers/constraints? • What risks to success emerged? Were they addressed/ mitigated and how? • What 'transferable' learning for other contexts?

Source: Modified from author's teaching materials

to review findings and agree which recommendations were to be taken forward for the intervention's design.
- In-parallel evaluations have their preparations best started during the development and design of the intervention itself, often well-ahead of any roll-out or formal start. This helps to align what is to be done in the evaluation with judgements the designers and funders will be making on issues such as required monitoring information, data sharing protocols (and agreements), and performance review points. Where the evaluation planning starts later, and perhaps after roll-out of

the intervention, method choices may be more constrained and possible efficiencies from tapping monitoring or shared data may be lost altogether.
- Ex-post evaluations need to tread a fine line in judging best timing. This will require a balance between the competing demands of not delaying for too long after an intervention has concluded for relevance and to tap 'fresh minds' for retrospective review, and deferring the evaluation start to a time when it can capture optimum evidence of later impacts and consequences.

Right timing needs to be purpose-led, so evaluators will need to fully engage key stakeholders in making many of the necessary judgements, as well as managing expectations of the opportunities and limitations of those choices (an issue returned to a little later).

Resourcing the evaluation: internal or external?

An early judgement in preparation for the evaluation will be if it is to be carried out internally (in-house) or commissioned for external delivery. External evaluation is characteristically seen as 'best' because it is regarded as more likely to deliver an independent assessment and provide for stakeholder credibility. In practice, there are different pros and cons for internal and external delivery (Table 12.2) which affect choice, although the most common influence is likely to be budget allocations.

Budgets for evaluations are invariably fixed, often well-ahead of method judgements. This may be driven by earlier 'business case' processes (for the intervention) or within a wider evaluation strategy, grant-bids or through wider budgeting decisions. Experience suggests the quality of budget judgements will vary greatly with an organisation's evidence and insight culture, as well as its funding assets. If there is no budget allocation for the evaluation, it will need to be conducted 'internally', or not at all. Nonetheless, internal evaluation is sometimes a preferable choice where, for example, they call on deep exploration of internal data systems or prioritise internal transferability of findings and acquired (evaluation) capability.

Where there is a choice between 'internal' and 'external', purposeful evaluation will be conscious of perceptions of

Table 12.2: Some pros and cons of internal vs external commissioning

	Pros	Cons

Internal and self-evaluation	• Lower (or no) costs to commissioning body
	• Capable of fast starts (no procurement delays)
	• Unlikely to be constrained by data access/protection issues; faster data access
	• Deeper 'internal' knowledge of available data systems, intervention and organisational culture
	• Existing relationships with (some) stakeholders, access to participants and more engagement leverage
	• Greater control over methodology focus and delivery
	• Potential for direct follow-through/leverage into decision-making
		• Available staff may lack sufficient skills or experience
		• Greater challenges to evaluator in critique (from findings) of intervention design/practice
		• Intensified risk of:
		  • Pressure on evaluators on appropriate method choice
		  • Uncontestable mission/scope creep
		  • Diminished external credibility; may not be seen as impartial
		  • Possible timing/resourcing delays or disruption (if other internal priorities arise)

External (contracted) evaluation	• More likely to be seen as impartial; trusted environment for generating positive and negative findings • Safety for participants to provide critical insights • Greater range of evaluation or other specialist skills/expertise (for example, specific techniques) • Greater (contractual) control over on-time delivery • Greater scope for drawing on wider comparative knowledge or relevant evaluation/research • As an invested activity, findings may have a higher profile with decision-makers	• Will require a significant budget allocation • More likely to be constrained by data access issues, delays or data protection regulation • Less contractor control of delivery responsiveness (risk of underwhelming delivery) • Lacks deep 'internal' understanding/insights on intervention • Narrower existing contracts or relationships; less leverage • Likely longer lead time into the evaluation start, including from mandated procurement process • Requires contract/contractor management capacity by commissioner

Source: Modified from author's teaching materials

impartiality. External resourced evaluations are commonly referred to as 'independent evaluations'. These are assumed to be impartial, although this does not automatically follow. Much will depend on planning for evaluator selection, including the transparency for any perceived conflict of interest. It is more challenging to cast an internal evaluation as impartial because, in one form or another, the funding or delivery body for the intervention will be regarded as 'marking their own homework'. Steps can, however, be taken to boost impartial positioning, by planning for separation of design and delivery from the evaluation, by external appointments to a steering group, or use of external peer review of methods and/or findings.

The decision on 'internal' or 'external' is consequently more nuanced than it might seem. There are many different pros and cons, which go much deeper than whether a sufficient budget is available. These factors may need to be weighed carefully against one another in the early stages of preparation.

Purposeful stakeholder engagement

Evaluation is more likely to flourish where it is optimally collaborative, especially in building necessary planning and delivery connections with stakeholders. While the value of stakeholder engagement may seem self-evident, evaluation circumstances commonly result in engagement being too narrowly defined, or achieved, to deliver that value. Deciding what is 'necessary' requires balancing 'technical' judgements with less readily defined 'political' considerations. Applying those judgements to successful engagement has been described as mastering: ' ... the black arts of [stakeholder] collaboration' (Kujala et al, 2022). This part of the book looks at its practice for purposeful evaluation, focusing on the practical issues and pitfalls, not the more theoretical aspects which have dominated much of the wider literature.

'Optimal collaboration' with stakeholders is rarely straightforward and evaluators may have more ambition for it than commissioners. An all too easy mistake to make is to rush into early judgements about who, how and when. This needs to be guided by a clear understanding about engagement purpose: just how are stakeholders to add to the evaluation journey and support its utility?

Some early engagement may already have been put in place, perhaps for prototyping or intervention design. For evaluation planning, judgements on engagement are likely to need to be more ambitious with an early need to:

- define a clear purpose for engagement and what it adds to the evaluation;
- establish any subsidiary objectives for engaging all, or specific stakeholders;
- set the necessary engagement scope and limitations.

Defining engagement purpose

The most obvious point of departure for stakeholder engagement is to start with where stakeholders need to be engaged in subsequent delivery of the evaluation or for critical collaborative relationships. Although there may be some specific requirements, this starts with the intended evaluation method and anticipating:

- necessary provider or participant motivation for involvement, including briefing;
- what available information needs to be accessed on the intervention, and any arrangements needed for data-sharing;
- required access to participants for securing necessary evidence and insights.

To this needs to be added the question of which stakeholders are needed to gather organisational or individual insights on the context of the intervention and its intention, and perhaps on prior or ongoing activities. For the credibility of the evaluation, this will likely need to tap diverse perspectives from providers, charities, voluntary or public services, and from those with lived experience (of which more later).

Establish subsidiary objectives

Within the overall engagement purpose there may be subsidiary needs for 'niche' stakeholder contributions. Instead of a one-size-fits-all approach to stakeholder engagement, this may call for a branched approach with different inputs from different stakeholders at different points of time. For example, if the evaluation needs to draw on existing data held by a single coordinating body, stakeholders' contribution may be limited to early-stage specification, and agreeing data-sharing protocols. They may have little or no interest (or contribution to make) in reviewing content for interview schedules, case study selection criteria, or preliminary findings and implications.

Setting engagement scope and limitations

With the exception of developmental evaluation (Chapter 6), applying any evaluation method will have some, probably non-negotiable, boundaries for what (external) stakeholders can influence. Legacy issues, commercial or other sensitivities from funders may also set limitations on who can be engaged. These engagement boundaries need to be clearly defined, with any implicit boundaries made explicit. Evaluators will rarely have a free hand in defining those boundaries, but there are usually creative ways of remedying practical, or commissioner-set, constraints. In a recent evaluation advisory role to a cross-national recruitment initiative for language teachers in schools, the author proposed teacher trade unions be invited onto a multi-stakeholder working group. Political considerations were said to make this impractical; instead, the subsequent evaluation built in early scoping interviews with selected unions, a solution which the commissioners and evaluators saw as an acceptable compromise.

Practical engagement of stakeholders

With a clear (and viable) purpose for engaging stakeholders agreed, decisions need to be made on how to make best use of them. Various guidance[1] is available, although centred mostly on engagement in research where the stakeholder contribution to utility comes less to the fore. For purposeful evaluation, practical stakeholder engagement is likely to need to address five recurrent particular issues:

- What is the necessary engagement scope for stakeholders and inclusion potential?

- How to best position engagement choices to account for any engagement 'legacy'?
- Where are the likely risks for engagement and how these can be avoided?
- How to engage using proportionate and inclusive processes?
- What is the appropriate level and mode of participation?

Which stakeholders; what potential?

Scoping may have identified a range of stakeholders that could usefully be engaged; if not, it pays to start with wider ambition and narrow down priorities from a long list. Table 12.3 sets out some of the prospective candidates.

Different mixes of these (and other) stakeholders will suit different evaluations and their approaches. Judgements on priorities for engagement will need to reflect how and where they add value, rather than to just be opportunity (or resource) driven. If the 'priorities' list is extensive, this can be accommodated by looking at different modes or timing of participation for different stakeholders (of which more later).

Reviewing engagement 'legacy'

Purposeful evaluation will recognise that stakeholders are not going to be automatic recruits. Their willingness to engage may be conditioned by any past experience of working with the commissioning body, its partners or the evaluators themselves. Such legacy issues need to be anticipated, allowing for:

- Those with past, positive engagement experience might be ready to volunteer (where they have capacity to do so) if they recognise prospective value from their own (or organisational) involvement. To tap this latent motivation, the evaluator may need to make the case for what that engagement value might be.
- Others may have less positive past experiences or be influenced by inter-organisational rivalry or tensions. Here, evaluators will need to consider if and how to make a sound, persuasive case for their involvement. Without this, they may not engage or (if they do) may be disruptive to the necessary quality of collaboration.

Table 12.3: Potential stakeholders for evaluation planning and development

Stakeholder	Contribution
Commissioners or partner bodies	• Commissioning bodies, co-funders or partners • Lead agents for the intervention and/or evaluation
Intervention 'architects' (designers and developers)	• Will have a close understanding of intent and intended practice or other insights affecting focus
Policy or programme teams	• Hold the aspiration for the intervention • Will be looking for useable evidence on what's working, improvement and transferability to other policy agendas
Key analysts in commissioners/funders	• Analytical intermediaries between policy and decision-makers • May have end-responsibility for appraisal or the evaluation
Accountability bodies	• Scrutiny bodies within or external to commissioners • Hold responsibility/interest in assessing efficacy or accountability for programme funding and investments
Regulatory or standard-setting bodies	• Agencies or others holding a specific interest in quality or compliance issues
Contextual experts	• Academics, researchers, consultants or others with expertise in intervention context • Expertise in relevant evaluation techniques or practice
Providers or provider representative bodies	• Delivery (or representative) bodies for the intervention • Insights on organisational-management practice for the intervention
Intervention practitioners	• Practitioners, professional or practitioner representative bodies; trade unions • Insights on front-line practice and delivery relevant to the intervention
End users	• Direct and/or other beneficiaries of the intervention • Lived experience insights (including outputs, outcomes and unintended consequences)
'Consequence' stakeholders	• Representative bodies, interest groups or charitable bodies (not directly involved in intervention) with active interest in its outputs/outcomes

Source: Author's teaching materials

- Some may have no past experience, either of engaging with the commissioning body or of cross-stakeholder collaboration within evaluation (or both). The second of these can be especially challenging, where the evaluation methods may be seen as technically demanding of their knowledge (for example, economic or theory based-evaluation).

Stakeholder collaboration cannot be taken as a given. Looking at engagement legacy, and positioning any subsequent invitation, briefing and the engagement 'ask', can help motivate at least some of the likely 'doubters' or reinforce existing relationships. Commissioning bodies will likely have a close interest in how this is to be managed by the evaluators, and may have a key role to play in it.

Assessing risks

Risks to engagement go beyond willingness to collaborate and will probably rise with the complexity of the intervention. Some of the more common risks are:

- lack of stakeholder motivation, recognition (of their relevance) or confidence in their prospective contribution;
- inter-stakeholder rivalries or conflicts of interest (is their engagement a threat or an opportunity to timely and responsive evaluation preparation?);
- unrealistic expectations of what is needed from (or boundaries to) their contributions;
- discontinuous engagement, stakeholder attrition or drop-out from collaboration;
- disruptive individuals who do not provide sufficient 'constructive' critical insights in any collaborative discussions;
- inappropriate or ill-informed representation of stakeholder perspectives or interests by engagement nominee.

Evaluators will find that timely (pre-engagement) consideration of likely risks will be time well spent. This can allow time for adjustments or for other mitigations to be put in place to ensure that stakeholder engagement draws on 'right brains – right mode – right time'. It can also help with early warning of any engagement difficulties which might subsequently arise and inform what are realistic demands to place on stakeholders and necessary communications. Many of these risks can be reduced by well-placed pre-engagement briefings to inform (and be transparent about) what is to be done, for whom or what for, with who else, and when (a preliminary timetable can help intensify any staged requirements).

Proportionate and inclusive processes for engagement

As with all preparations for an evaluation, stakeholder engagement needs to pay close attention to the resources available. This includes the capabilities and availability of those being asked to contribute: the engagement 'ask' should be proportionate to the demands and circumstances of their 'day jobs', personal responsibilities or knowledge. Most stakeholders best placed to contribute are likely to have multiple demands on their time, so the quality and continuity (where it is needed) of engagement needs to treat them as assets to be harnessed judiciously. Proportionality in engagement also needs to reflect aspiration for inclusion, to appropriately reflect diversity of stakeholder interests and needs, especially where: 'It is important to not only engage with your high influence stakeholders but to encourage and seek participation from stakeholders who may not be frequently heard or who may be harder to reach' (Victorian Government, 2018). This may mean it is necessary to customise engagement arrangements to better enable some stakeholders to participate, taking into account:

- constraints to sustained and effective stakeholder involvement;
- capabilities, capacities and (any) cultural preferences of different stakeholders;
- differences in intensity or focus of communications, information or briefing needed for different stakeholders.

Inclusion may be particularly challenging where engagement seeks to involve some lived experience from potential or actual participants, especially where this covers 'hard to reach' groups and those with limited agency or access constraints. This might call for creative solutions, such as modified access, or perhaps proxy representation.

Level of participation

Practical engagement will also need care and attention to the appropriate level and mode of stakeholder participation. Preparation for some evaluations may call for an early 'one-hit' approach, perhaps through a small number of key stakeholder interviews or a small-group meeting. This is helpful for intensive evaluation. In other cases, it may require something more involved and continuous, especially where stakeholders' early participation may be followed by some ongoing role in steering the evaluation (Chapter 13).

If an evaluation takes place in complex or evolving circumstances, or where stakeholders have different interests, or contribution potential, a variety of engagement levels and modes might be used. If time allows, and where there are multiple stakeholders, a two-track arrangement might be considered for:

- 'stakeholder coproduction' (tier 1), involving a smaller number of more deeply involved, well-selected stakeholders; and
- 'stakeholder engagement' (tier 2) to widen participation, but involving less intensive 'light-touch' participation.

This dual track approach can be useful in providing a layered opportunity (Table 12.4) to combine the otherwise conflicting needs for depth of engagement from some stakeholders, while also widening reach to others.

Done well, stakeholder engagement in evaluation preparation will be a cornerstone to raising credibility and confidence in the eventual findings. This may be critical where some of those stakeholders will likely have a role to play in assessing what implications from the evaluation findings are taken forward. Purposeful stakeholder engagement consequently deserves some care and attention: it provides

Table 12.4: Coproduction and engagement in stakeholder participation

	Tier 1: Coproduction	Tier 2: Engagement
	Higher intensity inputs from small numbers of stakeholders	Low intensity inputs from wide range of stakeholders and others
Participation level	• Small number of well-selected, knowledgeable stakeholders • Involvement usually of organisations via individuals • High motivation for sustained participation • Deeper (possibly multi-stage) involvement • Focus on preparation ideas building; detailed review	• Larger number of individual or organisational contributors • Light-touch, low-intensity engagement • Participation is optional for those invited • Focus on scrutiny/endorsement of evaluation approach or specific proposal
Possible participation options	• Small group working (in-person, online or hybrid) • Panel-based 'deliberative' review of (draft) working papers, method proposals, and so on • Individual stakeholder interviews	• Multiple segmented 'review' groups • Invited cross-stakeholder consultation event(s) • Issue-based, specific requests for contributions (or review) • Web-based, open-access consultation

Source: Author's teaching materials

potential capital to endow the subsequent use and utility of evaluation evidence.

Making designs proportional

Most commissioners will expect the design for an evaluation to be proportional; many will explicitly ask for it. Cost-efficiencies are the main driver, with most evaluations likely to be expectation-heavy but resource-light. To this may be added tight timeframes, especially in 'test and learn' micro-evaluations where decision-makers, who may themselves be under pressure to make early judgements, expect a lot within a limited period of time. Both are persisting and intensifying pressures.

Although commissioners may expect proportionality, experience shows that beyond asking for a 'fit for purpose' or 'cost-effective' design, they are unlikely to clarify just what they expect of it. This leaves those preparing for design and delivery with a vague or ambiguous requirement. This is also one area where evaluation literature is not helpful. Although strong on encouraging proportional designs, it lacks much attention to guiding what is meant or needed for its practice. In practice, what are, and are not, 'proportional' design choices will always be a matter of professional judgement, bringing together resourcing, data capacity, intervention circumstances, and evaluation intent.

At the heart of making judgements on proportionality is that the methodology should provide for as much scope and scale of evidence as is necessary – but as little as possible. This calls for 'optimally minimising' a design which might be codified to four broad axioms for making proportional choices (Table 12.5).

Table 12.5: Principles for proportionate design of purposeful evaluation

A code for proportional design choice:	Where a proportional design ...
Axiom 1: To achieve or exceed a minimal level of accuracy to assess what is being evaluated	Provides evidence-gathering approaches, scale and levels of analysis that are sufficient to enable a minimum (or higher than minimal) level of accuracy to meet the evaluation objectives
Axiom 2: To relate robust resource allocation within a methodology to the likely consequence for the evaluation	Ensures that the distribution of available resources within the evaluation emphasises those aspects which require the greatest intensity of allocation reflecting priority issues for decision-making and any specific evidence generation (or analytical) challenges (such as, accessing 'hard to reach' groups).
Axiom 3: To provide for responsive evidence with the potential for analytical credibility within decision-making	Aligns design judgements on necessary 'robustness' of findings, to how the evidence is to be used and what for. An evaluation methodology is proportionate where its process and evidence provides sufficient confidence to decision-makers that findings, and implications drawn from them, are a credible basis to inform necessary decisions
Axiom 4: To ensure the methodological choices as implemented are relevant to the intervention situation.	Ensures design mix, choices and implementation are relevant to the intervention's aspirations, its intended delivery focus, participant situation and circumstances.

Source: Modified from author's teaching materials

The last of these (relevance to situation) may require especially careful positioning. Here, some of the more common issues to be taken into account will be:

- scale of the intervention, in terms of participants, geographical or situational reach of what is being evaluated;
- potential for inappropriate disturbance to the actions of the intervention or to its participants;
- relative maturity or novelty of the intervention and its circumstances;
- complexity of the causal situation likely to influence the intervention and its outcomes;
- decision-making sensitivity of the problem, issue or challenge which the intervention is aimed at addressing.

Scale of the intervention

Evidence intensity is likely to be inversely related to the scale and reach of the intervention. Evaluating a test-and-trial project of peer-mentoring 100 young first offenders in one pilot community might need to survey or interview all beneficiaries and all mentors. This high intensity approach would be proportionate, given the small scale of the intervention and the need to capture a sufficient range of insights. In contrasts, for a similar but much larger-scale cross-community programme this intensity would be disproportionate.

Potential for inappropriate disturbance

A proportionate design will ensure method choices minimise disturbance to the intervention or participants from judgements on its scale or evidence collection approach. For the larger-scale cross-community young offenders mentoring programme (as in the previous paragraph) including interviews with a large sample of beneficiaries and mentors would likely be inappropriately disruptive; a more proportionate approach might be to interview only a small, stratified sample. If those 'depth' interviews were to anticipate two-hour individual interviews, this would also likely be disproportionate disturbance (and lead to high drop-out rates and uncertain validity).

Relative maturity of the intervention

Where an intervention is mature, a lot will probably already be known about its diversity, participant responses, influencing and other factors. In contrast, for a novel intervention much more will be uncertain (or unknown). Evaluation of less mature programmes or those with high levels of innovation will likely need greater depth and breadth of evidence to increase confidence that inherent uncertainties will be better informed, so this will also see an inverse relationship between maturity and the necessary intensity of evidence.

Causal complexity

Complexity evaluations (Chapter 10) will face multi-faceted cause–effect relationships, influencing how the intervention operates and contributes to outcomes. Complexity ratchets up evidence demands (multiple variables; intended and unintended consequences) and proportionate approaches will require more design subtlety and a wide range of both dependent and independent variables in evidence capture (and analysis). Returning to the young offenders pathfinder illustration, any reduction in repeat offending as an outcome is likely to be affected by many influences outside the initiative itself. A proportionate approach to reflect that causal complexity might require engagement with schools/colleges, health services, police and other local service providers, parents or guardians. If the same intervention had been running for many years, an evaluation might slim down the range of its evidence capture to draw on likely richer in-programme monitoring and legacy data.

Intervention sensitivity

Some evaluations may involve interventions in highly sensitive circumstances for decision-makers (or public perception) where proportional designs are likely again to need higher evidence intensity. A more streamlined design could fail to provide sufficient reassurance and confidence to decision-makers needing to take high profile decisions in sensitive circumstances. So, if the young offenders pathfinder pilot is targeted on a locality with a reputation for high recurrent levels of youth knife crime or gang violence, the evaluators might judge it proportionate to build in interviews with a wide range of community organisations, local lobbying groups and focus groups with a cross-section of past victims of youth crime, residents and other affected individuals.

Judgements on proportionality go much deeper than cost-effectiveness and will call on the evaluators' technical ability to balance needs and circumstance, perhaps trading off aspects of breadth, depth and priorities for focus.

Anticipating the evidence and analysis needs

Central to any evaluation are research-based techniques for collection, processing and analysis of necessary evidence about what is being evaluated. Many of these techniques will be familiar to readers. Our focus here is not on the methods themselves, but on how preparation for the evaluation translates earlier planning on objectives and inquiry focus (Chapter 3) into specific, essential evidence requirements. As with much in purposeful evaluation, this aspect of preparation requires an agile and iterative approach, combining the evaluators' technical insight and knowledge with framing necessary choices through stakeholder engagement.

Figure 12.1 sets out a loose, staged, practical 'eight-step' approach which draws those two insights together in an intuitive, critical pathway approach. It provides an adaptive, iterative, framework approach to assessing evidence needs and priorities, flexed to circumstances with embedded critical engagement of key stakeholders.

Going through these stages may take a little time but will ensure preparation of evidence requirements does not rely entirely on the evaluators' interpretation of needs and assumptions about how best to meet them. By iteratively drawing in (staged) key stakeholder insights, the process provides for better placed judgements on sourcing, minimising subsequent risks from unanticipated data quality, timing or access challenges. The stages are outlined briefly here:

Step 1

This involves harnessing the earliest planning (Chapter 3) leading to the evaluation objectives and inquiry focus so as to articulate

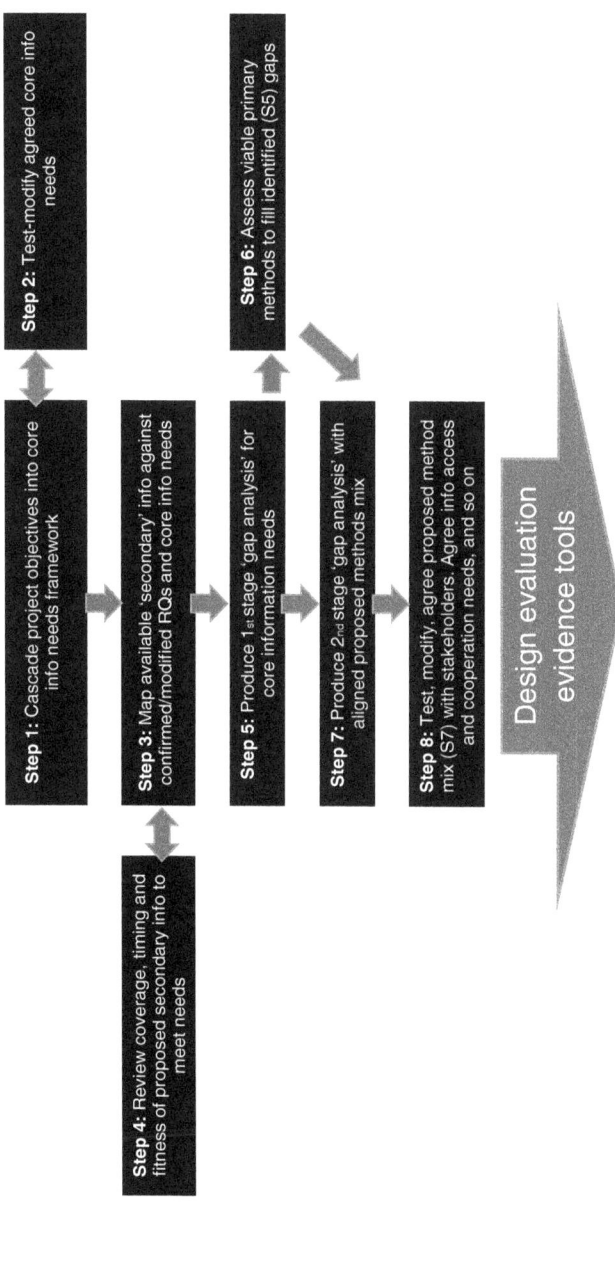

Figure 12.1: The eight-step model to setting evidence needs

Source: Modified from author's teaching materials

more specific 'research questions' (RQs). These will constitute the core evidence needs for the evaluation and represent an overarching 'core evidence framework' from which to specify more specific needs.

Step 2

That core evidence framework is shared with key stakeholders to sense-test it for expectations, purpose-fit and comprehensiveness. Feedback may identify modifications to the RQs, supplementary information or evidence needs relevant to the objectives or for evidence priorities within the RQs.

Step 3

Any evaluation will need to make best use of available 'secondary' data (such as monitoring, administrative data, 'big' data sets), where it is appropriate to needs. Step 3 maps likely secondary sources against the core evidence framework and specific RQs, and sense-checks their appropriateness. This will review the 'RQ fit' of the proposed secondary source for currency, scope, classification, quality, and access to identity information (where needed) to determine suitability and if they may need to be replaced or supplemented by primary methods (steps 5–7).

Step 4

The scrutiny of secondary data utility (step 3) may be compromised by imperfect information (to the evaluator) about limitations. To counter this, the step 3 'map' and assumptions are shared and reviewed with data providers to pick up any inaccuracies about presumed quality of those sources.

Step 5

An updated core evidence framework (from step 4) provides for a preliminary 'gap analysis' of where evidence requirements are not likely to be met by existing sources and which need additional (primary) data collection methods. The implied primary source needs must be conditioned by capacity, budget or time constraints, and may need to be refined (or excluded[2]) where resources are insufficient. This 1st stage gap analysis goes further to propose indicative evidence collection methods (and scale) to fill the gaps, recognising that some ways of collecting evidence (such as surveys; interviews) may use one method to cover a number of RQs.

Step 6

The penultimate feedback loop with key stakeholders tests the preliminary gap analysis (and idealised primary sources) from step 5 to surface any likely evidence quality or utility gaps, or inconsistencies with evaluation priorities and viability. Where resources do not meet those needs, timeframe or budgets may require adapting, or (more likely) stakeholders will inform reprioritisation (or streamlining) of the evidence required.

Step 7

Provides a 2nd stage gap analysis, building in any necessary refinements from step 6. This may involve necessary refinement of the secondary-primary balance, and specific primary evidence methods setting out approach, scale of activities, selection and access issues. It represents the anticipated needs-based focus and approach to evidence collection.

Step 8

The concluding step involves final feedback from users and key stakeholders on the 2nd stage gap analysis and method proposals. Feedback will provide for the progressing towards any specific evidence collection tools. It will also provide the departure point for partners or third parties to be brought in (if not already involved) to agree necessary access to data, data sites or for establishing necessary data-sharing formalities or protocols.

The eight-step approach is a simple and intuitive framework to translate objectives and RQs into viable evidence needs, but to this must be added further evidence to unpick findings. Four additional evidence requirements recur here:

- What comparative data are likely to be needed?
- What key 'independent' variables should be provided for in the 'primary' methods?
- How to allow for and assess unintended consequences?
- What is needed to verify and assess reliability and validity?

Comparative data

Virtually all evaluations will need some comparative data to assess relative change for outputs or outcomes, or (for impact evaluation) the attributable contribution to observed effects (Chapter 5). These data may be from intervention baselines on the pre-activity situation being assessed, or changes over time within the intervention, or for different external benchmarks, such as what happened comparatively to control groups or selected comparisons (Chapters 8 and 9).

Independent variables

Interventions in social settings will be dealing directly or indirectly with people who are unlikely to be homogeneous. Even where a specific 'needs' group is targeted, there will be potentially conditioning differences among them, to be unpicked in any analysis through factoring in selected independent variables. For beneficiary-centred interventions, this might typically be collecting data on age, gender, ethnicity, location, educational attainment and a host of other potentially relevant conditioning issues for analytical breakdowns. For other types of participating units (schools, businesses, service agencies) different independent variables will be needed. If these requirements are not anticipated at the preparation stage, they can rarely be adequately accommodated later on.

Unintended consequences

Unintended consequences (Chapters 9 and 10) are also an importance consideration to be anticipated for analysis, especially for most modes of impact evaluation. They may be critical also for Development Evaluation or 'test and learn' approaches. Evidence necessary to allow and adjust for these will also need anticipating if the evaluation is to provide a rounded picture of what has been achieved by the intervention.

Evidence verification

Evidence does not speak for itself, and users will expect, or otherwise deserve, analysis to critically assess both data reliability and validity. This may require early anticipation in the preparation stage for what focus, and approaches are to be adopted for quantitative data, to test for internal validity and, where relevant, also for generalisable potential (external validity). Where qualitative data are involved, consideration may also need to be given to how illustrative or inferential evidence are to be validated.

All this may seem a lot to achieve when demands to get an evaluation underway may be pressing. In practice, this more considered approach need not take much more time, but it builds in necessary engagement and some reflection, to optimise the design and delivery choices.

Some purposeful tips

Method choice for an evaluation is followed by the groundwork needed for its delivery. The attention and consideration given to judgements made here can make or break how purposeful the subsequent evaluation becomes. There are some common pitfalls to avoid:

- Be realistic about preparation time; if the start timeframe for the evaluation is tight, anticipate where stakeholder input adds most value, and set timing and turn-around to reflect this.
- Stakeholder engagement needs ambition and embedding in preparation for purposeful evaluation guided by:
  - Early consideration of engagement purpose to shape subsequent judgements and a proportional process;
  - Effective selection, where ambition is important but where more is not necessarily better. Stakeholder criticality and potential, as well as motivation, aptitude and availability, will vary greatly, and will need to be reflected in engagement decisions and processes;

- Consideration of stakeholder legacy, where past experiences can condition motivation for constructive engagement.
- Cost and other pressures may see host organisations opting to conduct evaluations internally. This can work well in high intensity and other appropriate circumstances, but it has particular risks for purposeful evaluation, from inadequate or poorly communicated role separation and compromised perceptions of impartiality.
- Preparation needs to unpick both any ambiguities about what constitutes a proportional approach to the evaluation and points to where not all proportionality requirements will pull in the same direction. Any conflict of needs, or of stakeholder expectations, of a proportional design will require likely trade-off between intensity and focus.
- Well-placed choices will have to be made for the most purposeful focus for evidence to meet objectives. Where demands exceed resources, any necessary reduction in ambition will need to be matched by condensing stakeholder expectations of what the evaluation takes into account, and with what confidence.

In purposeful evaluation, many of these issues centre on how well stakeholders are engaged to meet the 'needs' of both the technical and political requirements of the evaluation. Negotiated trade-offs are often inherent to balancing this mix, to optimally distil from the evidence what needs to be captured and how.

13

Managing challenges and delivery

Introduction

The recipe for a purposeful evaluation is simple. It mixes realistic goals with on-time delivery and fit-for-purpose delivery process (and deliverables) which have integrity, are well-engaged, and clearly and well communicated. Most evaluators, however, if not operating in fully controlled (trial) circumstances, will find it less than straightforward to ensure all those elements join up as and when needed. Managing challenges and change are inherent to ensuring 'success', and it will be a lucky evaluator who does not encounter at least some disruption to planned delivery and quality.

Purposeful evaluation recognises that, of themselves, solid planning and preparation, sound method choice and application are unlikely to guarantee a smooth pathway to delivery. This commonly calls for 'agile' management to respond constructively to change and disruption by combining early anticipation, well-placed governance or steering, and sound risk-foresight to inform adaptiveness. This chapter looks at how those capabilities can be drawn into, and drawn upon, in managing for a purposeful evaluation.

Managing for change and responsiveness

Managing an evaluation has much in common with the diligence needed for effective project management in other situations, but it also places additional demands on analytical knowledge to quality assure and resolve technical issues. Beyond those foundations, effectiveness is a mixture of style, structure and systems. This chapter cannot look across all of those; instead, it focuses on the capability and practice needed to respond to challenge and disruption.

A starting point is to recognise that challenges and disruptions happen in the best planned, positioned and prepared evaluations. The measure of 'effectiveness' in managing an evaluation is not a lack of disruptions occurring, but how those that do arise are anticipated (within planning and subsequent monitoring) and satisfactorily addressed. Disruption risks are many and varied. These commonly include routine disturbance to, for example: anticipated engagement with key players or participants, or access to them; secondary data challenges, delays or flaws; and, changed evidence collection circumstances. Others may occur from 'outside' the evaluation, such as when (all too often) an intervention's starting purpose, priorities or what is needed of (or available to) its evaluation change over time.

In these circumstances, the evaluator 'sticking to plan' is rarely an option. However, the room for manoeuvre may be limited, especially for intensive evaluation or where evaluation budgets and timetables are inflexible, ratcheting up the need for agility in finding timely responses consistent with the resource boundaries. A lot will hinge on issues beyond the scope of this book, including the experience, management style and forged relationships of project leadership, but there are some common features to help in keeping the evaluation responsive to change and on a purposeful track, and especially:

- scheduling an evaluation workplan with adaptable potential;
- foresight on likely disruptions and risk management;
- engaged and responsive steering and governance;
- building project management agility in adapting to changing circumstances.

These will themselves be built on the effective use of any clearance and compliance requirements early in the management of the evaluation. These are our starting point.

Managing clearance and compliance procedures

All evaluation involves an obligation on those specifying, designing, delivering and/or managing evaluations, to make judgements on what is consistent with commissioner procedural requirements, robust, and ethical (Chapter 4). An early requirement for funders, or later for evaluators, will be negotiating a necessary clearance or compliance process, to sign off whatever method of 'balance' is proposed. This typically involves either:

- a formal process for clearance of an evaluation methodology and/or for its ethical delivery;
- a code of practice on principles and/or standards, perhaps set by a professional or other external body.

The first of these involves a formal, usually mandated, requirement of method clearance before an evaluation can commence. The second is a looser framework of guidance or standards ensuring professional credibility. Navigating one (or both) of these is a managed process which often co-locates research robustness and ethical quality (see Chapter 4).

Formal clearance procedures

Different commissioning organisations have different arrangements for method clearance; some have none at all. Where arrangements do exist, they may involve a joint clearance process covering research method and ethics, or a separate ethical clearance process as is common in the health and medical fields. Both will typically involve a formal submission of details of the proposed approach (and sometimes draft evidence-gathering tools).

By their nature, evaluations are likely to find ethical clearance the more intensive and challenging. Clearance usually centres on probing arrangements for identifying and ensuring appropriate attention to risk of harm and consent processes, with particular attention paid to any engagement of vulnerable individuals. Some funders set different ethical compliance requirements for different sorts of studies. One large health service provider in the UK, for example, mandates ethical clearance where the evaluation is of a clinical or therapeutic trial, but not where it evaluates service delivery. If there is no funder requirement for ethical clearance, the evaluator's own organisation may have its own process, as is typically the case in a university.

Clearance processes take time in both preparation and due process, which some might regard as inconvenient. Purposeful evaluation needs to see such processes more constructively – as an impartial, standards-based sense-check of meeting necessary standards. Although clearance may cause some start-up delay, evaluators may be able to finesse the process by integrating clearance with a phased workplan (Example 19).

Example 19: OPTIMISING WORKING WITH CLEARANCE PROCESSES TO PROVIDE FAST STARTS FOR AN EVALUATION

A cross-university team was evaluating a harm minimisation programme for land-based gambling in the UK. An outline methodology anticipated early stakeholder scoping interviews and a rapid evidence review (RER) on markers of gambling harms. This was to inform a later survey of providers, offering support services and a series of semi-structured interviews (and case studies) with 'problem' and 'at-risk' gamblers for participants and comparator evidence.

The evaluation funding body did not require ethical clearance, but as the evaluation was university-led it required clearance from the university internal 'research ethics' clearance panel. The team recognised the planned interviews with 'vulnerable' problem and at-risk gamblers would present substantial ethical risks in selection, briefing, consent and for embedding post-interview support. They anticipated that part of the evaluation methodology would be a particular focus for the clearance panel and likely to cause a delayed start to the intensive seven-month timetable. The solution, ahead of ethical submission, was to divide the intended methodology into two complementary phases. The first involved the scoping interviews, RER and provider interviews, and the second the selection and conduct of the gambler interviews.

Project clearance was submitted for both phases at the same time, with approval secured speedily for the first phase which commenced on schedule. Panel feedback on the second phase involved resubmission for that phase with fine-tuning (on interview briefing and consent arrangements); this was subsequently approved. The study was completed on time.

External codes of practice

There are numerous codes of practice relating to assured standards, including ethics in research and evaluation (often combined). Those of most significance sit with national or cross-national bodies, such as the American Evaluation Association, UK Evaluation Society, European Evaluation Society, and African Evaluation Association among others. There are also codes in many professional institutions where research is a common feature of practice, such as professional bodies for market research (for example, the UK Market Research Society).

Codes of practice may be set out as overarching (broad) principles, but may also include more specific statements, or standards of practice. The American Evaluation Association has five principles, and 26 guidelines within those. The African Evaluation Association also has five general principles, with 21 specific guidelines (six on ethics). Codes are not 'clearance' hoops to be jumped through, but guidance on necessary practice. This presents two challenges for evaluators:

- Which code of practice to follow?
- How to interpret and apply the guidance in specific evaluation circumstances?

'Which code of practice?': Codes of practice share many similar principles, but these are expressed differently with contrasting levels of detail. An evaluation commissioning body may specify compliance to a specific code of practice, but others may only ask for 'good' research or ethical practice (or make no reference at all). Where the choice falls to the evaluator, the evaluator may align to a specific professional affiliation or to a subject-specific code (for example, education initiatives) if the intervention falls within a particular subject field. Beyond that, the evaluator will need to be aware of what code options there are, so that picking the most appropriate can help to boost confidence or trust in subsequent findings.

'How to interpret and apply the guidance': Codes of practice are not tick-boxes; however, whatever code or standard is to be applied, it is not likely to offer detailed guidance on compliance. The evaluator, or those acting for them, will need to interpret how broad standards or principles are to be applied to a specific evaluation situation. For example, the American Evaluation Association's five 'headline principles' include a requirement for 'systematic inquiry [where] evaluators conduct systematic, data-based inquiries'. This is unlikely to cause much difficulty of interpretation, but 'Competence [where] evaluators provide a competent performance for stakeholders' may prove much more challenging to unpick.

The purposeful evaluator is well advised to always remember there are very good practical reasons behind making best use of clearance or guidance processes. Doing so helps to anticipate and minimise risks and pitfalls, that might otherwise affect the credibility of eventual findings.

Scheduling the workplan

In the author's experience, the greatest single contribution of delivery management for an evaluation is the transformation of the intended methodology into a viable, sequenced and comprehensible workplan. This is more than a delivery template; it becomes a crucial tool for responding to changing circumstances and disruptions.

Not everyone might agree with this critical placement; some evaluators may prefer a looser, more incremental approach, open to creativity and for scheduling the work as and when it is needed. The author's experience suggests quite the opposite; the workplan is a guiding – not controlling – framework, putting together the specific 'nuts and bolts' for the constituent parts of the evaluation to deliver what the method anticipates. It is the end result of the metamorphosis from evaluation 'type', through a proportional method mix and judgements on the inquiry and evidence focus, into a plan for its end-to-end implementation.

An effective workplan is not a straitjacket. Where the evaluation is likely to face emerging pressures and changes, it needs to be dynamic and adaptable; the workplan an evaluation starts with is rarely exactly the same as the one it concludes with. It translates the agreed methodology into an overarching, nuanced, sufficiently directive, framework for implementing that method by setting a start-to-end sequence for 'what to' and 'when by'. When team delivery resources and capacity are clearer, it will add 'who by' to set responsibility for each component part, transforming the workplan into a tool for monitoring and managing the project trajectory.

A structured, directive workplan may seem a big ask, but putting it together follows on naturally from the agreed evaluation methodology. The challenge with a workplan is not so much when to do it, but how to do it well. There is a lack of detailed guidance specific to preparing a directive evaluation workplan. Embedded tools in IT operating systems, proprietary project management systems and specialist software can help but are only as good as the substance and detail put into them. To ensure necessary detail particular attention needs to be paid to a process which defines:

- each of the constituent stages (work packages) of the evaluation methodology;
- the more detailed tasks needed within each stage, and the sequence of delivery for each of them, reflecting any evidence-gathering, analysis or output inter-dependencies;
- the specific method inputs required for each task to be delivered, with allocated responsibilities or accountability for delivery.

Developing the workplan in this way consequently moves from the general (stages) to the particular with specific 'key inputs' usually expressed as achievement milestones (Table 13.1). When the key input milestones are defined, tested against the anticipated methodology for any gaps in detail and clarity, and set out

Table 13.1: From work packages to workplan

Workplan element	Likely content	Notes
Stages of workplan	• Initial scoping (if needed) such as scoping interviews; data or literature review • Design and clearance of engagement, evidence capture or analytical tools • Components work packages of evidence capture and processing • Project review elements (for example, steering groups; phased progress review) • Analysis and deliverables (progress, interim and summative reports, and so on)	Stages will reflect the pre-determined inquiry focus and method choice Evidence capture includes secondary data (such as, collation and review of monitoring or admin data), primary sources (such as, observation, surveys, interviews, case studies, and so on)
Required task groups	• Defining main actions needed for each stage to be completed • Setting a framework for the broad design and delivery building blocks • Anticipating 'action' dependencies between the stages	Tasks will be intermediary between the component stages and individual sequenced inputs required, to ensure responsive and purposeful delivery
Key input milestones	• Breaking down each task into delivery elements (key inputs) to complete stages • Sequencing inputs into a (first to last) schedule across stages and reflecting duration needed for each input and any dependencies.	Each task is likely to involve multiple inputs Workplan utility hinges on the nuance in setting and appropriately sequencing inputs to delivery milestones

as a 'start to end' logical sequence, the evaluation will have a customised workplan.

Method stages

The agreed methodology will probably have anticipated broad stages and dependencies between them, perhaps as method 'phases' or 'work packages'. This will be the first and most straightforward part of workplan-setting; here, simpler evaluation may have just three or four stages, something complex will have more. Longitudinal evaluations may repeat similar stages at different periods (for example, entry cohorts, annualised delivery).

Workplan tasks

Setting the tasks for the workplan refines the evaluation stages of the evaluation. For example, if an evaluation needs a self-completion sample survey of participants (a stage), this will be likely to need several different 'tasks', including perhaps:

- identifying, agreeing and accessing an appropriate sample frame;
- developing and agreeing a sampling protocol to reflect scale and quality needs;
- applying that protocol to select a scaled, consistent, utilisable sample;
- develop and test a survey tool consistent with whatever survey delivery approach or e-platform is to be used;
- commence and administer the survey including quality assurance (for example, eligibility or logic checks) and reminder stages;
- establish any coding requirements, including assessing response fields for the required data processing;
- set and agree an analysis and data reporting protocol to reflect primary analytical requirements and analyses in appropriate formats;
- deliver analysis to the protocol.

Differentiating stages to tasks provides the subsidiary workstreams within which the key input milestones will be set.

Key input milestones (KIMs)

KIMs provide the nuance that is needed for the workplan by setting out the 'nuts and bolts' for responsive delivery for each and every task, together with the necessary join-up. Although referred to as 'inputs', they combine both things to be done (inputs) and what derives from them (outputs). Inputs may involve both start and completion milestones (for example, a survey launch and a survey end-date as two inputs), with all placed in a 'first to last' delivery sequence. The sequencing will reflect necessary task durations and any dependencies between different stages (for example, a literature review might need to inform selection criteria or interview schedule content). KIMs are not limited to what is to be done by the evaluation team and will include any inputs needed from commissioners or stakeholders (for example: signing off evaluation tools; case study selection criteria; or providing timely comments on draft reports).

There is no mystique to putting together a sound workplan. It draws on common-sense application of research knowledge with some sensible scrutiny that everything adds up and is viable. Looking at it in terms of stages – tasks – key input milestones help to break down what is needed (and when). The final workplan can also provide for the need for the content to be readily shared with others (the evaluation team, collaborators, commissioners, stakeholders).

Risk foresight and management

Risk management starts early to 'foresight' what might occur; forewarned is forearmed. Risks previously anticipated can be more readily spotted if and when they occur during the evaluation, and can then be acted upon more speedily and before they become too disruptive. Risk foresight also provides an opportunity for management of an evaluation to anticipate countermeasures for many of them. This may come early for externally contracted evaluation, where commissioners often require an assessment of delivery risks at the tendering stage, perhaps set out as a 'risk register'. Those conducted 'internally' can miss out on that opportunity altogether.

Risk foresight needs care and attention, and the author's experience as an evaluation advisor shows that they often lack sufficient insight or ambition. Foresight cannot anticipate all likely challenges, but that is no reason not to go as far as possible. This may suggest modifications to the evaluation approach (before it starts) to avoid some of the delivery risks, so the earlier this is put together the better. For example, if a risk is identified of there being too few (or skewed) interview volunteers, the proposed evaluation methodology might be revisited, to add in motivation payments, widen eligibility or to provide for a larger reserve selection list.

Risk registers need to be dynamic to respond to any changing circumstances in or for the evaluation. Starting registers need to be regularly reviewed and updated; long duration or longitudinal evaluations may need a series of updated risk registers. While the foresight process needs to be as thorough as is practicable, the registers themselves do not need to be overcomplicated. Synthesised foresighting can be reduced to a single document to set out:

- Risk identification – what disruption could occur to the anticipated evaluation process, evidence quality and schedule?
- Disruption assessment – what is the likelihood that the risk could occur; and, if it did, what would be its broad effect for the scope, quality or timing of the evaluation?
- Anticipated contingencies – what could be put in place, either to avoid or minimise the risk occurring (for example, modification of the planned method or delivery schedule) or, if it did occur, contingencies to mitigate its disruption to the evaluation?

Risk registers are only as useful as the quality of thinking that goes into them for identifying – assessing – and anticipating. A framework for tackling this is outlined in Table 13.2.

The anticipation stage (third column of Table 13.2) is what transforms foresight into a crucial management tool for the agility of an evaluation. Here, it is not necessary to put contingencies in place for all of the possible (identified) risks, and this effort is usually focused on those assessed as 'high-high' or 'moderate-high' risks (for likelihood and consequence). Not all will be capable of remedial action, but many will be.

Planning for contingencies is at the heart of risk management. Unless the project manager is very unlucky, most of the identified and assessed risks will not take place or will prove insignificant, but for those that do, those managing the evaluation will be in a better place to speedily recognise them and adapt to minimise unnecessary (later) disruption.

Oversight, steering and governance

Funding and procurement processes may put a lot of weight on the evaluation process, so many will have embedded oversight arrangements. Oversight may be about funding accountability but, more constructively, it can also act as a validating forum,

Table 13.2: A practical framework for risk-foresighting an evaluation

Identified risks	Assessed risks	Anticipated contingencies
Identifying risks should be as comprehensive as possible (that is, those which could occur, not which are most likely or intrusive)	Broad assessment of identified risks for possible occurrence and likely consequence to evaluation if the risk were to occur	Outline proposals for any contingencies to be put in place to avoid or mitigate level or effects of risks on the evaluation if occurring
• Start up risks (such as, contractual or budgetary delays; slow clearance) • Procedural risks (such as, delay to data-sharing agreement or other access protocols) • Resourcing risks (such as, in-team illness, injury, absence, or job changes) • Implementation risks from disruption to timely or quality delivery (such as, low or skewed survey response, few interview volunteers, and so on) • Exogenous risks to delivery (such as, industrial action; travel/weather disruption at key points of evidence gathering; and so on)	• What is the *likelihood* each identified risk will occur? (Note: considered general assessment of 'low,' 'moderate,' or 'high' probability of occurrence) • If risks were to occur, what will be the *likely effects* to the evaluation or its intended workplan (inputs/delivery)? (Note: Assessment of consequences for timely delivery of evaluation tasks, any knock-on consequences to other tasks, likely impact of scope or quality if not mitigated)	• Can the risk be prevented by an adapted scope or methodology; how? • If prevention is not possible what (if any) contingencies could be viably applied to respond to or minimise disturbance if risk occurs? • Are there indirect/knock-on consequences to other aspects of the evaluation of the mitigation being applied? • Is there a 'mitigation gap' for risks that cannot be countered; which risks? What consequence for timing/quality if these occur?

contributing to the credibility of the evaluation process and its findings. Ensuring the effective composition of oversight is consequently important to purposeful evaluation.

Unless those conducting the evaluation are part of the commissioning body (that is, internal evaluation), evaluators may believe that they have no role in oversight composition. This is short-sighted. Oversight may in effect be 'policing' evaluators' delivery, but it also has a positive contribution to make to evaluation responsiveness, as well as providing insights on emerging challenges. Those conducting the evaluation are consequently well-advised to seek some influence on what representation and expertise are drawn into oversight and its process.

Oversight can come in many different shapes and sizes, conditioned by funders' due process and perhaps the size or sensitivity of what is being evaluated. For smaller or very intensive evaluations, this may be limited to ad hoc review between the (funding) contract manager and the project lead of the evaluation. Such light-touch arrangements put an emphasis on very well-developed relationships and communications. Where more formalised arrangements are put in place this may be through high-level governance or steering groups (and occasionally both), where these have different implications for oversight (Table 13.3).

Governing bodies, where they exist and are relevant to an evaluation, do not negate the need for a separate steering group, who will themselves be guided by the high-level deliberations. If both are in place, evaluators will have a much closer engagement with steering groups and probably little with high-level governance bodies. The steering groups may be constituted wholly internally

Table 13.3: Governance and steering roles in an evaluation

Governance body	Steering (or working) group
High-level 'executive' membership from a programme board or strategy group concerned with a wider agenda to which the evaluated intervention is contributing	Close contact group, variously including funder representatives, partners, policy interests, and key stakeholders. May also involve an independent or 'peer' advisor
• Defines or provides executive sign-off of evaluation goal and objectives • Sets boundaries and any (broad) rules of engagement for the evaluation • Sets high-level expectations of the project, including ambition for stakeholder engagement • Provides direction for any changing project needs, or major differences to circumstance • Receives high-level findings • Reviews, responds to (and harnesses) any evaluation recommendations	• Advise on (sign-off on) project design, scope, feasibility, evidence priorities • Arbiter of timetable/adjusted timing and periodic review of evaluation progress • Quality assure evaluation tools • Staged guidance for engagement, quality and utility issues • Provide or influence data, provider, participant access • Forum for engagement of stakeholders or relationship with wider interests • Detailed quality review of progress, interval, and final deliverables

within the funding body, but they will commonly include at least some external representation, and their oversight will be (much) more regular and frequent than governance bodies. They are also likely to be a focus for addressing any change within the project, such as delivery going off-track, or where new requirements or response to changed circumstances are involved.

Where they suggest new or modified requirements, steering groups will often themselves be agents of change in the evaluation. This can itself be disruptive, if it involves 'mission drift' from often well-intentioned but 'off-purpose' proposals. These situations need very careful handling. In the author's experience, these can often be addressed by (constructively) asking how the proposed change contributes to the agreed goal and evaluation objectives. Where the suggestion is agreed to be well-aligned, then a modification to the evaluation scope, and perhaps workplan, is justified; where not, the steering group will usually acknowledge it as 'nice to know' but not essential. This underlines the value of solid objective-setting and expectation management.

Whether through governance or steering, at the heart of oversight are mechanisms for well-placed progress review. Arrangements may be set by the funding body for frequency of review, review points (often steering meetings), and progress reporting, but there is often scope, and value, for the evaluators themselves to influence mechanisms, in particular for:

- Oversight frequency: Review points are commonly set at regular intervals to keep a phased 'finger on the pulse' of the evaluation – perhaps monthly or every quarter. Fixed intervals are often not in the best interests of the evaluation where key decision points for the evaluation method, next steps, or emerging implications are more likely to be at specific points in the workplan, not at regular defined intervals. Evaluators have a role here in proposing more relevant review points.
- Review mode: Oversight typically hinges on some form of progress reporting by synthesis, presentation or progress reports. These requirements come in different shapes and sizes, and may not always be useful for assessing progress or steering an inquiry. Whatever progress review is required, oversight will be better placed where these ensure they provide a picture of the whole

project 'trajectory', to review what has happened and what is yet to be done with a (brief) assessment of gaps, any emerging issues of concern for delivery, and proposed resolutions.
- Composition: Commissioners will probably set any oversight membership, but where this includes external bodies, they may be open to evaluators making constructive proposals on how to enhance composition. Oversight needs an appropriate range of (different) insights from steering or working group members; where evaluators can see gaps, the arrangements may lack important voices or representation, perhaps limiting expertise or the wider credibility of eventual evaluation findings.

Evaluators who see oversight as a largely policing function may be reluctant to take a proactive role in shaping the arrangements. This is not in the best interest of purposeful evaluation, and experience suggests few commissioners will not be open to well-placed suggestions about mechanisms or gaps in composition. Not all evaluator suggestions will be endorsed, but some may well be. Example 3 (Chapter 2) illustrated how commissioners responded positively to the evaluation team's suggestion for adding representatives from a distributed community network to steering arrangements, with these representatives' involvement later enhancing access to participants and cross-community confidence.

Keeping it agile

The more complex the intervention situation, the more multi-faceted the evaluation approach, and the longer its timeframe, the more likely it will be that delivery challenges will occur. Method agility and responsiveness to necessary change, through active evaluation management, are part and parcel of making, and keeping, an evaluation purposeful.

That agility is grounded in the combination of a responsive and adaptable workplan with adequately foresighted (and potentially mitigated) risks, and constructive engagement with the agents of oversight. These are instruments for adaptation; effectiveness in managing challenges depends on how the evaluator harnesses them (alongside their technical and relationships skills) through due diligence and timely actualisation.

Due diligence

With a nuanced workplan in place, tools allocated, and well-demarcated (team) roles, responsibilities and skills, the evaluator may be confident only a light touch is needed to ensure the evaluation remains on track and is responsive to disruption. They may also be keen to emphasise trust in often highly skilled and experienced colleagues (or contractors) in taking forward the detail. While recognising the need for empowering colleagues, this light touch is likely to be imprudent; workplan, resource and team management needs a quality of due diligence by the evaluation lead to capitalise on the preparation and planning.

A lack of due diligence commonly results from insufficient in-project scrutiny, with two common misconceptions. The first is conflating devolved with delegated authority. The evaluator lead may delegate allocated evaluation inputs, and even whole tasks, to specific individuals, but in doing so, they do not devolve authority for their delivery to them. That authority, and accountability for it, remains with the project lead and managing it needs due diligence

The second misconception is that scrutiny is a staged process. However, snags and challenges do not arise on a phased basis: early identification and responses to minimise disruption need continuous attention to workplan milestones, intra-team communications, and also externalities that might affect delivery. This persistence in scrutiny takes nothing away from team empowerment, but it does ensure a granular and progressive attention to the timeliness and quality of inputs being delivered. It goes beyond monitoring of 'are we where we expected to be at now?', to continuously review the project's forward trajectory against the workplan and any changing circumstances.

Actualisation

Timely actualisation is about how evaluation responds to any apparent or likely performance gaps. Day-to-day project pressures or other priorities mean it is all too easy to defer response. We may succumb to 'wishful thinking' that identified disruptions may be temporary and go away of their own accord. There may be occasions where it is justified to 'wait and see', but it is more often ill-advised. Slippage in workplan delivery, or response, means a problem deferred is too often a problem intensified down the line.

Effective actualisation also needs to avoid trying to fall back on 'easy' fixes to disruption. Slow progress, perhaps on some aspects of evidence-capture or engagement, may be 'easily' resolved by an extended timeframe or an enhanced budget. However, it is unwise to assume either will be readily available. Even if either were an option, it could take some time to agree, causing further delay and intensifying knock-on problems to other aspects of the evaluation. Evaluators are better advised to be creative in identifying early solutions within available resources and conditioning the workplan correspondingly, with the risk register a first port of call for contingencies.

Agile responses call for disruption resolution based on:

- thinking laterally to recast parts of the workplan to create time for whatever adjustment is to be implemented;
- watching out for sequencing/dependency implications for other inputs in the evaluation, and asking whether there are likely knock-on effects which may also need adjustment;
- recasting the project's interim key input milestones or timing of task dependencies to provide adjustment space in the workplan without delaying eventual delivery;
- anticipating any quality consequences of the solution and adaptions, and seeing whether appropriate mediations for those can be put in place;
- engaging commissioners and perhaps others in agreeing the 'fix' and any necessary trade-offs within the workplan.

Managing challenges, change and disruption in evaluation is about resolution, not avoiding or apportioning blame. How purposeful a concluded evaluation is will likely be more adversely affected by a lack of timely actualisation than by a successfully modified initial workplan.

Some purposeful tips

Most evaluation is usually placed under a restrictive time burden for its preparation, start, timeframe or conclusion. The real challenge, however, is not lack of time, but in managing the use of the time available, including in timely responses to emerging challenges. There are some practical tips which can help with this.

- Evaluations need to start with the expectation that, even with effective planning and preparation, change and challenges are a likely and often inevitable consequence of operating in a dynamic situation for evidence-gathering, context and purpose.
- Purposeful evaluation places a premium on minimising emerging disruption through engaged, timely and agile responses, built on the preparatory effort put into work planning, risk foresight and proactivity in oversight.
- Any temptation to rush or even neglect clearance and compliance requirements when responding to set-up or start pressures is ill-advised. Time put into these is an investment in necessary focus and credibility, providing also a safety-net when delivery challenges later emerge.
- The utility of workplans is based on the care and attention going into them; this provides returns going beyond resource distribution and project monitoring, to provide a framework for trajectory review and guiding timely adjustments to risks.
- Risk registers provide for a 'negative' workplan: to foresee as far as possible what issues might disrupt the actual workplan, and to provide a fast-response framework for addressing any identified challenges if and when such problems arise.
- Evaluators need the confidence and skills to be proactive, wherever possible and necessary, in guiding oversight mechanisms and composition to support constructive scrutiny and provide insights to aid responses to in-project disruptions and change.

It is a lucky evaluation which is able to conclude with the same workplan as the one with which it started. Responding to change and disruption is, consequently, just another of the challenges the evaluator needs to face. The purposeful evaluator will recognise that tackling them is about resolution, not blame.

PART V

Presenting and mobilising evidence

A wise man proportions his belief to the evidence.
David Hume

14

Delivering the evidence

Introduction

Purposeful evaluation has a resolute commitment to informing decision-making, where the agent of change is the evidence and how it is shaped, represented and communicated. That evidence does not speak for itself, and well-purposed deliverables are needed to direct and enhance its 'voice'. A solidly purposed evaluation stands or falls on its reporting; if poorly positioned, reporting can compromise confidence in what is being evidenced, and any prospects for its use.

For purposeful evaluation, that positioning involves not only responsiveness to the evaluation's formal objectives but also negotiating a use-responsive pathway between the many tensions involved in synthesising findings into a narrative readily understood by (and useful to) decision-makers. Much of this book has been concerned with the many possibilities for purposefully shaping and delivering intent-based evidence; this chapter goes further to look at its effective representation. It is followed by a final chapter focusing on wider dissemination and communications issues for optimising evidence use (Chapter 15).

What deliverables, for whom and when?

The starting point for purposeful reporting is clarity on what deliverables are expected and viable. Funder guidance on this can be minimal, stating little more than what type of report(s) is required, necessary timing and perhaps indicative length. This is not a sound starting point for reporting utility. This is compounded by a funding trend towards favouring brevity, with unrealistic limitations set for reporting length. This may help with assimilation, but intensifies reporting challenges in rehearsing necessary detail and substantiation where some evaluators have called for a 'theory of evidence for evaluation' (Donaldson et al, 2015) to better balance utility with representation.

In practice, evaluations have a diverse range of options for effective presentation of findings, including oral[1] as well as written reporting, at different phases of the evaluation, for different purposes and different audiences, and using different vehicles for representation. Characteristically, funders will be seeking some form of summative reporting, but this may fall short of what may be needed to support decision-making especially in test and learn or developmental situations. Here, an important distinction needs to be made between concluding reporting, knowledge transmission and knowledge exchange (issues returned to in the final chapter).

The first reporting challenge for purposeful evaluation is not synthesis of evidence but better defining what is expected, and needed, of its (subsequent) reporting. This may go beyond clarification of perhaps vague or ambiguous requirements to be proactive in proposing to remix, or add to, that requirement. This is not to ignore funders' expressed needs, but to clarify and build on these to ensure responsiveness to the evaluation's delivery and use. For some commissioners, this may seem like 'heresy', and it is certainly unwise for the evaluator to unilaterally rewrite or define what is to be delivered, for whom, how, when and to what conditions. Nonetheless, the evaluator will be closest to the evidence, its strengths and limitations, and that experience should be important in assessing how best to present findings for use and utility.

A simple starting point is to bring together (and agree), with the funders, the necessary reporting clarifications and proactive proposals into a suitably positioned reporting (or deliverables) plan (Table 14.1). This complements and extends funders' initial 'ask' to set out what is being delivered, its scope, for whom, with what parameters and priorities, and to what sequence and timing. It also provides an early opportunity to set out an indicative guide to the

Table 14.1: Indicative content for the reporting plan for an evaluation

	Indicative content
Deliverable(s)	• What is being delivered; status (for example, draft) • Identified separately from, for example: inception report; progress reports; interim report; draft/final report; executive summary report • Including any supplementary deliverables (for example, case study report; infographic presentation; machine-readable survey data file)
Status (at delivery)	• Confidentiality; distribution restrictions; intellectual copyright; and so on • Intent for wider distribution or publication
Received by and distributed to	• Initial recipient(s) for the deliverable • Intended and referred distribution • Any supplementary access including wider access (for example, website; social media) • Intended audience
Timing (receipt and review)	• Expected date of delivery to initial recipient • Distribution delivery (when by) • Review dates (such as, receipt of comments on drafts) • Sign-off, clarification or query arrangements
Anticipated scope and requirement	• Focus or boundaries of deliverable (for example, for a progress or interim report, what period is to be covered) • Requirements (if any) for conclusions or recommendations • Any priority focus (such as, for evidence reporting or recommendations) • Statement of anticipated content (for example, for reports this might include an indicative structure or essential content to cover) • Indicative requirements for page/word length and any specific formatting requirements • Substantiation of evidence needed – proof, likelihood or potential • Any required or proposed supplementary or supporting documentation or material

Source: Modified from author's teaching materials

anticipated content (for each deliverable). Putting this together as a deliverables requirement can go some way towards the 'theory of evidence' anticipated by Donaldson and colleagues (2015).

The plan could be set out as a structured narrative, or as an extended matrix[2] (the author's preference) with a bullet-point summary for content set out separately for each major deliverable.

Reporting plans will refine anything set out in the contract or funder reporting requirement to provide a whole project overview, informed by an early collaboration between funder(s) and the evaluator (with initial drafting usually led by the evaluator).

By setting out the overall architecture for deliverables, the plan can anticipate any gaps in, or additional opportunities for, reporting or outputs, and is also an opportunity for funder and evaluator to engage with key stakeholders' expectations and needs. Framing the reporting plan is a collaboration with commissioners and perhaps through them with key stakeholders. This combines the evaluator's knowledge of the design, evidence, and analytical tools (and possible limitations), with funder/user insights on the likely utility and need for evidence, sensitivities involved and audience(s), including institutional arrangements to be negotiated to harness the evaluation findings.

This necessary collaboration may not be comfortable for evaluators preferring complete independence in reporting processes and content. Users, however, will not favour little or no influence on reporting process. Purposeful evaluators will do well to recognise that, to users, there is a risk that evaluation findings may be uncomfortable for those who initiated the evaluated intervention, and could be at odds with policy, practice or organisational intentions. Users will be likely to play a more constructive role in absorbing 'negative' findings where they are confident it is not just the evaluation design which is fit for purpose, but the reporting process as well.

The deliverables focus within the reporting plan will necessarily vary (substantially) from one evaluation to another, but is likely to involve some combination of:

- outputs for effective management of the evaluation (usually progress reports);
- developmental and interim outputs, including for phased factual reporting;
- summative factual reporting (in either comprehensive and/or summarised forms);
- condensed (summary) reporting and synthesis deliverables;
- supplementary outputs centred on specific factual content, supporting data or additional knowledge exchange contributions.

These are the more likely choices open to funders and evaluators for the delivery and presentation needed for purposeful evaluation. Each of these are looked at in the rest of this chapter.

Progress review and reporting

Chapter 13 looked at some of the challenges for assessing project progress where well-placed progress reporting helps to keep a finger on the pulse of delivery. Progress reporting points are an opportunity, and necessary focus, for diagnosing and sharing delivery issues or shortfalls, and likely resolution, by setting out:

- a 'point of time' review of where the delivery of an evaluation is at (set against where it was intended to be); and
- an assessment of the delivery trajectory towards the intended end-point and any emerging challenges to quality or timing.

Progress reports which focus only on the first of these risk neglecting the evaluation's forward trajectory. Both the state of play and direction of travel are important in retaining funder and user confidence that the evaluation is at, and going to, where it needs to be. Progress reports are just that: an assessment of progress on the evidence journey. They will *not* be looking at emerging findings; where an evaluation needs these at intervals in its timetable, this calls for interim reports (considered a little later).

Although the difference between 'progress' and 'interim' may seem self-evident, it is not always so clear for funders or users; different organisations may use the same term to mean different things or have different expectations of each. As an illustration, only recently the author, leading an evaluation for a multi-national organisation, provided the first of a series of required 'progress reports'. This was subsequently greeted with hesitant enthusiasm because it did not provide any early findings! For this organisation, 'progress' assumed both a trajectory review and a presentation of early findings. With these expectations clarified, subsequent 'progress reports' in that evaluation were shaped as interim reports (but with an expanded progress review built in).

Progress reports (without findings) need to be positioned in relation to what they are looking at and how they are to be used. Simple or short duration evaluations may require only oral reporting and a review between the evaluation lead, accountable management, policy leads (for internal evaluation) or funder/contract manager (for commissioned projects). More commonly, progress reports will involve some form of written narrative, which might include one or more of: inception reports; traffic light reports; progress reports; or, progress statements (Table 14.2).

Where they are needed, inception reports will provide necessary feedback on the start-up phase of an evaluation, perhaps only a few weeks after they commence. They are important for not only setting the groundwork of what's to be done but also as an opportunity to raise any further clarifications and start to build the necessary constructive relationships with funders and users.

Table 14.2: Narrative progress reporting options (or combinations)

Report mode	Likely scope and utility
Inception reports	• Developed at a short (appropriate) interval after evaluation start-up • Review of early progress in development, design, scoping for evaluation focus, viability (of initial requirement), and timing • Exploring implications for refining the evaluation scope or adjusting intended approach
Traffic light reports	• Short key points assessment of state of play achievement in workplan • Provides (across evaluation) a rolling assessment of areas of shortfall or concern within workplan • Uses red (alarm) – amber (concern) – green (satisfactory) colour notation for progress against key inputs
Progress reports	• Longer narrative format (usually 5–10+pp) setting out a summary of ambition and current state of play • Sets out a narrative review of (any) workplan shortfall, with an assessment of consequence • Also provides a next steps assessment for subsequent stages of workplan, including any remedial actions for shortfalls
Progress statements	• Synthesised form of summary report (3–5pp) using matrix format to condense statement of progress • 'Completed', 'delayed', or 'pending' indicator for each key input milestone • Also provides short explanatory statement of any gaps and proposed remedial actions with next steps implications

Source: Modified from author's teaching materials

Each of the other progress reporting options has different pros and cons. Traffic light or 'RAG' (red/amber/green) reports are the most heavily synthesised but, in attributing a colour 'rank' to each anticipated input in the workplan, can miss important nuance and create doubtful distinctions between what is 'green' (all OK), 'amber' (cautious or incomplete progress), and 'red' (item of concern). Progress reports offer a fuller assessment of the state of play but are more demanding to produce; they can consume a disproportionate amount of project resources when they are required frequently. Progress statements (the author's preference for all but very large-scale evaluations) offer much that a full progress report provides in a more synthesised and less resource-intensive format.

Interval and interim reports

As the name suggests, these are interim analyses of preliminary findings produced typically at specified intervals in an evaluation. Although unlikely to be required in very intensive evaluations, they can be a vital ingredient of purposeful evaluation where decision-makers need early, mid-term, stage or cohort evidence. They are crucial to formative evaluation, where decisions need to be taken about, for example, funding review or decision points for intervention scale-up or roll-out, and often for improved processes to increase intervention efficiency. Making best use of interim reports calls for:

- Well-positioned timing, where findings are delivered to a schedule allowing sufficient time to act on findings and implications.
- Adequate allocated resourcing to reflect interim reports needing a lot more effort than progress reporting to assemble, make sense of, and report stage or preliminary evidence from an ongoing inquiry.
- Commissioners and funders to take a judicious and purpose-led approach in seeking interim reports, as well as in clarifying their necessary focus, high-utility timing, and priorities for contribution to (interim) decision-making.
- Adequate and timely evidence, where evaluators need the confidence to push back, when an interim report is being asked

for prematurely but there is insufficient adequacy of evidence to provide for confident (if preliminary) assessment.

Interim reports are usually in narrative form, but they might also be delivered through presentations to user workshops. In either situation, funders may be asking for evaluators to make initial recommendations. There is good reason to be cautious about going beyond preliminary findings to propose early recommendations. Early, and even mid-term evidence risks being atypical by looking just at early participation or progression (for example, early participant cohorts). Its scale might be too limited for sufficient confidence or inadequate for necessary disaggregation, meaning it is unable to (yet) identify what might be important differences for emerging outputs or outcomes for key sub-groups. Evaluators could consider adding a 'preliminary' label to any such interim recommendations, but there is a risk of this conditionality being overlooked by decision-makers keen to act on early findings.

A final consideration is that, unlike progress reports, interim reporting needs considerable forethought and guidance from funders on its necessary focus, evidence priorities, structure and substantiation. These issues are much the same as those for final reports, outlined next.

Summative (final) reporting

Purposeful evaluation will necessarily place a strong emphasis on end-results set out in concluding or summative reporting. This is both the most testing and rewarding part of any evaluation. Putting these reports together demands discipline and rigour in the selection and representation of evidence to meet the inquiry objectives and RQs, but also for its utility. Judgements made here will make or break how purposeful an evaluation is likely to be (or not).

The evaluator will be helped greatly in getting to (and over) this high bar, where there is clarity on its use and utility. Curiously for such an important part of any evaluation, there is often only a vague steer from users about this. A well-informed reporting plan can provide much of what is required but, where this does not exist, clarity needs to go further than timing and review processes, to set out:

- the necessary focus and intended audience;
- boundaries or priorities for what is needed;
- the anticipated content and an (at least) indicative structure for essential content;
- anticipated substance (page/word length) and substantiation (see later);
- any required supporting documentation.

Some prefer to work with more open reporting briefs, feeling it gives greater scope to pursue and represent whatever key points or interests emerge from findings. While taking nothing away from the evaluators' need to be evidence-led in reporting, there are dangers in this more open approach, for both evaluators and commissioners. In particular:

- Signing off reports from open approaches is more likely to be iterative, with more 'to and fro' between evaluator and funder to resolve necessary content and structure needs.
- If budgets are tight, this iterative process is wasteful of resources and will place added burdens on the commissioners or funders in reviewing and commenting on (often) successive drafts, and in difficult revision conversations with evaluators.
- The more open process may require several redrafting stages, leading to an extended timeframe, with subsequent delay to decision-making processes.
- Having multiple redrafts, and consequent delays between first drafts and a final, signed-off and distributed report, risks the data (and analysis) becoming out of date or its relevance being sidelined by changing circumstances or priorities.
- Redrafting delays also risk a loss of credibility and confidence in the evaluator and/or the evaluation process, and consequent findings.

For purposeful evaluation, these more open approaches to drafting involve significant and unnecessary risks. Avoiding them requires paying early attention to establishing sufficient guidance and clarity between commissioners and evaluators.

Different funders, and circumstances, will call for different responses to an appropriate structure for a summative report, although with some common ground (Table 14.3).

A recurrent issue for use-orientated summative reports is how to handle the description of method, where the evaluator is likely to prefer fuller description and the commissioning body something more condensed. A possible approach, accommodating both, is for a brief method outline in the introduction section, supplemented by a fuller method annex which provides:

- a stand-alone statement of method linked to the evaluation objectives and research questions (RQs);
- a brief descriptions of reasons for comparative choice of design or approach;
- a summative workplan or timetable for the main stages (narrative, graphical or tabular);
- a summary of evidence-gathering emphasis and priorities, tools, output and outcome measures/indicators (and any eligibility issues or exclusions);
- description of analytical focus and methods, including verification, validity and reliability testing, with any key supporting variance or sensitivity analyses, and so on;
- review of method effectiveness, with critical appraisal of (summary) strengths and weaknesses, against intended quality and use.

Narrative style and tone are important for any communication, but have greater prominence for representing potentially confusing, multi-faceted findings in maximising confidence and credibility in concluding reports: 'For the reader, reading becomes a problem of translocation as well as one of comprehension ... the impenetrability of specialised language leads to scepticism about the motives of researchers, and thereby, to devaluing of results' (Locke et al, 1998).

Funders are likely to interpret this principally as an issue for brevity in reporting. This can lead to tensions between managing the legitimate need for reporting to be appropriately concise and the capacity for sufficient detail, explanation and (caveated) caution about findings, implications and strength of evidence. If an evaluation is to be purposeful, the resolution for summative

Table 14.3: Indicative structure and content for a summative evaluation report

Stand-alone report section	Indicative content
Preface, etc	• Contents list; pagination • Acknowledgements and preface/foreword (as necessary)
Summary	• Synthesised summary of report with 'read-across' sub-sections (to signpost to main report sections) • Content reduced where possible to extended bullet points
Introduction	• Brief statement of commissioning body/other funding and evaluation rationale/intent for use (users?) of evaluation • Background to what is being evaluated and focus, priorities or scope (Note: Include or signpost to 'theory of change. where available) • Evaluation aims/objectives; any boundaries or limitations to coverage • Short description of method (Note: Usually supported by longer annex) • Summary of report structure and content signposting
Evidence (descriptive) analysis	• Single section in short reports; multiple sections for fuller analysis (Note: With multiple sections, each may represent a specific objective, key theme, such as impact, VfM or method strand) • Balance coverage of key evidence with evidence quality/scope and absorption potential of audience (Note: May be helped by proportionate use of illustrative interview quotes or synthesised case studies) • Data presentation style agreed with the users (for example, graphical + summary tabulations) (Note: Detailed tabulations usually in annexes) • Footnotes for detailed caveats and essential citations (Note: Avoids a bibliography)
Interpretation and conclusions	• Separated from evidence/data section(s) to differentiate reported 'fact' from evaluator 'interpretation'. (Note: For shorter main report, add 'overview' sections (bullets?) at end of main-body sections) • Provides cross-cutting (triangulated) analysis across sections • Conclusions and interpretations (judgements) set against individual evaluation objectives or criteria (that is, answering the detailed RQs or broad questions the evaluation is expected to address)

(continued)

Table 14.3: Indicative structure and content for a summative evaluation report (continued)

Stand-alone report section	Indicative content
Proposals or recommendations	• Stand-alone, precision statements of evidence-based and justifiable implications for decision-making • Each clearly signposted to evidence in descriptive analysis • May also include suggestions for further evidence or research (only where directly relevant to proposed actions)
Annexes	• Multiple annexes presented in sequence with reference in main body • Possible addition of copies of evaluation instruments • Providing essential supporting material/data/evidence to support main-body presentation/analysis • Might include: formal evaluation brief; review of methodology; selected illustrative case studies; evidence validity testing results; supporting data/key tabulations and p-tests); lists of engaged participants (if not confidential) (Note: Where there are multiple/long annexes, consider replacing some/all with a separate Technical Report)

Source: Modified from author's teaching materials

reporting lies in *how* language is used and not just in reducing the amount of it. This involves working outside the comfort zone of the 'specialised language' which researchers and evaluators commonly use between peers. In particular, it needs robust attention to narrative style, sensitivity and needs of the anticipated audience, with some of the common considerations set out in Table 14.4.

Purposeful use of language is helped greatly if the evaluator takes a little time, when reviewing drafts, to place themselves in the shoes of those likely to read and interpret the report.

Condensed and summary reports

Most 'end of evaluation', summative reports, are likely to be accompanied by some form of condensed summary of findings. Put together well, it can provide a signpost into the detail contained in the fuller report, and invite readers who might otherwise not go deeper to explore further. Preparing this may not need as much time and effort as the full report, but it presents

Table 14.4: Appropriate language and style for purposeful summative reporting

Purposeful aid ...	What to do?
Minimise use of jargon Jargon breaks up narrative flow, slows comprehension, and can confuse and alienate unfamiliar readers	• Consistent editing for use of technical terms and abbreviations for what is/what is not common parlance • Where possible replace technical terms with easier to comprehend language or (at a minimum) provide explanation in the text • A glossary of terms is useful but not a substitute for minimising use of jargon
Emphasise use of commonplace language Commonplace language increases accessibility and will be recognised by a wider readership	• Reduce description and explanation to well-placed 'lowest common denominator' language • Readers who are specialists will not object to simplified language; those who are not, will be confused or suspicious where jargon is used
Avoid use of pejorative or potentially prejudicial language Unintended prejudice in language alienates readers and risks destroying credibility of the evaluation	• Be conscious of the risk of unintended meaning or negative connotations; replace with impartial terms • Risks are most acute when dealing with evidence about, or involving, culturally sensitive settings • Consider use of an independent editor or peer reviewer to identify and desensitise narrative.
Be sensitive to any inappropriate generalisation findings Oversimplifying the representation of findings may streamline narrative but risks credibility in the sensitivity of analysis, and its conclusions	• Interrogate draft narrative for incautious use of generalisation or oversimplification in findings • Inappropriate generalisation is a particular risk in complex settings or for heterogeneous groups • If data on differences is not available (or of insufficient strength), point out possibility of different outcomes/experiences for some groups/situations
Using up-to-date description for categorised data/terms Use of non-current terms reduces confidence evaluators are applied, up to date, or situation aware	• Ensure currency of terminology or descriptive categories for data where terms change over time • Risks are greater in policy or practice settings, or where users are likely to have a high level of cultural awareness or sensitivity
Rigorous attention to strength of evidence in prioritising and representing findings	• Avoid prioritising 'interesting' but insufficiently sound findings; if used, accompany with well-placed caveats (such as explanatory or cautionary footnotes)

(continued)

Table 14.4: Appropriate language and style for purposeful summative reporting (continued)

Purposeful aid ...	What to do?
Users like straightforward conclusions but evidence representation can rarely be reduced to that that level	• Where evidence is 'robust' be open to nuanced and/or alternative explanations for causal association
Appropriate precision in representing quantified data to reflect evidence strengths Users may see highly generalised data description as 'weak' findings	• Where evidence involves small sample sizes or low 'n' counts, evaluators should replace imprecise terms (for example, 'a few', 'most' or 'many') with clearer numerate indicators (for example, 'around one in 10', 'a little over a half', 'approaching three in four users')
Consider use of qualitative 'highlights' to illustrate key points of quantified analysis Users often relate strongly to lived experience illustration. This can aid understanding and confidence	• Integrate use of evidence-based quotes (such as from participant or practitioner interviews) to illustrate quantified evidence (if evaluations are mixed mode) • Be selective with illustrations; they are not generalisable evidence, but can serve to bring clarity and credibility into findings

Source: Modified from author's teaching materials

its own substantial challenges, in consciously designing a user-orientated focus, choosing an appropriate representation, and essentialising its narrative. Part of that design is a choice between various summary options:

- summary report
- executive summary
- synthesis report

Summary report

This is a mini-report, provided usually as a stand-alone, separate product to the main report for the purposes of supporting wider transmission of an evaluation. Public bodies, for example, increasingly opt for placing a summary (and not the main) report on their website to meet any obligations for open access to publicly funded research or evaluation. For the evaluation, the main value of summary reports is in meeting any client or funder requirements and for wider dissemination of the evidence and its implications. Summary reports will be shorter than the full report, but they will require a substantial narrative to condense the background, findings and any recommendations, perhaps supported by selected graphics or figures from the main report. The 'right' length for a summary report will vary; the author has produced summary reports varying from under 2,000 words to over triple that length.

Executive summary

This will probably 'front' the summative report and will be an embedded and not separate product. Its value goes beyond providing an easy-to-read, short summary to preface the main findings in signposting readers to those parts of the main body likely to be of particular interest to them. Signposting is particularly important for purposeful evaluation, offering those receiving the full report an opportunity for (self-determined) pointers to those aspects of the evidence most likely to be important to current agendas, issues or decision-making needs. Decision-makers themselves, and those guiding them, may be unlikely to give detailed attention to all of the main body of even a summative report; the executive summary therefore provides a road map to focus their attention on what they see as most current and relevant.

Minimising the length of an executive summary is consequently more important than for a stand-alone summary report. It will need to balance a well-judged selection of what it is important to cover, with overall brevity. It is quite likely to rely on mainly (extended) bullet point syntheses for its narrative, perhaps condensing findings to around 800–1,500 words.

Synthesis report

This is a special form of condensed reporting which goes beyond summarising an evaluation's evidence, to look across or combine key points of evidence from different reporting processes or phases. This might be relevant to evaluation reporting, where there have been several summative reports at different times, such as for a 'longitudinal evaluation' where different cohorts of entrants or time periods have been separately evaluated and reported. A synthesis report sets out the main points of each separately reported source and looks across them for cross-cutting findings (such as, reporting similarities and differences), identifying implications of likely reasons for convergence (or divergence).

There are other vehicles which might be relevant to condensed reporting. This might include evaluators producing a shortened report, or evidence-based 'policy brief', on a specific theme or policy issue of particular currency (see Example 20).

Example 20: USING SYNTHESIS REPORTING – A THEMED EVIDENCE POLICY BRIEF FROM THE IMPACT EVALUATION OF THE UK'S TEACHING AND LEARNING RESEARCH PROGRAMME

Some years ago, the author led a collaboration to conduct the impact evaluation of the 10-year Teaching and Learning Research Programme (TLRP) funded on behalf of the UK government (see Example 4, Chapter 3). The evaluation looked across a multi-project, funded research programme aimed at widening Higher Education Institutions' (HEI) capacities (and collaborations) for supporting publicly funded education-related policy and applied practice research.

As part of the programme, co-funders set up an external Programme (TLRP) Coordination Unit to monitor project progress, and support inter-project dialogue, collaboration and knowledge exchange. This also aimed to boost capabilities and provide in-project learning across the 70 project teams and 700 researchers involved, including coordinating 20 initiatives of cross-programme thematic analysis.

At the (draft) summative reporting stage (for the wider programme evaluation), co-funders identified particular interest in the effectiveness and impacts of the Coordinating Unit, because one funding body was planning to set up a similar coordination body for a cross-institution programme on international development policy research. In parallel with the revised draft main report, the evaluation team additionally reviewed the main body of survey and interview data and drew together a separate 'policy brief' on TLRP learning, for cross-project 'central unit' coordination. This set out synthesised evidence on enabling relationship-building with and between projects, with conclusions for future cross-programme collaboration mechanisms in multi-project, policy-geared research programmes.

Condensed and summary reporting consequently involves judgements on appropriate modes and how to best use them. What reporting vehicle to use may be out of the hands of the evaluator, but judgements on evidence selection, representation and style will remain (mostly) with the evaluation team and can have a significant influence on how the wider evidence is used. Different vehicles are often used in combination to optimise take-up and transmission of findings for different audiences, or for users with different interests or capabilities. In the example of the Teaching and Research Learning Programme evaluation above (Example 20), reporting involved: a 140-page full report; an embedded 4-page executive summary; a separate 10-page summary report, aimed at the wider HE sector; the 15-page policy brief (as mentioned); and a slide deck for internal communication.

Anticipating supplementary delivery requirements

Evaluators may also be asked to go further than narrative reporting in one form or another, to support dissemination of findings or wider knowledge exchange. This might involve one or more of:

- visual synthesis of key evidence through, for example, infographics;
- supporting materials drawn from parts of the evaluation;
- data-based outputs, perhaps for subsequent use and manipulation by users;
- tools to enhance practice, including evidence-based guidance for practitioners.

Infographics

The popularity and use of simple graphic or pictorial visual representations of data and information (infographics) has intensified with the availability of often free, and easy-to-use, infographic apps and other ICT tools. Although not a substitute, they can be a useful supplement to other forms of condensed reporting, by using modified isotypes or pictorial representation of highly synthesised (usually single point) data on selected findings or key data contrasts. These can have particular value to widen accessibility to key findings, or to audiences who may be unfamiliar with conventional data representation. They also have a specific use in cultural circumstances where communication is to 'readers' with languages other than that used in reporting.

Supporting materials from evidence

Where qualitative evidence such as focus groups, ethnographic observation or case studies are part of the evaluation approach, funders and users may be looking for a separate representation of these. Such evidence may play a minor part in summative reporting and users may value more prominent representation. This might include, for example, a separate report of a participant survey or drawing together individual comparative case studies (usually anonymised), perhaps with a synthesis assessment to complement the main report.

Data-based outputs

Where evaluations employ large-scale surveys, segmented 'big data', or participant diagnostics in evidence collection, funders will often ask for manipulatable data files as a separate deliverable. For example, if a participant (self-completion) questionnaire or telephone interview survey is conducted, funders may ask for a whole-data syntax file (or spreadsheet for smaller surveys) to access the data for subsequent use and manipulation. Such files need to be cleaned, anonymised, and presented in any pre-set, usually encrypted, machine-readable format (such as SPSS) and with user-guidance on access, content, structure, and technical classifications (such as variable or code designations).

Practice tools

On occasions, funders may also be looking for specific tools derived from evaluation evidence to support practitioners. This might include, for example, action packs, practice checklists, or toolkits on specific issues to guide improved practice. In the earlier (hypothetical) illustration of an evaluation of a youth employability programme, a supplementary requirement might be to harness the evidence on retention enablers (and constraints) to produce a 'good practice' toolkit for programme providers on minimising drop-out rates.

The pressure on evaluators to minimise the length of reports appears to be intensifying the demand for supplementary requirements. Here, we have looked only at the most likely additional deliverables; users may also be looking to support a range of additional delivery through dissemination, and this is looked in the next chapter.

Substantiating the findings

Reporting is a selective process; not all evidence can be, or deserves to be, represented and evaluators will be expected to be scrupulously conscious of evidence relevance and strength in making choices on what to select or prioritise. On its own, careful selection of what is reliable and appropriate will be insufficient for users, especially where there are sensitive findings, such as evidence challenging precepts or efficacy of policy or practice. In these situations, users expect and deserve appropriate substantiation of the findings. Nearly 250 years ago, Dr Johnson put it simply: 'A story is a picture ... if it be false, it is a picture of nothing.' Evaluators will not knowingly be providing a 'false' picture, but if not enough is done in substantiation, it will risk being seen as 'a picture of nothing'. A practical consideration hangs over evaluation reporting for how much (and what) substantiation is appropriate for the data used, the outputs or outcomes being assessed, and utility circumstances. What is appropriate will also need to take into account users' ability to absorb substantiation, including the differences between:

- Proof of effect: This will be the most robust level of demonstration that what is being proposed by evidence is valid. It provides decision-makers with certainty, usually through statistical demonstration from reliable quantified data that a specific cause–effect association is valid. RCTs will be engineered to provide this level of proof and many impact evaluations and some economic evaluations will aspire to this. In cases where the methodology is legitimate, substantiating proof of effect will need to demonstrate a high level of internal validity in the relevant data.

- Likelihood: Evidencing this is the fall-back option for quantitative analysis where data and circumstances cannot provide for the high levels of validity needed for proof of effect. Substantiation here will provide for statistical demonstration that an evidenced association is sufficiently strong as to be plausible (not be likely to occur by chance), and that other possible influences (confounding variables) are not likely to account for what is observed. For complexity evaluations, this may be the highest level of substantiation which can be aspired to, although it is likely to be sufficient for many practical decision-making circumstances.
- Potential: Findings may draw attention to a possible association but one where the evidence is insufficient to establish likelihood or confidently eliminate other influences. This may be the case, for example, where evidence is based on small 'sample' sizes. Demonstrating potential might be the best that can be achieved for substantiating 'high possibility' cause–effect associations which either need to be acted upon cautiously, or where further evidence is needed to improve the substantiation.

What is needed across these will depend on the intended use of the evaluation evidence as established early in the evaluation, and how this was applied to method choice. Evaluators may need to act to caution funders and users where they are seeking, perhaps, proof of effect where the circumstances of the intervention, resources available, method possibilities, and data scope cannot provide it.

The quality of evidence cannot be taken at face value and reporting needs to take account of two underpinning, elemental concepts of quality of designs for both quantitative and qualitative evidence:

- reliability of the methods or overall design; and
- validity of evidence or data.

In essence, 'reliability' assesses the trustworthiness of data, in evidencing the extent to which an evaluation design or specific method provides for consistent results. It assess how well-founded the indicators, measures, or data used is, in representing the issues about which they are giving information. For 'validity', an important distinction needs to be made between internal and external validity (Table 14.5), where internal validity is concerned with the strength of evidence perhaps for cause–effect associations being assessed within an intervention, and external validity looks at the strength of evidence for transferring findings from within the intervention to other situations.

Table 14.5: Substantiation and internal and external validity for an evaluation

Common quality risks	Evaluation reporting needs
Internal validity: Demonstrating the extent to which evaluation results are a trustworthy reflection of what is being evaluated	
• Situational change during the evaluation reducing data consistency or coherence • Behavioural changes during intervention by/affecting providers or participants • Changes in measurement, recoding (or measurers–observer/rater changes) • Inappropriate or unmediated flaws in evidence scale, sampling or selection • Flaws in (any) randomisation, control integrity or comparator quality	• Identification of effects of measurement variability or constraints • Identifying unadjusted 'internal' 'cause–effect' confounding influences in reporting • Demonstrating appropriate use of parametric or non-parametric testing for internal validity in the analysis
External validity: Demonstrating the evaluation results can be confidently generalised to another similar context or situation	
• Atypical intervention comparative situation or context of evaluation evidence • 'Transferability' weaknesses from (any) external comparator selection in evaluation (such as, for counterfactual) • Atypical evaluation measures or indicators for relevance to other situations • Scale biases (such as, likely changed effects between local/pilot transition to roll-out)	• Clarity on internal measures/ assumptions in evaluation design • Identified limitations of evaluated evidence for anticipated (or likely) transfer situations • Clarity on likely transfer constraints (such as, prospective external changes)

Source: Updated from Parsons, 2017

Demonstrating the quality (and any limitations) of internal validity will always be important to an evaluation and also in demonstrating reliability for proof of effect or confidence in the likelihood of a cause–effect association. External validity is important in demonstrating reliability only where findings are expected to be generalisable to other situations; this is commonly the case with pilot interventions or to test and learn situations aspiring to scale-up or roll-out.

This is not the place to delve into specific tests for validity: there is an extensive literature, practical guides and manuals advising non-statisticians. However, evaluators need to recognise the key distinction between 'parametric' and 'non-parametric' tests in the confidence offered, especially where a proof of effect is being assessed. Parametric tests offer the highest level of confidence in validity and include tests for regression, correlation or intervariable comparison (for example, p-values or t-tests). Where data do not meet the greater parametric demands,[3] non-parametric methods can be used, although with lower levels of confidence. For qualitative data, tests of causal association can be used such as through qualitative comparative analysis (QCA), reducing tested associations to numeric coding (which in turn can be reinforced by using Bayesian methods).

Some purposeful tips

There is a trend towards more, and more diverse, deliverables from evaluation, often accompanied by other supporting materials to avoid over-lengthening a final 'main' report. This is beneficial to the utility of evidence, but places greater pressures on evaluators to provide for resource-intensive production of different deliverables within usually tight timeframes and budgets. Some of the issues to be taken into account include:

- Early attention to preparing an endorsed delivery plan (for reporting) helps define and clarify requirements and minimise later risks to quality and responsive delivery.
- Purposeful reporting may need to go beyond contracted deliverables, where the evaluator needs to propose modified or additional outputs which add value to utility.

- Funder requirements for progress reporting cannot be assumed to be well-judged; evaluators need confidence to propose more purposeful arrangements, including more appropriate timing and proportional scope.
- Evaluators should seek clarifications, and not make assumptions, about what is needed for deliverables, including for the scope of early findings and preliminary recommendations (if needed).
- Methodology needs explanation and rehearsing of any limitations, but this may be at odds with funders wanting to minimise report length and/or method detail. Evaluators are advised to be creative in making room for sufficient description and caveats.
- Brevity can be both 'friend and foe' to effective reporting and needs sensible determination and use of supplementary products. Brevity on its own cannot make a report accessible; rigorous attention needs to be given to quality assurance of narrative reports, style and use of language.
- Users may be sceptical about (some) reported findings, especially where they are challenging or not 'positive'. Effective substantiation is required to build necessary trust and confidence in findings, with the approach to establishing validity carefully positioned against how the evidence is to be used and who by.

Reporting is more than responsibly setting out findings and perhaps recommendations. It is the vehicle through which understanding of, and confidence in, use-orientated evidence, is transformed into the potential for evidence-informed subsequent actions. To optimise the chance for reports and other deliverables to be purposeful, evaluators need to look at reporting not as a concluding activity, following analysis and interpretation, but as a whole project activity, needing early preparation and use-sensitive product and process management.

15

Optimising evaluation influence

Introduction

The rise of AI, and controversy about its best (or any) use, is the most recent demonstration of how technology for generating and communicating evidence continues to grow at a dizzying pace. Support for those taking 'evidence-based' decisions can now come from a plethora of sources including pseudo-evidence from lobbying, interest groupings and disparate sources within social media. Evaluation evidence, where it exists, will be just a part of the perhaps numerous influences open to decision-makers.

Evaluation evidence may consequently struggle to have its voice listened to. Even well-placed evidence may struggle to be heard against more palatable or louder voices. Purposeful evaluators need to avoid cynicism that this is naturally the case. As a leading opinion former in medical science recently put it to the author: 'Evidence [in public policy] may take time, effort and persistence to make its mark, but good evidence will eventually get there.' This chapter focuses on how to optimise opportunities for making that mark; it draws unapologetically, and heavily, on the author's own experience and practice.

Improving use and utility

The practice of systematic evaluation, in many areas of public policy, has been boosted by ideas of 'evidence-based' decision-making which emerged from 'evidence-based medicine' in the

1980s. In the later 1990s, this began to be applied to other areas of public policy, notably in the UK,[1] Australia and parts of Europe, and was a central tenet behind the creation of the UK's 'What Works Centres'.[2] Yet, despite the policy rhetoric and an extensive academic literature exploring and categorising what is 'evidence-based', evidence continues to find itself facing competitors who may have more pull on decision-makers (Figure 15.1).

Evidence-based policy is better considered as 'evidence-informed' policy, where decision-makers and those mediating information will draw on multiple sources, many of which will not be evidence-based. The author's experience of working within, and for, public bodies shows recurrent conditioning influences on how, and how much, evidence informs decisions. Influencing scope may be limited by aspiration, where decision-makers invested in an intervention (often also the evaluation funders) may be focused on evidence to confirm that it was 'a good idea' and a sound investment. In those situations, evidence looking at the bigger picture of how well it works, its relative performance, or whether it represents clear added value may be seen to be threatening.

A second recurrent influence is the relative accessibility of evaluation reporting for presenting evidence and its implications.

Figure 15.1: Influencing change

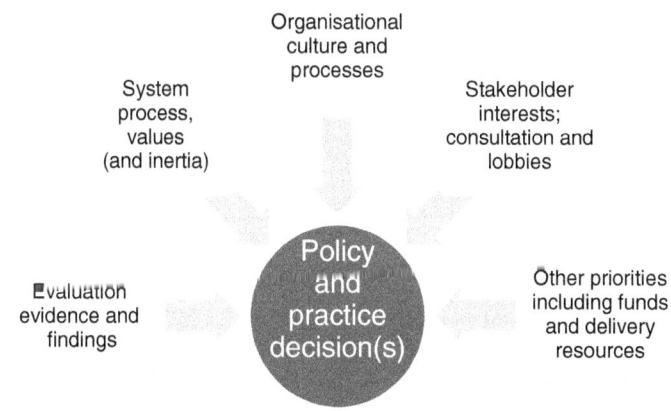

Source: Modified from author's teaching materials

Evaluators will be concerned to present a detailed, nuanced picture of evidence, influences, and actual and potential interconnections, as well as methodology constraints and evidence substantiation. However, this requires time to generate, validate and assemble suitable evidence, as well as communicating it. Those making judgements often need speedier feedback as well as more straightforward 'answers': does the intervention work or not? In public policy, issues can move on speedily; any open window of opportunity for influence can close long before evidence is assembled and transmitted.

Purposeful evaluators consequently need to start with some humility that the odds are often heavily stacked against decisions being fundamentally 'evidence-based'. If evaluation is to be purposeful, evaluators need to go further than what is necessary to meet reporting and deliverables requirements. This involves exploiting the potential for a more proactive role in communicating both emerging and summative evidence and its implications.

Going beyond end-reporting in an evaluation will not be universally welcomed. Evaluators have come to see their role as ending with a signed-off report, with the torch then passing to users to weigh the evidence and its implications. This idealised role separation fits easily with the natural comfort zone of evaluators as producers and analysts of reliable evidence. It also reflects practical resourcing issues, with funding for the evaluation concluding with end deliverables. Users are also more likely to be comfortable with this conventional division of roles between 'evidence provider' and 'evidence user', with the evaluators' role ending with factual reporting.

Evaluators will also be conscious of any implications for their impartiality and independence, and will be rightly cautious about making any direct contribution to decision-making based on 'their' evidence. However, there is a crucial difference between compromising impartiality by directly contributing to taking decisions, as opposed to acting as an agent for the evidence to inform decision makers while standing back from any final decision-making. The evaluator acting as evidence agent goes beyond a passive role as evidence provider to actively gearing evidence representation towards utility with more nuance and creativity in evidence transmission.

Given the influencing difficulties for evidence in decision-making, purposeful evaluation will need to actively optimise its role in articulation of those findings. Implications drawn from evidence are rarely binary ('yes or no'; 'high or low') or as straightforward as users may be looking for. Findings may be nuanced; available methods and practical constraints can mean levels of 'proof' are less than absolute. In these situations, the evaluator will be closest to the data, limitations and subtleties in interpretation; and well-placed to unpick implications affecting decision-making.

With confidence, purposeful evaluators will recognise there is much that can be done, before and after reporting, to optimise evidence use and utility without compromising independence. Doing so calls for more than an evaluation with relevance to intent reflected in sound method choice, robust application and reporting. It puts an emphasis on creative proactivity in articulating findings and implications with effort and persistence in going beyond 'good' reporting.

Situating opportunities for influence

The opportunities for maximising the use of the evaluation evidence will vary greatly with the circumstances, in particular with:

- the context of anticipated decision-making;
- the type of the evaluation conducted;
- users' specified needs for deliverables and dissemination.

Taking account of these circumstances early in the evaluation, will give a reliable guide on the likely need and scope for optimising the influence of evidence.

Decision-making context

Opportunities for evaluation influence will depend largely on how the evidence generated is to be mobilised. An early contribution to codifying different opportunity circumstances was made by the eminent US evaluation theorist Carol Weiss (Weiss, 1979). Others have explored classifying circumstances under which research (and evaluation) evidence is used in medical research (Sackett et al, 1996) and outside (Nutley et al, 2003, 2007; Bannister and Hardhill, 2015; Rossi et al, 2004; Parsons and Thomas, 2015). This book is not bounded by any one classification of decision-making contexts, but looking across these insights suggests evaluators will find themselves in one of four decision-making contexts, each with different implications for intended evidence use (Table 15.1).

In the first two situations, evidence-directed or policy justification contexts, the potential for optimising the use of

Table 15.1: Evidence needs, circumstances and scope for evaluation influence

Decision-making context	Use of evidence for ...	Situation
Evidence-directed decision-making	Evaluation results are expected to be directly applied to a specific decision based on specific performance achievements	Instrumental evidence needs for interventions targeted with a required level of delivery, or targets, facing an interim or concluding review for budget or other continuation decision
Policy justification evidence	Evaluation results are used to reinforce political or ideological determination for an intervention. Emphasis on showing the intervention works, not whether, or how well, it works	Increasing public rights of access to publicly funded evidence (such as, OPEN Government (US) Act, 2007; UK Freedom of Information Act, 2000) mean this is more likely to be a hidden influence on setting inquiry boundaries for what can/cannot be looked at
Mandated evidence-based review	To meet statutory or other mandated obligations for evidence at a fixed period, or at the close of funding for an intervention	May apply to a fixed period review of funding accountability, or for a policy implementation review
Multi-evidence source (plural) decision-making	Evaluation evidence contributes to a multi-source evidence review (drawn from a wide range of sources)	Evaluation evidence to be used alongside other decision influences. Sources are likely to be evidence-based (such as, evaluation, attitude survey, performance data, and so on) and also opinion-based (such as, interest lobbying, stakeholder representations)

evaluation findings (beyond the reporting itself) is nil or negligible. It is greater for plural contexts, where decision-makers will be juggling evaluation evidence with other influences, and where there is scope to raise the profile of evaluation evidence, as the main, or only systematic evidence they will draw on. The potential is probably strongest in mandated contexts, which provide greater potential for those providing the evidence to optimise its leverage in subsequent decision-making.

Evaluation type and approach

What form an evaluation takes, will influence any scope for a proactive role in helping decision-makers unpick evidence and implications. This is likely to be limited where an RCT is employed, since the evidence and level of proof will largely speak for itself. Here, beyond well-justified findings, there is little or no scope for further interpretation or promoting use of findings by the evaluator. Most evaluations, however, will employ evaluation types and approaches geared to more complicated circumstances, often using multi-source, multi-mode evidence, and, for impact evaluations, counterfactual design and reviewing effects of confounding variables. This provides greater risk for user confusion, misinterpretation, misunderstanding or distrust, and correspondingly more need for the evaluator to provide further explanation or interpretation.

Particular considerations affect the potential for evidence use in meta-evaluation and other forms of evidence synopsis. These have become a significant contribution to evidence-informed policy and practice in the clinical and wider medical fields and in international development. Expert and structured review across a number of systematic evidence sources can be a powerful tool in influencing decisions, by minimising risks associated with reliance on any one empirical source. However, this mix of sources can cause decision-makers confusion if it does not position (inevitable) differences between different source findings robustly and transparently.

User-evaluator relationships

Developmental evaluations, test and learn approaches, some in-house evaluation, and others with direct and extensive user-evaluator co-operation, will probably have an 'open door' when it comes to promoting understanding and use of evidence. Proactive evaluators will be keen to exploit those opportunities and act in clarifying and promoting evidence implications within decision-making processes. These opportunities will, perhaps, have the greatest scope for influence in formative evaluation, requiring interim reporting with staged or preliminary findings and implications for change or improvements in an intervention.

In other circumstances, commissioning or funding processes too often constrain such relationships; users may also not be open to post-reporting contributions from the evaluation team. Even where there is a willingness to extend the influence of evidence on decision-making opportunities post-reporting, any additionally resourced contributions by the evaluator may encounter procurement rules or lengthy recontracting. In practice, this means timely contributions will often need to be pro bono, if evaluators have the discretion or flexibility to do this.

This brief review of user contexts shows the opportunities for maximising the use of reported evidence will vary with the situation within which the evaluation takes place. Being aware of these different contexts will help evaluators – acting always as the analyst, not the decision-maker – to anticipate those opportunities, and position and balance their independence with scope for more active post-reporting contributions to optimise evaluation utility.

It remains to look at how evaluators can help commissioners and funders to take maximum advantage of whatever opportunities may exist for evidence to be utilised. In reality, the contribution of evaluation evidence to decision-making remains obscure (Chapter 1). For any decision situation, it is difficult to decipher (retrospectively) if and how research or evaluation evidence has made a contribution, when those decisions will have been an amalgam of influences and the process behind combining them often obscure. There has been considerable debate (and concern) in the evaluation community and among funders about pathways to evidence influence. In recent years, this has seen a focus on how practices of knowledge mobilisation (Bannister and Hardhill, 2015) contribute to evidence-informed practice. This chapter does not aim to contribute to that ongoing but important debate, but suggests that optimising evaluation evidence can exploit a layered approach combining:

- evidence articulation
- evidence transfer
- evidence promotion

Each involves different aspirations and audiences. Probably all three are most effective when used in an appropriate combination, as part of a coherent approach: each of these approaches is now explored.

Capitalising on evaluation articulation

Chapter 14 looked at deliverables and, specifically, reporting, as the primary vehicle for articulating evidence. This is a long established foundation for presentation of evidence and its implications but, as already noted, is often insufficient to mobilise evidence use. Two aspects in evidence articulation in reporting are worth special attention in strengthening the potential for evidence use:

- the formation and presentation of evidence-based recommendations;
- building confidence and trust in the evidence, and analysis, presented.

Evidence-based recommendations

A fulcrum for how purposeful an evaluation can be is likely to be the quality of evidenced proposals for action or recommendations. This involves recognising an important distinction between conclusions and recommendations; a report may ask for one or the other, but often both. Conclusions will be a narrative exploration of issues and observations arising from findings; they are *not* a summary of what is found (a common mistake when drafting conclusions), rather the evaluators' evidence-based, cross-cutting commentary. In contrast, recommendations will flow from these and provide actionable, evidence-based proposals to point decision-makers towards implications for actions.

Recommendations are a critical opportunity to capitalise on the evaluation purpose. Unfortunately, writing applied recommendations may not always be within the comfort zone of evaluation teams. Some of the common risks are: lack of clarity in the proposed action; lack of directed intent (who is meant to act, when, what or who for and how) or realism; or providing aspirational recommendations which lack sufficient evidence to justify the proposal. Table 15.2 sets out some broad principles for tackling the more common challenges facing the positioning and expression of recommendations.

Recommendations consequently need not only substance and realistic direction but also appropriate brevity. Resolving this tension between detail versus brevity can be a substantial drafting challenge, but recommendations which fail to successfully address this may

Table 15.2: Guidelines for preparing actionable recommendations

Narrative principle	Where a recommendation needs to be ...
Comprehensible	• Capable of accurate understanding by decision-makers and -takers (that is, those likely to judge or implement action(s) needed to respond to what is proposed) • Understood also by those seeking to influence those making those judgements
Concrete and specific	• Precision statement of what action is intended and for whom • Including defined focus, eligibility or boundaries, timeline for action (broad), and any other specifics, defining necessary scope • Setting out what actors (such as organisations) the recommendation is directed at, and/or whether intended to implement action
Evidence-informed	• Evidence-geared • Including only those areas for action where there is a sufficient evidence-base to rationalise what is needed (Note: This might signpost to supporting rationale in 'conclusions')
Purpose-centred	• Relevant to the intervention's ambition or intent • Responsive to likely implementation circumstances
Actionable	• Capable of reasonable implementation within the broad scope and focus proposed • Taking into account actors' capacity and capability

Source: Modified from author's teaching materials

lack direction, credibility or comprehension for decision-makers. Careful drafting can only go so far: recommendations also need to be sensitive to currency with decision-makers. This requires the evaluator to have a strong sense of issues on, or approaching, the agenda(s) of those setting policy and practice. This does not mean recommendations can only relate to 'current' issues, but ensuring the currency of some is more likely to attract interest in others.

A probable final consideration is the extent to which collaboration needs to inform setting recommendations, where pre-reporting engagement between evaluator, funders and key stakeholders is likely to increase influence. Starting early can capitalise on opportunities for discussing the nature of recommendations and clarifying goals, when preparing an evaluation. Clarifications here may significantly influence method choice. These, and later discussions, inform needs and focus and should not compromise the impartiality of how evidence is translated into recommendations. This is important when setting, and managing, pre-reporting discussions of preliminary or draft recommendations, perhaps set out (pre-draft reporting) as anticipated options.

Recommendations are the primary portal through which evidence informs actions, and they need care, attention and time to shape them. Michael Patton's long standing advice was to: 'Allow time to do a good job on recommendations, time to develop recommendations collaboratively with stakeholders, and time to pilot-test recommendations for clarity, understandability, practicality, utility and meaningfulness' (Patton, 1990: 326).

Building trust in the evidence

Evidence that is not trusted by users will not be acted upon and can have adverse effects for whatever is being evaluated and the evaluator. Trust is likely to be influenced by many factors which go well beyond how what is presented, evidence quality and its substantiation (Chapter 14). It will be particularly influenced by issues which are, at least partly, in the control of the evaluator including:

- Rigour in attention to the likely comprehension of evidence representation. This is underpinned by avoiding confusion, or

scope for misunderstanding; the fall-back option for users who do not understand what is presented will be to doubt sincerity.
- Legitimacy in the selection and representation of findings which are plausible, well-founded assessments of the evidence and associated implications.
- Integrity in representation based on the evaluator's freedom and confidence to report what is important or significant even where these may be uncomfortable for users.
- Sensitivity to organisational dynamics (such as for funders, providers) and both the intervention and participant circumstances.

A final consideration in trust is with the purposeful engagement of funders, users and stakeholders, through the 'beginning to end' evaluation process. Previous chapters have shown this is a recurrent issue for purposeful evaluation, where trust in findings will be conditioned by the relationships forged with key players and how they are mobilised to the benefit of its robust delivery. For purposeful evaluation, this starts early with preparation and expectation management, and continues through the various opportunities for engagement through implementation and reporting.

Evidence transfer

However well recommendations are presented and trust built in them, gaining leverage and influence from an evaluation's findings can be a 'slow burn' activity. Evaluators may have little or no direct involvement after reporting, but their investment in the findings will see many being keen to support post-report dissemination beyond immediate users and stakeholders. Conventionally, this has centred on dissemination through:

- papers or articles in academic or professional journals looking at component parts of the findings from the evaluation;
- contributions to books (including chapters in edited collections);
- proactive dissemination or issue exploration through social media, blogs, or podcasts;
- contributions to aligned conferences, themed seminars, or workshops;

- engagement in professional or other networked knowledge exchange opportunities.

The aim in all cases will be wider knowledge transfer and exchange, beyond a user community having direct access to the evaluation report or associated deliverables. Reaching wider audiences will involve some form of accessible – usually opportunistic – presentation and/or publication within the public domain. Not all evaluators, of course, will have the time or motivation to contribute proactively to evidence transfer, but many will and may be well-versed in the possibilities for tapping wider dissemination channels. These transfer mechanisms will have likely multiplier effects for extending awareness, knowledge and use of the evidence, by enabling findings to be picked up through web-searches or promoted by others through, for example, citation.

While many funders will offer an open door for conventional dissemination, this is not always the case. There are some limitations, which may be imposed by funders from the outset of an evaluation, including dissemination delays, perhaps until after a commissioning body has published the evaluation report (or summary) or provided access on its website. It may also contractually defer any dissemination permissions until user determination on actions to be taken in response to findings or recommendations, all of which can take some time. There may also be restrictive covenants constraining publication, although in fully democratic societies practising open government, such limitations are more likely to involve only a requirement for formal notification of publications.

Dissemination also rarely provides the opportunity to look across the full spectrum of the evaluation evidence. It is most likely to be focused on specific aspects of the evidence, or themed issues within the fuller evaluation. The formats and scope required by even academic journals, and their quality control processes, can also substantially limit the ambition, depth and breadth of what is being disseminated.

Evidence promotion

Evidence transfer is a long-established pathway for knowledge exchange and has a role to play in wider dissemination. Many evaluators will be well-versed in traversing these opportunities, but these transfers may not be the most appropriate vehicle for timely and responsive promotion of evidence influence. Other than blogs or podcasts, most evidence transfer opportunities take some time before the evidence sees the light of day. For some, the processes (such as journal targeting, preparation, likely peer review, revision and eventual digital or print publication) are likely to involve substantial delay to any timely stimulus to decision-making.

There are various opportunities post-reporting which go beyond conventional dissemination and are better placed for capitalising more speedily on the evidence. Where evaluators are able and willing to take advantage of them, they offer a more diverse approach to promoting evidence, perhaps by:

- awareness-raising of the occurrence of the evaluation and provenance of its (broad) findings;
- general promotion of the reported (broad) findings to contribute to wider confidence in and credibility of the evidence;
- targeting particular findings, issues or implications, perhaps tapping aspects of topical interest or currency;
- exploring and explaining findings of particular complexity, and perhaps positioning these in a wider policy or practice context.

Some of these aspirations may overlap with dissemination objectives, but their focus, process and mode will be different. The emphasis with evidence promotion is on speedy and accessible communications, building and sustaining a momentum for findings: it calls for a different approach and tools. Table 15.3 sets out some of the evidence promotion possibilities open to most evaluations, where the funding arrangements and stakeholder environment are receptive to going further than reporting and dissemination.

This is not an exhaustive list. Tapping these – and similar fast turnaround opportunities – calls for creative opportunism. Unlike dissemination, this is not confined to an end-of-evaluation activity. Where there is scope, evaluators can progressively engage with users, and perhaps wider stakeholders, to build understanding of emerging findings. To this could be added, phased, distributed

Table 15.3: Pre- and post-reporting promotion options

Medium	Audience and reach	Method(s)
Policy/practice briefs	- Cascade briefing (users/stakeholders) - Wider policy, practice or professional audiences, including specialist consultants	- Briefs tailored to specific or priority audiences - Emphasise 'implications' and proposals (evidence-based)
Newsletters/e-bulletins	- Policy advisors, consultants and practitioners in niche/specialist groups - Priority audiences or wider coverage	- Harness stakeholder contacts to access specific newsletters, and so on
Post-report presentations (oral) – online, face to face, or hybrid	- Wide reach where open access (targeted where an invited event) - Internal to funder (policy team, advisors, account managers, and so on). - Post-reporting external audience events	- Internal (user) briefings, launch events, roll-out workshops - Roll-out events (with embedded evaluation element) - Dedicated invitation events for sector or professional bodies - Presentations at negotiated events (run by others)
User/stakeholder 'peer' network events	- Internal (funder/stakeholder) professional or practitioner focus	- Targeted workshops of standing peer forums - Internal network events suitable for mini-presentations
User/stakeholder (or evaluator) websites	- Wide access 'publication' pathway to meet public duty or open access requirements - In-house roll-out for user/core stakeholders - Provider managers, practitioners and consultants	- Website summary or summary report publication (with or without link to full report) - Customised web-material from evaluation deliverables (such as: case study profiles; toolkit; or summary recommendations)
Blogs, podcasts	- Wide reach for peers - Potential to reach non-engaged practitioners	- Harnessing existing blogs for speedy (partial) dissemination - Targeted blog/podcast on specific evidence issues/themes - Scope for rolling agenda of blog contributions to drip-feed findings

(continued)

Table 15.3: Pre- and post-reporting promotion options (continued)

Medium	Audience and reach	Method(s)
X and various social media	- Wide reach for non-practitioner audience and stakeholders - Wider access also to provider managers/practitioners - Potential access to otherwise hard to identify/reach users	- Low investment; wide distribution but highly condensed 'single messages'
Visualisation	- All - Valuable in cross-cultural circumstances	- Isotype representation of data, causal pathways (enhanced infographics), and so on - Interactive visualisations - Video outputs

Source: After Parsons, 2017

press releases and briefings, as a potentially easy way for speedily reaching a very wide audience for rapid transfer potential of high-level findings. This could involve open or selective press releases, or targeted briefings to specific outlets or journalists. In the author's experience, these may be a ready fall-back for wider promotion, where viable, within any funder restrictions, but due to media overload have less currency than in the past.

The author has previously suggested that going beyond reporting involves a move away from a conventional dissemination focus to a communications-led approach, better placed to accommodate the changing way in which decision-makers and those working with them acquire and search for knowledge (Parsons, 2017). Rapid spread of information online, including through social media, is now a fact of life, so embracing the multiplicity of online communication possibilities is important to widening evidence mobilisation. The same technology has also offered easy access and use of visualisation methods, capable of reaching wider audiences and opening doors to time-pressed users.

Going beyond reporting may not be open to all evaluations, but it has potential for most and can add greatly to achieving intent and purpose. Not all evaluators (or funders) will feel comfortable with a proactive approach to evidence promotion. It also needs to accommodate the implications for the skills of the evaluation team and post-evaluation resourcing, especially where additional resources are needed. Nonetheless, proactivity in communicating findings helps evaluators strengthen the potential for findings being constructively used.

A call for action

This book started off with suggesting evaluation is something simple, made complex by its many different choices. For purposeful evaluation, a critical consideration adding to that complexity is how to go about optimising the influence of evaluation findings. We might ask, is this a complication too far; should evaluators leave influencing to funders and engaged users, and let reporting speak for itself? This is a question which needs asking. It is also an appropriate end to a book which suggests that even perfect choice and use of methods will not, of itself, enhance evidence use, unless the preparation for, engagement with, application of, and reporting of what comes from those choices are purposefully driven.

In an era of rising aspirations for evidence-based (or evidence-influenced) policy, political institutions, public interest bodies and others are often explicitly committed to using the best available evidence in decision-making. This is not universal, nor will all organisations 'walk the talk' of such commitments, but it is an increasingly common feature where public interest actions are guided through democratic governance. Some countries have seen government action to boost evaluation evidence use; this includes the UK, through the joint HM Treasury and Cabinet Office Evaluation Task Force and its linked Evaluation Trial and Advice Panel expert network. As a result, more evaluation is being conducted, often with ambitious expectations, but paradoxically this co-exists with enduring concerns that the evidence they generate is not achieving the influence anticipated; it remains often sidelined or neglected in decision-making.

Conventionally, this poor exploitation of evaluation evidence is seen to reflect other more prominent influencing channels, and perhaps an often immature 'managing' culture for harnessing evaluation evidence in many organisations. Both can be significant and only slowly eroding barriers but, just as 'Rome was not built in a day', embedding evaluation cultures and substantially raising evidence profile and use will take time for capabilities and practices of evidence use to change.

Those change responsibilities are not confined to organisations commissioning and using evaluation. Addressing the challenges to ratcheting up the influence of evidence will make slow (or no) progress without those shaping and delivering evaluations, generating, translating and presenting evidence which is responsive and has high potential for informing decision-makers and decision-making. A more engaged and collaborative approach to providing for, and harnessing of, evaluation findings is called for. Here, this author has come to conclude that evaluators themselves need to play a more proactive role.

Purposeful approaches to evaluation provide a framework for developing such collaborations and enhancing the prospects for more and better evidence use. It builds on a whole-project approach to preparation, planning, method choice and application, as well as a multi-layered approach to articulating, disseminating and promoting findings. It can also fit well with emerging user concerns for evaluation processes which are more intensive, agile and responsive to shortening decision-making cycles. This does not call for a new model for the practice of evaluation; it builds on much that is already recognised as better evaluation practice. However, much of that 'better' purposeful practice is fragmented and can be held back by commissioning and funding processes.

This book consequently concludes with a 'call to arms' for funders and evaluators to look towards energising 'purposeful evaluation'. With it, the commissioning and conduct of evaluation can play their respective roles, in bringing about a momentum of change to the culture and practice needed to take advantage of the windows of opportunity opening up for evaluation use and utility in evidence-influenced policy and practice.

Notes

Chapter 2

1. Additional notation from Parsons, 2017.
2. This is not to suggest 'theory of change' is a recent innovation; the concept has been around in different guises for some time but has only more recently become a common feature of evaluation practice.
3. There appear to be no published definitions of coproduction in evaluation. From the wider literature on coproduction in public and other services, it would emphasise a managed process of mutual respect and valuing of contributions across (different) stakeholder perspectives, responsiveness to contributory capabilities and capacity to engage, and reciprocity of benefit for the coproducers.
4. This involves a two-layered arrangement of a small central group discussing specific issues, with the agenda shared with an actively engaged wider group (perhaps in real-time online). The wider group initially observes discussion, later adding comments, perhaps using an online whiteboard or chatroom.

Chapter 4

1. The legal definition will vary internationally. In developed economies it is often 16 years but may be lower in other countries or subject to conditions.
2. Data pseudonymisation replaces identifiers with obscured or fake identifiers, which mean the individual's data can still be linked to participants, but only through a proxy identity, such as an encoded tag or unique serial number.
3. Useful starter advice on better practice for research or evaluation data security is provided by the UK Data Archive in *Managing and Sharing Data* (Van den Eynden, 2011).
4. More specifically, organisational impartiality refers to the evaluation host body (or part of it) whereas behavioural independence refers to the individual(s).
5. This will require a declaration of an absence of conflicts of interest or, where potential conflicts have been identified, the evaluation commissioners assess these as not relevant to the evaluation circumstances.
6. There is no 'what is diversity' template for an evaluation but common markers would take account of gender, race, ethnicity, sex, caste, sexuality, class, affluence, faith, language, disability, and age, as well as the intersectionality across them.
7. This is a helpful online tool from the UN Women Training Centre that provides concepts and definitions with gender perspective structured

according to thematic areas. It can be accessed at: https://trainingcentre.unwomen.org/mod/glossary/view.php?id=36&mode&lang=en

Chapter 6

1. Developmental evaluations may be the only form of evaluation where a team managing or delivering the intervention might be best placed to also conduct the evaluation. This will trade off impartiality and independence against closeness to practice and speed of response to adaptation evidence.

Chapter 7

1. Terminology often changes faster than underpinning concepts. The UK government's guide to evaluation of public policy and publicly funded programmes, the *Magenta Book*, in its fifth version (2011) referred to 'economic evaluation'; its revision (2020) preferred the label 'value for money evaluation'.
2. These terms have been argued over by economic theorists for decades and are set out here as condensed explanations, simplified to make them more accessible.
3. This is not the same metric for all economic valuations. The selected metric will often be a currency unit selected to reflect what is appropriate for the evaluation purpose.
4. Monetising social value outcomes is challenging and can be controversial. Economists suggest a range of considerations for how to go about setting social value using 'revealed' or 'stated' preferences. For those looking to cut through the complexities, a practical guide is provided in HM Treasury's *Green Book* (HM Treasury, 2013; updated 2024).
5. An accessible and shorter account is provided by Fox et al, 2017: 132–7.

Chapter 8

1. The author is not in a position to verify this but is grateful for colleagues suggesting that Dehue (1997) pointed to a control trial by the psychologists Robert Woodworth and Edward Thorndike who collaborated on a therapy trial published in 1901.
2. Evaluation theorists have set out some of the more philosophical considerations of if and where an RCT is justified. This book focuses on more practical, technical considerations, while acknowledging deeper issues such as 'equipoise'.
3. Options may involve selection by, for example, systematic random allocation, blocked stratified randomisation, or machine-derived random number allocation.
4. Not all interventions being trialled will automatically expect sizeable effects (for outcomes). Many public sector programmes may be expecting only marginal gains, but when produced at scale, even small effects can add up to significant public expenditure efficiencies.

Notes

5   There is no shortage of generic guidance on sample size calculations. Software packages can help (for example, Optimal Design), but the best aid is an individual experienced in sample size determination.
6   This is statistically stronger than a post-test comparison of the remaining randomised groups.
7   Equipoise is defined in different ways, but the balance of harm and utility is a common principle often applied to justifying medical and health RCTs.
8   Not all adjustment methods are themselves bias free. Intention to Treat analyses (ITT) can better focus adjustment on those 'As treated' (ITT-AT) or 'As per protocol' (ITT-PP). Other methods include Complier Average Causal Effect (CACE) approaches (Torgerson and Torgerson, 2008b).

Chapter 9

1   Alan Krueger died 18 months before, after serving under President Obama as Assistant Secretary of the US Treasury for Economics Policy and later Chair of the Council of Economic Advisors.
2   PSM estimate selection probability (from observed unit characteristics) for units in the intervention and (proposed) non-intervention (comparator) groups. As an ex-ante method, it can identify selection biases and help to create a better aligned comparator. See: Gertler et al, 2016: 144–8.
3   The Maryland Scientific Method Scale (SMS), developed at the University of Maryland (Sherman et al, 1997), can assess pre-evaluation design weaknesses, with the advantage that evaluators can use this to demonstrate comparator quality to users and stakeholders ahead of an evaluation start.

Chapter 10

1   The ideas of Rudolf Carnap and others in inductive logic influenced developments in scientific realism from the 1920s.
2   Different labels apply to this broad territory with different method expressions, but a unifying undertone separates them from more conventional experimental and quasi-experimental approaches. These are collectively referred to in this book as 'theory-based evaluation'.
3   Coryn and colleagues acknowledged others from North America could have been added.
4   This a regrettable generalisation with some notable exceptions, including for international development where in the UK, for example, the former Department for International Development supported TBE methodological development (Stern et al, 2012).
5   This stems largely from the publication in March 2020 of the revised *Magenta* guidance on evaluation practice, drawing attention to theory-based methods as an option, supported by an extensive supplement on theory-related complexity evaluation methods.
6   There are different theory frameworks which range from rudimentary approaches through 'logic modelling' through the context-mechanism-outcomes (CMO)

configurations of Pawson and Tilley's *Realist Evaluation* (1997) and John Mayne's 'results-expectations frameworks' and subsequent 'contribution stories' (Mayne, 2001, 2008, 2011). A valuable and comprehensive guide looking across different approaches is Funnel and Rogers' *Purposeful Programme Theory* (2011).

7   Also variously referred to as logic charts, logic maps, intervention logic models and, in modified form, as log frames,
8   See for example: *Building and Using a Theory of Change: A Practical Introduction*, a practitioner familiarisation and development course offered by the Social Research Association.
9   For example, Punton and Vogel's C+I+M = O configuration (2020).
10 Mayne also explored the use of behaviour change models including COM-B in CA theory testing (Mayne, 2015).
11 Other configurational methods exist; these are the two most likely to be credible for commissioners.
12 There are various descriptions of the method, but a commonly cited description of applying process tracing in a research and not evaluative context can be found in Collier, 2011.

Chapter 11

1   After Archibald Leman Cochrane, the Scottish physician and advocate for medical RCTs, whose work led to the creation of the Cochrane Library and the Cochrane principles for working across prior RCTs to guide practice.
2   The six-stage process as summarised here may appear intuitive but requires expert and cautious application; evaluators not experienced in this area are advised to take advantage of a range of 'Cochrane' based training that is available.
3   As developed for the Research Methods Programme of the UK Economic and Social Research Council.

Chapter 12

1   Among many published guides, three are of particular value: the United Nations Evaluation Group principles and practice for stakeholder engagement (UNEG, 2017); toolkits from the Australian Federal Victoria State Government (Victorian Government, 2018) and from Bryson and colleagues (Bryson et al, 2011).
2   Excluding primary data may involve some methodological trade offs or streamlining of evaluation objectives; either will need endorsement by funders.

Chapter 14

1   Oral reporting is not considered in any detail here and usually supplements a written report (interim or summative). It may also include more creative forms of evidence presentation, such as posters, poetry, drama or creative visuals, which can be of particular value where the evaluation involves strong community representation and engagement.

Notes

2   The matrix format is readily accessible and set out in four columns – deliverable; received by; timing; scope and requirement – and with a row for each separate required deliverable.
3   Both p-values and t-tests assume independence of observations, homogeneity of data variance within each (tested) group, and also normal or close to normal distribution of the data. These conditions may not be present in practice and non-parametric tests provide an alternative if less confident assessment.

Chapter 15

1   In the UK, evidence-based policy was one of the tenets of the December 1999 White Paper on Modernising Government.
2   The What Works Centre network was first set up (and since expanded) in 2013. It has been seen as an important stimulus to the generation, transcription and communication of policy-related data and evidence in various policy domains (Sanders and Breckon, 2023).

Bibliography

American Evaluation Association (2018) *Guiding Principles for Evaluators*. Washington, DC. https://www.eval.org/About/Guiding-Principles

American Evaluation Association (2025) *AEA Guiding Principle D2*.

Apgar, M., Hernandez, K. and Ton, G. (2020) 'Contribution analysis for adaptive management', *ODI Briefing/Policy Paper*, September 2020. Accessed at: https://odi.org/en/publications/contribution-analysis-for-adaptive-management/

Archibald, T. (2019) 'Seeds of failure', in K. Hutchinson, *Evaluation Failures: 22 Tales of Mistakes Made and Lessons Learned*, Sage, pp 35–42.

Armstrong, R., Gelsthorpe, L. and Crewe, B. (2014) 'From paper ethics to real-world research: supervising ethical reflexivity when taking risks in research with the risky', in K. Lumsden and A. Winter (eds) *Reflexivity in Criminological Research: Experiences with the Powerful and Powerless*, Palgrave Macmillan, pp 207–19.

Bannister, J. and Hardhill, I. (2015) 'Knowledge mobilisation and the social sciences: dancing with new partners in an age of austerity', in J. Bannister and I. Hardhill (eds) *Knowledge Mobilisation and the Social Sciences: Research, Impact and Engagement*, Taylor & Francis.

Bashir, N. (2020) 'The qualitative researcher: the flip side of the research encounter with vulnerable people', *Qualitative Research*, 20(5): 667–83.

Befani, B. and Mayne, J. (2014) 'Process tracing and contribution analysis: a combined approach to generative causal inference for impact evaluation', *IDS Bulletin (Special Edition)*, 45(6): 17–36. https://doi.org/10.1111/1759-5436.12110

Boruch, R., Weisburd, D., Turner, III, S., Karpyn, A. and Littell, J. (2009) 'Randomized controlled trials for evaluation and planning', in L. Bickman and D.J. Rog (eds) *The Sage Handbook of Applied Social Research* (2nd edn), Sage, pp 147–81. https://doi.org/10.4135/9781412985574

Bown, S.R. (2005) *How a Surgeon's Mate, a Mariner and a Gentleman Solved the Greatest Medical Mystery of the Age of Sail*, St. Martin's Griffin.

Britten, N., Campbell, R., Catherine, P., Donovan, J., Morgan, M. and Pill, R. (2002) 'Using meta ethnography to synthesise qualitative research: a worked example', *Journal of Health Services Research and Policy*, 7(4): 209–15.

Bryson, J.M., Patton, M.Q. and Bowman, R.A. (2011) 'Working with evaluation stakeholders: a rationale, step-wise approach and toolkit', *Evaluation and Programme Planning*, February, 34(1): 1–12.

Campbell D, T., and Stanley J. C. (1963) *Quasi Experimental Designs for Research*, Houghton Miffin.

Card, D. and Krueger, A.B. (1994) 'Minimum wages and employment: a case study of the fast-food industry in New Jersey and Pennsylvania', *The American Economic Review*, 84(4): 772–93.

Cartwright, N. and Hardie, J. (2012) *Evidence-Based Policy: A Practical Guide to Doing It Better*, Oxford University Press.

Chaplin, D.D., Cook, T.D., Zurovac, J., Coopersmith, J.S., Finucane, M.M., Vollmer, L.N. and Morris, R.E. (2018) 'The internal and external validity of the regression discontinuity design: a meta-analysis of 15 within-study comparisons', *Journal of Policy Analysis and Management*, 37(2): 403–29.

Chelimsky, E. and Shadish, W. (1997) *Evaluation for the 21st Century: A Handbook*, Sage.

Chen, H.T. (1980) 'The theory-driven perspective', *Evaluation and Program Planning*, 12 [special edition]: 299–306.

Chen, H.T. (1990) *Theory-Driven Evaluations*, Sage.

Chen, H.T. (1994) 'Theory-driven evaluation: needs, difficulties and options', *Evaluation Practice*, 15(1): 79–82.

Chen, H.T. (2015) *Practical Program Evaluation: Theory-Driven Evaluation and the Integrated Evaluation Perspective* (2nd edn), Sage.

Chen, H.T. and Rossi, P.H. (1980) 'The multi-goal, theory-driven approach to evaluation: a model linking basic and applied social science', *Social Forces*, 59(1): 106–122.

Clark, A. and Dawson, D. (1999) *Evaluation Research: Introduction to Principles, Methods and Practice*, Sage.

Collier, D. (2011) 'Understanding process evaluation', *Political Science and Politics*, 44(4): 823–30.

Cook, T. and Campbell, D. (1979) *Quasi-experimental Design and Analysis Issues for Field Settings*, Houghton Mifflin Company.

Coryn, C.L.S., Noakes, L.A., Westine, C.D. and Schroter, D.C. (2010) 'A systematic review of theory-driven evaluation practice from 1990 to 2009', *American Journal of Evaluation*, 32(2): 199–226.

Cousins, J.B. and Leithwood, K.A. (1986) 'Current empirical research on evaluation utilization', *Review of Educational Research*, 56(3): 331–64.

Cronbach, L.J. (1982) *Designing Evaluations of Educational and Social Programs*, Jossey-Bass.

Datta, L.E. (2007) 'Looking at the evidence: what variations in practice might indicate', *New Directions for Evaluation*, 113(March): 35–54.

Davies, R. (2013) *Planning Evaluability Assessments: A Synthesis of the Literature with Recommendations*, Department for International Development Working Paper 40, DFID.

DeAngelo, G. and Hansen, B. (2014) 'Life and death in the fast lane: police enforcement and traffic fatalities', *American Economic Journal: Economic Policy*, 6(2): 231–57.

Dehue, T. (1997) 'Deception, efficiency and random group', *Isis: An International Review Devoted to the History of Science and Its Cultural Influences*, 88(4): 653–73.

Donaldson, S.I., Christie, C.A. and Mark, M.M. (2015) *Credible and Actionable Evidence: The Foundations for Rigorous and Influential Evaluations*, Sage.

Drummond, M., Schulper, M., Torrence, G., O'Brien, B. and Stoddart G. (2005) *Methods for the Economic Evaluation of Health Programmes* (3rd edn), Oxford University Press.

Fernainy, P., Cohen, A.A., Murray, E., Losina, E., Lamontagne, F. and Sourial, N. (2024) 'Rethinking the pros and cons of randomized controlled trials and observational studies in the era of big data and advanced methods: a panel discussion'. *BMC Proceedings*, 18(Suppl 2): 1.

Ferretti, S. (2023) 'Hacking by the prompt: innovative ways to utilize ChatGPT for evaluators', *New Directions for Evaluation*, 2023(178–9): 73–84.

Filmer, D. and Schady, N. (2009) *School Enrolment, Selection and Test Scores*, Policy Research Working Paper 4998, World Bank.

Fletcher, G. (2015) *Addressing Gender in Impact Evaluation: What Should be Considered*, A Methods Lab Publication, Overseas Development Institute; Better Evaluation.

Fox, C., Grimm, R. and Caldeira, R. (2017) *An Introduction to Evaluation*, Sage. https://doi.org/10.4135/9781473983151

Funnell, S.C. and Rogers, J.R. (2011) *Purposeful Programme Theory: Effective Use of Theories of Change and Logic Models*, Jossey Bass.

Gertlerl, P.J., Martinez, S., Premand, P., Rawlings, L.B. and Vermeersch, M.J. (2016) *Impact Evaluation in Practice* (2nd edn), World Bank.

Guba, E.G. and Lincoln, Y.S. (1986) *Fourth Generation Evaluation*, London.

Guillemin, M. and Gillam, L. (2004) 'Ethics, reflexivity, and "ethically important moments" in research', *Qualitative Inquiry*, 10(2): 261–80. https://doi.org/10.1177/1077800403262360

Haynes, L., Service, O., Goldacre, B. and Torgerson, D. (2012) *Test, Learn, Adapt: Developing Public Policy with Randomised Controlled Trials*, Cabinet Office.

Higgins, J.P.T., Thomas, J., Chandler, J., Cumpston, M., Li, T., Page, M.J. and Welch, V.A. (2019) *Cochrane Handbook for Systematic Reviews of Interventions* (2nd edn), The Cochrane Collaboration; Wiley Blackwell.

Hitch, C.J. (1960) *On the Choice of Objectives in Systems Studies*, The RAND Corporation.

HM Treasury (2013) *The Green Book: Appraisal and Evaluation in Central Government*, updated 2024, HM Treasury.

HM Treasury (2020) *The Magenta Book: HM Treasury Guidance on What to Consider when Designing an Evaluation*, HM Government. https://www.gov.uk/government/publications/the-magenta-book

IAPP (2007) *IAP2 Spectrum for Public Participation*, International Association for Public Participation. http://c.ymcdn.com/sites/www.iap2.org/resource/resmgr/imported/spectrum.pdf

Kamstra, J. (2020) 'Civil society aid as balancing act: navigating between managerial and social transformative principles', *Development in Practice*, 30(6): 763–73.

Kara, H. (2020) *Creative Research Methods: A Practical Guide* (2nd edn), Policy Press.

Kemmis, S. and McTaggart, R. (2005) 'Communicative action and the public sphere', in N.K. Denzin and Y.S. Lincoln (eds) *The Sage Handbook of Qualitative Research*, Sage, pp 559–603.

Kilpatrick, D.L. (1959) 'Techniques for evaluating training programmes', *Journal of the American Society for Training and Development*, 13: 21–6.

Kujala, J., Sachs, S., Leinonen, H., Heikkinen, A. and Laude, D. (2022) 'Stakeholder engagement: past, present, and future', *Business and Society*, 61(5): 1136–96. https://doi.org/10.1177/00076503211066595

Leeuw, F.L. and Donaldson, S.I. (2015) 'Theory in evaluation: reducing confusion and encouraging debate', *Evaluation*, 21(4): 467–80.

Lewis, D. (1973) *Counterfactuals*, Blackwell.

Lipsey, M.W. (2007) 'Method choice for government evaluation: the beam in our own eye' *New Directions for Evaluation*, 113: 113–5.

Locke, L., Silverman, S. and Spiroduso, W.W. (1998) *Reading and Understanding Research*, Sage.

Ludwig, J. and Miller, D. (2007) 'Does head start improve children's life chances? Evidence from a regression discontinuity design', *Quarterly Journal of Economics*, 122(1): 159–208.

MacDonald C. (2012) 'Understanding participatory action research: a qualitative research methodology option', *The Canadian Journal of Action Research* 13(2): 34–50.

Mark M., Green J. and Shaw I. (2006) 'The evaluation of policies, programs and practices', in I. Shaw, J. Green and M. Mark (eds) *The Sage Handbook of Evaluation*, Sage.

Markiewicz, A. and Patrick, I. (2016), *Developing Monitoring and Evaluation Frameworks*, Sage.

Mason, S. and Hunt, A. (2018) 'So what do you do? Exploring evaluator descriptions of their work', *American Journal of Evaluation*, 40(3): 395–413.

Mathison, S. (2008) 'What is the difference between evaluation and research and why do we care?', in N.L. Smith and P. Brandon (eds) *Fundamental Issues in Evaluation*, Guilford Publishers, pp 183–96.

Mauthner, M., Mauthner, M.L. and Birch, M. (2002) *Ethics in Qualitative Research*, Sage. https://doi.org/10.4135/9781849209090

Mayne, J. (2001) 'Addressing attribution through contribution analysis: using performance measures sensibly', *Canadian Journal of Programme Evaluation* 16(1): 1–24. Earlier version at: http://www.oagbvg.gc.ca/domino/other.nsf/html/99dp1_e.html/$file/99dp1_e.pdf

Mayne, J. (2008) 'Contribution analysis: an approach to exploring cause and effect', *ILAC Methodological Brief*. https://web.archive.org/web/20150226022328/http://www.cgiar-ilac.org/files/ILAC_Brief16_Contribution_Analysis_0.pdf (archived link)

Mayne, J. (2011) 'Addressing cause and effect in simple and complex settings through contribution analysis', in R. Schwartz, K. Forss and M. Marra (eds) *Evaluating the Complex*, Transaction Publishers.

Mayne, J. (2015) 'Useful theory of change models', *Canadian Journal of Program Evaluation*, 30(2): 119–42. Accessed at: https://evaluationcanada.ca/system/files/cjpe-entries/30-2-119_0.pdf

Mello, P.A. (2012) *A Critical Review of Applications in QCA and Fuzzy-set Analysis and a 'Toolbox' of Proven Solutions to Frequently Encountered Problems*, American Political Science Association, 2012 Annual Meeting Paper. Accessed at: https://ssrn.com/abstract=2105539

Mies, M. (1993) 'Towards a methodology for feminist research', in M. Hammersley (ed) *Social Research: Philosophy, Politics and Practice*, Sage.

Montrosse-Moorhead, B. (2023) 'Evaluation criteria for artificial intelligence', *New Directions for Evaluation*, 178-179: 123–34.

Moore, G.F., Audrey, S., Barker, M., Bond, L., Bonell, C., Hardeman, W. and Baird, J. (2015) 'Process evaluation of complex interventions: Medical Research Council guidance', *British Medical Journal*, 350.

Nicholls, J., Lawlor, E., Neitzert, E. and Goodspeed, T. (2012), *A Guide to Social Return on Investment*, Social Return on Investment Network.

Norvig, P. and Russell, S. (2010) *Artificial Intelligence: A Modern Approach*, Pearson.

Nutley, S., Walter, I. and Davies, H. (2003) 'From knowing to doing: a framework for understanding the evidence-into-practice agenda', *Evaluation*, 9(2): 125–48.

Nutley, S.M., Walter, I. and Davies, H.T.O. (2007) *Using Evidence: How Research Can Inform Public Services*, Policy Press.

O'Leary, B., Kvist, K., Baylis, H.R., Derroire, G., Healey J., Hughes, K. and Pullin, A. (2016) 'The reliability of evidence review methodology in environmental science and conservation', *Environmental Science and Policy*, 64: 75–82. https://doi.org/10.1016/j.envsci.2016.06.012

Oakley, A., Strange, V., Bonell, C., Allen, E. and Stephenson, J. (2006) 'Process evaluation in randomised controlled trials of complex interventions', *BMJ (Clinical Research ed)*, 332(7538): 413–16.

OECD-DAC (2010) *Glossary of Key Terms in Evaluation and Results Based Management*, Organisation for Economic Co-operation and Development/Development Assistance Committee (DAC), OECD-DAC. https://doi.org/10.1787/632da462-en-fr-es

Ovretveit, J. (1998) *Evaluating Health Interventions*, Open University Press.

Parsons, D. (2017) *Demystifying Evaluation: Practical Approaches for Researchers and Users*, Policy Press.

Parsons, D. and Thomas, R. (2015) *Valuation of the Economic Impact of Social Science*, Economic and Social Research Council.

Patton, M.Q. (1990) *Qualitative Evaluation and Research Methods* (2nd edn), Sage.

Patton, M.Q. (2006) 'Evaluation for the Way We Work', *The Nonprofit Quarterly*, 13(1): 28–33.

Patton, M.Q. (2008) *Utilization-focussed Evaluation* (4th edn), Sage.

Patton, M.Q. (2011) *Developmental Evaluation: Applying Complexity Concepts to Enhance Innovation and Use*, Guilford Press.

Patton, M.Q. (2014) *Qualitative Evaluation and Research Methods: Integrating Theory and Practice*, Sage.

Patton, M.Q. (2018) 'A historical perspective on the evolution of evaluative thinking', *Evaluative Thinking*, 158: 11–28.

Pawson, R. and Tilley, N. (1997), *Realistic Evaluation*, Sage.

Pawson, R., Greenhalgh, T., Harvey, G. and Walshe, K. (2004) *Realist Synthesis: An Introduction*, ESRC Research Methods Programme, RMP Methods Paper 2/2004.

Pettigrew, H. and Roberts, H. (2006) *Systematic Reviews in the Social Sciences: A Practical Guide*, Blackwell. https://doi.org/10.1002/9780470754887

Picciotto, R. (2011) 'The logic of evaluation professionalism', *Evaluation*, 17(2): 165–80.

Pirracchio, R., Resche-Rigon, M. and Chevret, S. (2012) *Evaluation of the Propensity Score Methods for Estimating Marginal Odds Ratios in Case of Small Sample Size*, BMC Medical Research Methodology: Case reports.

Punton, M. and Vogel, I. (2020) 'Keeping it real: using mechanisms to promote use in the realist evaluation of the Building Capacity to Use Research Evidence program', *New Directions for Evaluation 2020*, (167): 87–100.

Ragin, C. and Rihoux, B. (2009) *Configurational Comparative Methods: Qualitative Comparative Analysis (QCA) and Related Techniques*. Thousand Islands. Sage, pp 71–82.

Ramanathan, R. (2008) *The Role of Organisational Change Management in Offshore Outsourcing of Information Technology Services*, Universal Publishers.

Rigterink, A.S. and Schomerus, M. (2016) 'Probing for proof, plausibility, principle and possibility: a new approach to assessing evidence in a systematic evidence review', *Development Policy Review*, 34(1): 5–27.

Rittel, H. and Webber, M. (1973) 'Dilemmas in a general theory of planning', *Policy Sciences*, 4(2): 155–69.

Rossi, P., Lipsey, M. and Freeman, H. (2004), *Evaluation: A Systematic Approach*, Sage.

Sackett, D.L., Rosenberg, W.M., Gray, J.A., Haynes, R.B. and Richardson, W.S. (1996) 'Evidence based medicine: what it is and what it isn't', *British Medical Journal*, 312(10).

Sanders, M. and Breckon, J. (eds) (2023) *The What Works Centres: Lessons and Insights from an Evidence Movement*, Policy Press. https://doi.org/10.51952/9781447365112

Schneider, C.Q. and Wagemann, C. (2012) *Set-theoretic Methods for the Social Sciences: A Guide to Qualitative Comparative Analysis (QCA)*, Cambridge University Press.

Schwandt, T. (2008) 'Toward a practical theory of evidence for evaluation', in S.I. Donaldson, C.A. Christie and H.H. Mark (eds) *What Counts as Credible Evidence in Evaluation and Evidence-based Practice?*, Sage, pp 197–212.

Scriven, M. (1991) *Evaluation Thesaurus*, Sage.

Scriven, M. (1999) 'The nature of evaluation, part I: relation to psychology', *Practical Assessment, Research & Evaluation*, 6(1).

Shadish, W.R., Cook, T.D. and Campbell, D.T. (2004) *Experimental and Quasi-experimental Designs for Generalized Causal Inference*, Houghton-Mifflin.

Sherman, L., Gottfredson, D., MacKenzie, D., Eck, J., Reuter, D. and Bushway, S. (1997) *Preventing Crime: What Works, What Doesn't, What's Promising*, US Department of Justice.

Simons, H. (2006) '*Ethics and evaluation*', in I.F. Shaw, J.C. Green and M.M. Mark (eds) *The International Handbook of Evaluation*, Sage.

State of Victoria (2005) *Effective Engagement: Building Relationships with Community and Other Organisations. Book 3: The Engagement Toolkit*, State of Victoria: Department of Sustainability and the Environment.

Stern, E., Stame, N., Mayne, J., Forss, K., Davies, R. and Befani, B. (2012) *Broadening the Range of Designs and Methods for Impact Evaluations*, Report of a Study Commissioned by the Department for International Development (DfID).

Stufflebeam, D.L. (1967) 'The uses and abuses of evaluation in Title III', *Theory into Practice*, 6(3): 126–33.

Suchman, E. (1967) *Evaluative Research*, Russel Sage Foundation.

Thornton, I. (2023) 'A special delivery by a fork: where does artificial intelligence come from?', *New Directions for Evaluation*, 2023(178–79): 23–32.

Ton, G., Mayne, J., Delahais, T., Morrell, J., Befani, B., Apgar, M. and O'Flynn, P. (2019) *Contribution Analysis and Estimating the Size of Effects: Can We Reconcile the Possible with the Impossible?*, Centre for Development Impact, Practice Paper 20. Accessed at: https://www.ids.ac.uk/publications/contribution-analysis-and-estimating-the-size-of-effects-can-we-reconcile-the-possible-with-the-impossible/

Torgerson, D.J. and Torgerson, C.J. (2008a) *Randomised Trials in Education: An Introductory*, Palgrave McMillan.

Torgerson, D.J. and Torgerson, C.J. (2008b) *Designing Randomised Trials in Health Education and the Social Sciences*, Palgrave McMillan.

Trevisan, M. and Walser, T. (2014) *Evaluability Assessment: Improving Evaluation Quality and Use*, Sage. https://doi.org/10.4135/9781483384634

UNEG (2017) *Principles for Stakeholder Engagement*, United Nations Evaluation Group, UNEG SO2: Use of Evaluation.

Van den Eynden, V., Corti, L., Woolard, M., Bishop, L. and Horton L. (2011) *Managing and Sharing Data: Best Practice for Researchers*, UK Data Archive, University of Essex.

Victorian Government (2018) *Stakeholder Engagement Toolkit*, Department of Health and Human Services. https://dhhs.vic.gov.au/publications/stakeholder-engagement-and-public-participation-framework-andtoolkit

Weiss, C.H. (1972) *Evaluation Research: Methods for Assessing Program Effectiveness*, Prentice-Hall.

Weiss, C.H. (1979) 'The many meanings of research utilization', *Public Administration Review*, 39(5): 426–31.

Weiss, C.H. (1998) *Evaluation: Methods for Studying Programmes and Policies* (2nd edn), Prentice Hall.

Wilson-Grau, R. (2015) *Outcome Harvesting*, Better Evaluation. Retrieved from http://betterevaluation.org/plan/approach/outcome_harvesting

Index

References to figures appear in *italic* type; those in **bold** type refer to tables. References to endnotes show both the page number and the note number (305n5), and where required for clarity, the chapter number (ch1).

A

accountability 15–16
  bodies as potential stakeholders **230**
action research type model 194
activities 101
  and processes **128**
actualisation 260–1
adaptive learning and methods 110, 189, 194, 196, **197**
added-value indicator 132
additionality 177, **178**
administrative or close match eligibility comparators 165
African Evaluation Association 249
AI *see* Artificial Intelligence
American Evaluation Association 8, 66, 73, 249
  professional code of 65
annexes **276**
Artificial Intelligence (AI) 20
ask, challenging the initial 48–51, 55, 64
assessment 35–6, 113, **208**, 210, 216, 255, 307n3(ch9)
assumptions 15, 34, 37, 49, 57, 60, 67–8, 75, 114–15, 119, 127, **135**, 136, 137, 138–9, 168, 169, 182–3, 184, 186, 188–9, 190, 195, 238, 240, **285**, 287
attribution 12, 17, 89, 91, 93–7, 98, 99, 140, 159, 161, 174, 175, 177, 179, 191, 192–3, **193**, 201
attrition (bias) 150

audience 266, **267**, 268, 273, **275**, 276, 281, 282, 295, **301**–2
auditing actions, outputs and/or outcomes 46
austerity-related social disturbance 199–200

B

before-and-after designs 165, 167, 174–5, 203
benefits 118, 121, 122, 123, 124, 125, 138, 142, 151, 175–6, **178**, 189, 212
bias 64, 72–3, 150, 154, 167, 177, 206, 207
blinding 141, 148, 150–1, 161
blogs **301**
boundaries 33, 138, 228
brevity in reporting 274, 276, 287
budgets and budget allocations/provision 157, 224, 241

C

CA *see* contribution analysis
call for action 303–4
Card, David 169
causal conditions and insights 188, 201, 202, 213
causal inference 191
causal model 186
cause and effect 20, 59, 93–7, 114, 183, 198, 199, 214, 237
CE *see* cost-effectiveness
CEAsR (context-expectations-assumptions and mechanisms-risks) profile 188–9

320

Index

challenges
　and delivery, managing 245–62
　and disruption 246
chance bias 149–50
change
　influencing *289*
　most significant 194, 196
　and responsiveness, managing for 245–6
choice of type 91–3
clearance and compliance procedures 247–50, 262
clinical and drug trials and research 151, 172, 177, 207, 288
　required standard of proof for 141
　see also and the gold standard *under* randomised control trials
close match eligibility **166**
cluster-RCTs (c-RCTs) 146
CMO configurations *see* 'context-mechanism-outcome' configurations
Cochrane, Archibald Leman 308n1(ch11)
Cochrane (charitable organisation) 206–7
Cochrane-based training 308n2(ch11)
Cochrane Collaboration 206
Cochrane compliant approaches **213**
Cochrane Library 308n1(ch11)
Cochrane principles 206, 207, 308n1(ch11)
codes of practice
　external 249–250
　on principles and/or standards 247
commissioners 15, 18, 21, 24, 30, 31, 36, 37, 40, 41, **45**, 47, 49, 51, 55, 59, 65–6, 72, 76–7, 85, 87, 92, 96–7, 99, 108, 110, 112–13, 114, 118, 119–20, 128, 137, 140, 153, 155, 160, 174, 184, 194–5, 203, 214, 215, 226, 228, **230**, 234, 254, 259, 261, 266, 268, 271, 273, 294, 305n5, 308n11
　see also primary users
commissioning, pros and cons of internal and external **225**
communication 23, 72, **74**, 76
comparator designs 95, 96, 160
comparison groups 97–8
complexity, causal 184–5, 236, 237
compliance 154, 208, 250

conclusions, drawing **215**, 295
confidence 57–8, 63, 72, 78, 125, 147–9, 179, 186
　see also humility
configurational methods 189, 198, **202**
confounding factors and variables 155–7
consent and consent briefing 68–9, 152
consequence stakeholders as potential stakeholders **230**
consequences and consequential changes 90, 91, 94, 101, **117**, 188, 242–3
constrained comparators and experimental designs 96, 165
constraints 19, 31, 49, 62, 77, 143, 176, 228
constructive co-production *111*
context 188, 190, 291–3
context-expectations-assumptions and mechanisms-risks profile *see* CEAsR profile
'context-mechanism-outcome' (CMO) configurations 190–1
contextual experts as potential stakeholders **230**
contingencies, anticipated 255, **256**
contribution analysis (CA) 191–3, **193**, 202
　key inquiry stages for *192*
contributors, protecting the 70–1
control groups 95, 97–8, 143, 147–51, 160
controls and control approaches 96, 142, 151, 161, 173–4
core evidence framework 240
cost-benefit analysis and evaluation 90, 125, 126, 127–8, **128**, 130–1, 133, 134–7, **135**, 138
cost-description analysis 129–30
cost-effectiveness 234
　analysis 126
　and CE–EC ratios **131**
　evaluating 130–2
　ratio **131**, 132
cost-efficiencies 234
costs 90, 122, 123–4, **129**, 130, 149, 244
counterfactual 17, **23**, 97–8, 99, 132, 140, 151, 159, 160, 165, 167, 171, 173, 183, 201, 202–3, 204, **285**, 293

c-RCTs *see* cluster *under* randomised control trials
cross-over designs 146, 158, 164
 see also step-wedge designs
CU *see* cost-utility
cultural competency, demonstrating **74**
cultural sensitivity 78
currency 123, 125
cut-off point and threshold 169, 171
cyber-security systems 71

D

data management **23**, 70, 71–2, 107, 172, 227, 242, 243, **277**
DE *see* developmental *under* evaluation
deadweight **178**
decision-makers 94, 106, 109, 111, 123, 142, 222, 237–8, 289
decision-making processes xiv, 11, 16, 19, 35, 66, 92, 206, 228, 265, **292**
deliverables, nature of, for whom and when 46, 265–9, **267**
delivery 60, 119, 221, 224
 of intervention, variation in **185**
 and (intended) sequence 188, 251
designs and designers 85–99, **128**, 143, 146, **230**, 234–8
DID *see* difference-in-difference
difference, valuing **74**
difference-in-difference (DID) 88, 162, 165–9, 173–4, 175
disruption 246, 255, 262
dissemination 299–300, 302
distance travelled contrast 167, 175
diversity 74–5, 76, 77, 305n6
 markers 79–80
dynamic approach and structure **111**

E

early-stage intervention development 197
e-bulletins **301**
ECR *see* effectiveness-cost ratio
effectiveness 111–15, **113**, 119, 245–6
effectiveness-cost ratio (ECR) **131**
end gains 90, 91, 94
end users 31, **230**
engaged quality plan/assurance process **117**

engagement 12–13, 228, 232–3
 legacy, reviewing 229–31
 purpose 226–7, 243
enhanced minimum wage (New Jersey, 1992), evaluation of impact of 167–8, 175, 176
equipoise 142, 152, 307n7
ethics and ethical dimensions 65–82, **117**, 142, 143, 151–3, 247–8
evaluability assessments 35–6
evaluand 3, 15, 32
evaluation
 for accountability 34
 accountability-based process 101, 103, 104
 action 186
 articulation, capitalising on 295–8
 contribution **23**
 coproduction of 40–1, 305n3(ch2)
 cost-benefit 127, 128, 130, 131, 134–7, 138
 cost-description 127, 128
 cost-effectiveness (CE) 92, 127, 130–2, 136, 151–2
 cost-utility (CU) 127, 133–4, 138
 delivery management for 227, 250
 design 14, 21, **23**, 75, 79, 95, 151, 183, 234–8, 268, 285, **285**
 for development 35
 developmental (DE) 46, 107, 108, 194, 195–6, 242, 306n1(ch6)
 economic **89**, 90, 121–39, **128**
 see also value for money *under* evaluations
 embedded 118
 empirical 4–5
 ethical dimension to 65–7
 evidence 14–18, 284, 291
 evidence-generating 205, 216
 evidence intensity 236
 ex-ante 127–8, 131, 205, 206, 214, 222–3, **223**, 307n2(ch9)
 experimental 95–6
 ex-post 127–8, 222, **223**, 224
 external (contracted) 222, 224, **225**, 226
 findings 34, 35, 233, 259, 268, 292–3, 303, 304
 focus needed, essential 32–4
 fully experimental impact 140–58
 governance and steering roles in an **257**

hybridisation for non-experimental 201–3
impact **81**, **89**, 90–1, 93–4, **128**, 155, 160–1, 195–6, 242
improvement process 103
inclusion of vulnerable and disadvantaged people/groups in 77–8
independent and impartial 46, 226 *see also* external *under* evaluation
indicative content for the reporting plan for an **267**
influence 288–304, *289*, **292**, **296**, **301**–2
in-parallel 222, **223**, 223–4
intensive 233
internal and self- 222, 224, **225**
judgements 65
for knowledge 35
leverage 16–17
method
choice for 221–44
methodology 251
and monitoring 13–14
non-experimental 95, 96–7
objectives 46, 52–3
optimally collaborative 226
optimising clearance processes to provide fast starts for an 248–9
organisational power dynamics in an 62–3
participative process 116–19
planning for 221
positioning scope of *33*
practical framework for risk-foresighting an **256**
principles of method choice for developmental **111**
process 88–90, **89**, 100–20
purpose and focus for the four types of evaluation **89**
purposeful 3–25, 29, 44, 46, 51, **54**, 55, 67, 94, 165, 176, **235**, 243–4, 245, 248, 262, 265, 272, 298, 304
purposefulness and purposing of 18–19, 62
quasi-experimental impact 159–80
realist 190–1, 193, **193**
reporting needs **285**
and research xiv, 3, 7–13, *8*, **10**, 14–15, **23**, 50, 65, 66, 76, 91, 110, 126, 149, 157, 160,

188, 194, 199, 203, 204, 205, 207, 216, **225**, 238, 249, 250, 254, 278, 291, 294 *see also* participatory action research; research questions
research and monitoring in 7–13
resourcing of the 224, **225**, 226
roots of 4–7
steering the 76–7
structuring of a rapid evidence review 211–12
substantiation and internal and external validity for an **285**
summative or formative 44–6, **45**
team, avoiding overconfidence (or neglect) in the evaluation 82
and theory of change, scoping 36–7
theory-based (TBE) 181–204
adaptive approaches to 194–7
configurational and case-based 197–201
developmental 194–6
fit of 184–6
preference, complexity push factors to justify **185**
pull factors 185–6, 203
push factors 184–5, 203
theory and 'wicked problems' 182–4
theory-based impact 181–204
timing of 222–4, **223**
in transition 19–23
type and approach 293
users' aspirations for 34–5
utility 6, 7, 67, 110, 294
evaluation intent, scoping the 31–7
evaluation objectives and expectations, managing 48–64
evaluation resources 57
Evaluation Trial and Advice Panel expert network 303
evaluation types 86, 87–91
evaluation utility 67
evaluations
budgets for 224
comparative (indicative) content of economic **135**
complexity 183–4, 201
cost-minimisation 130
decolonising 77
developmental process 109–11

in international development and aid programmes 77
longitudinal 252
participatory 40
performance process **105**, 107
piloting and small-scale **41**, 42, 165, 197
transfer and developmental 107–11
value for money (VfM) 122–3, 306n1(ch7)
see also economic *under* evaluation
evaluator safety 71
evaluators 4, 6–7, 11–12, 18, 22, **45**, 49, 51, 52, 53, 66, 72, 73, 95, 96, 112, 118, 140, 159, 174, 176, 228, 229, 238, 250, 256, 259, 268, 272, 273, 283, 287, 290–1, 293–4, 298
evidence 99
 building trust in 297–8
 communication and reporting of 82
 delivering 265–87
 formative 186
 outcome-based 16
 policy justification **292**
 process 93, 210
 required, reprioritisation of 241
 rigorous attention to strength of evidence **277–8**
 searching for and appraising **215**
 from summative assessment 210
 supporting materials from 282
 uniform collection of 144
 use and utilisation of 17–18, 92
evidence (descriptive) analysis **275**
evidence and analysis needs, anticipating 238–42
evidence-base and evidence-based assessment 97, 104, 205
evidence boundaries 217
evidence collection 57, 241
evidence demands 237
evidence examples or illustrations, incautious use of 78
evidence focus 35
evidence-gathering tools and methods 53, 61, 119, 178
evidence hierarchy xv, 15, 140, 143, 158
evidence needs, eight-step model to setting 238, *239*, 240–3

evidence promotion 299–300, 302–3
evidence quality 6, 7, 85, 241
evidence synthesis 206, 212, 213, 214, 217, 218
evidence transfer 298–9
evidence verification 243
expectations 55–8, 62–3, 64, 92, 188
experimental approaches 185
experimental designs, (fully) *see* randomised control trials
experimental inquiry 141
expert peer review 63
extension values 126
external advisors and expertise 76, 126
external data and datasets 172
external oversight 153
external transferability of evidence to inform other interventions 108
external validity 155, 171, 179, 243
externalities 126

F

factorial designs 146, 154 *see also* cross-over designs
fairness in evaluation 72–4, **74**, 111
fall-back designs and comparators, using 162, 174–6, 179, 184
field experiments and settings 141–2
findings
 communication of **23**
 extracting and synthesising **215**
 inappropriate generalisation **277**
 substantiating 283–6
fishbowl formats 305n4(ch2)
fit and viability, ensuring 58, 61–3
fit-for-purpose 234
fixed costs **129**
flexibility 161, 178–9, 193
formative feedback of evidenced implications **111**, 186
formative reporting 44, **45**, 46, 103–4
funds and funders 29–30, 55, 97, 162, 269, 270, 284, 294

G

gambling stakeholders 30–1, 43, 136, 163–4, 183–4, 197
gap analysis 240, 241

Index

gender, intervention perspective on **81**
gender as a (data) category 80, **81**, 242, 305n6
gender as a process 80, **81**
gender-based inclusion 79–80
gender dimensions 79–80, **81**
generative AI 21–3, **23**
geographical comparators, selecting 163–4
goals 52, 53, 64
governance bodies **257**
grid/template approach 216
group methods and workshops 42

H

harm avoidance 67–8, 152
harm minimisation 43, **69**, 248–9
Hawthorne effect 155–6
HEIs *see* higher education institutions
hierarchies of evidence xv, 15, 140, 143, 158
higher education institutions (HEIs) 50
HM Treasury and Cabinet Office Evaluation Task Force 303
hoop 198
humility 75, 157–8 *see also* confidence

I

identity safety and protection 70, 82
IMF *see* International Monetary Fund
inception reports 270, **270**
inclusion and ethical engagement 74–8
inclusion criteria **208**
inclusion in practice 75, 78, 79–80, 232–3
inclusive theory-based methods 189, 190–3
independence and impartiality 63, 72–3, 224
individual randomised control trials (i-RCTs) 88
individual stakeholder discussions, scoping through 42
influences 114–15, 188, 291–5, **292**
infographics 281, 282, **302**
informed consent and decisions 68–9
innovation 20, 110, 186

input-outcome relationships 131
inputs 101, 253, 254
inquiry 14–15, 46
inquiry focus, setting the 58–63, 217
insufficient but necessary (INUS) condition 201
intangibles 125, 126
integrated theory- based methods, pros and cons of **193**
integrity 72, 73, 82, 154, 158, 298
intent 19, 62, 64, 85, 216
interim reports 269, 271–2
intermittent application 164–5
intermittent comparators **166**
internal transfer for a next steps decision 108
internal validity 154, 155, 171, 179, 243
International Monetary Fund (IMF) 199
inter-organisational rivalry or tensions 229
interpretation and conclusions 275
intersectional
  considerations **74**
  dimension 77
  influences 75, 79–80
intersectionality 305n6
intervention 10–11, 15
  attending to backcloth to 47
  component parts of an *102*
  context and intent of 227
  integration of 186
  minimisation of disturbance to 236
  nature and circumstances of 92
  relative maturity of 236, 237
  status, significance and value of 92
  whether worked against expectations/targets 100
intervention architects as potential stakeholders **230**
intervention assumptions 186
intervention focus **81**
intervention gatekeepers 82
intervention logic models *see* logic charts
intervention management information 138
intervention mechanisms, uncertain efficacy or integration of **185**
intervention practitioners as potential stakeholders **230**
intervention sensitivity 236, 237–8

325

introduction 275
INUS condition *see* insufficient but necessary condition
inverse probability treatment weighting (IPTW) 177
IPTW *see* inverse probability treatment weighting
i-RCTs *see* individual *under* randomised control trials
iterative process 208, 213, 214

J

jargon **277**
John Henry effect 155–7
judgement, making and communicating (fair) 67, 72–4, 119, 126, 127, 138, 221, 222, 223, 224, 226, 227, 229, 235, 238
'just in time' responses 82
justifiable utility 151–2

K

key analysts in commissioners/funders as potential stakeholders **230**
key input milestones (KIMs) 251–2, **252**, 253–4
key performance indicators (KPIs) 61, 104, 106
KIMs *see* key input milestones
KPIs *see* key performance indicators

L

language 78, **277**
large group discussions, scoping through **42**
leakage **178**
'legacy' (time series) data 33, 175, 176, 205–6, 208, 214, 216
log frames *see* logic charts
logic 9, 137
logic chains *see* logic charts
logic charts 21, 49–50
logic models 59, 64, 187, 188, 203

M

M and E framework *see* monitoring and evaluation framework
machine-based learning (ML) 22
Magenta Book, UK 21, 36–7, 306n1(ch7)
Maryland Scientific Method Scale (SMS) 180, 307n3(ch9)
Maryland SMS *see* Maryland Scientific Method Scale
matched comparator designs, options for **166**
matched comparators and comparator groups 162–5, 175
matched variables and variable comparators 162–4, **166**
matching, quality of 172, 177
matrices 200, 201, 209–12, 267, 309n2(ch15)
Mayne, John 190, 191, 307n6(ch10), 308n10
MEL frameworks *see* Monitoring Evaluation and Learning frameworks
meta-analysis 214, 216, **217**
meta-ethnography 216, **217**
meta-evaluation 89, 91, 205–18
method(s) **301–2**
method agility 259–61
method choices 85–99, 243
method clearance 247–9
method inputs 251
method pathway 99, 158
method stages 252
metrics, setting purposeful 151–2
milestones, key input **252**
mission creep, managing 55–6
mixed mode methods 191, 201
ML *see* machine-based learning
monetisation of value 90, 123, 124–7, 306n4(ch7)
monitoring and evaluation (M and E) framework 56
Monitoring Evaluation and Learning (MEL) frameworks 14
most significant change (MSC) 196, 202
MSC *see* most significant change
multi-donor programme (Cambodia) 170
multi-evidence source decision-making **292**
multiple source evidence 196

N

narrative principles **296**
narrative progress reporting options (or combinations) **270**
narrative style and tone 274, 276
natural comparators 160, 161, 172
natural experiments 160–2

NDPB *see* non-departmental public body
necessary condition 201
needs 55, 99, 138
net outcomes and impacts 94
net present value (NPV) 134, 136
net value, adjusted methods of assessing 136–7 *see also* social return on investment analyses
newsletters **301**
'niche' stakeholder contributions 227–8
Nobel Memorial Prize in Economic Science 169
non-departmental public body (NDPB) 17
non-experimental approach 183 *see also* theory-based *under* evaluation
non-experimental assessment of impacts 194
non-experimental evaluation 95, 96–7, 201–3
non-experimental methods 197
non-intervention comparators and influences 176, 184
non-parametric tests 286, 309n3
NPV *see* net present value

O

objectives and objective-setting 51–4, 58–61, 64, **81**, 92, 227–8, 241, 244
OCDE *see* Organisation de Coopération et de Développement Economiques
OECD *see* Organisation for Economic Co-operation and Development
optimal minimisation of design **235**, 235–6
optimised multiple insights (and sources) **111**
opt-in–opt-out comparator **166**
Organisation de Coopération et de Développement Economiques (OCDE) 35
Organisation for Economic Co-operation and Development (OECD) 35
outcome effects/successes, unclear **185**

outcomes 60, 94, 101, **128**, 151, 154–5, 157, 179, 188, 190, 196
outcomes harvesting 194, **197**, 201, 202
outputs 16, 101, 105, 282
oversight, steering and governance 255–9, 262

P

PAR *see* participatory action research
parallel modalities **166**
parametric tests 286
participant duress, minimising the potential for 69–70
participant engagement 76
participant groupings 95
participant responses, dynamic and adaptive **185**
participant rights, protection of 70
participants, access to 227
participation 118–19, 233–4
participatory action research (PAR) 118
Patton, Michael Quinn 86, 109–10, 297
Pawson, Ray 181, 190, 214, 307n6(ch10)
peer challenge 194, 196–7
performance 104–7, **128**
performance evidence needs 107
performance measurement data 107
piggy-back discussion forums, scoping through 42
PIRs *see* post implementation reviews
planning lead-times 222–4
plural approaches 24, 155
plural contexts 293
plural decision-making *see* multi-evidence source decision-making
plural interpretation 19
plural (hybridised) mixed methods 201–2
plural perspective/view 4, 24
pluralist approach xv
pluralistic approach and evaluation 93, 100–1
podcasts **301**
point of time analysis 136
police officer layoffs on fatal road traffic accidents (Oregon, US), impact evaluation of 173–4

policy or practice briefs **301**
policy or programme teams as potential stakeholders **230**
policy makers 9, **45**, 106, 110–1, 122
political considerations and dimensions 57, 66, 226, 228, 244
post implementation reviews (PIRs) 109
post-report presentations (oral) **301**
power calculations and dynamics 62, 63, 149
preface **275**
pre-evaluation design weaknesses, assessment of 307n3(ch9)
pre-implementation comparators **166**
pre-participation consent briefing, indicative information for a **69**
pre-participation group 164–5
preparation and groundwork 221–44
primary evidence collection 107
primary sources and source needs 240–1
primary users 31, **38–9**, 40
  see also commissioners; users
problems, wicked and tame, solvable 58
process achievements 105
process-orientated methods 189
'process' quality indicators **117**
process tracing 198–9, 201, 202, **202**, 204
processes, why and when to evaluate what 100–4
prognostic factors, using 149–50
programme effectiveness, anticipating hidden influences on 114–15
programme theory 21, 181
progress review and reporting 269–71, **270**
progress statements **270**
promotion options, pre- and post-reporting **301**–2
proof 95
proof of effect 148–9, 159, 201, 283–4, 286
propensity score matching (PSM) 177, 307n2(ch9)
proportionality in engagement 232, 234–5, 238

proportionate design **235**
proposals **276**
protection through anonymity and confidentiality 70
protocols 144, 154, 206, 216
providers/provider representative bodies as potential stakeholders **230**
PSM *see* propensity score matching
public policy and programme interventions 181–2, 289, **289**, 303, 306n4(ch8)
purpose and purpose-setting 9–12, *10*, 29–47, 48, 49, 51–4, 59, 62, 64, 85–99
purposeful specification 52–3
purposing 37–40, 62, 64, 75–6, 101, 103

Q

QALYs *see* Quality of Adjusted Life Years
QCA *see* qualitative comparative analysis
QEDs *see* quasi-experimental designs
qualitative comparative analysis (QCA) 189, 199–201, 202, **202**, 204, 286
qualitative evidence 97, 106–7, 161, 216, 243, **278**, 286
quality 115–16, **117**, 119, 284
Quality of Adjusted Life Years (QALYs) 133
quantifiable measures 124
quantified data and quantifiable measures 124, **278**
quantitative evidence and measurement 97, 106, 243
quasi-experimental designs (QEDs) 95, 96, 97–8, 159–61, 163–80, 201, 202

R

RAG (red/amber/green) reports 271
  see also traffic light reports
Ragin, Charles 199
randomisation 143–7, 152, 161
randomised control trial, nine-step approach to a *145*
randomised control trials (RCTs) 95, 96, 97–8, 151–8, 160, 161, 171, 176, 177, 203, 216
  cluster (c-RCTs) 146

328

costs of 149
fit and design of 143, 145
and the gold standard 140, 141–3, 207
inappropriate responses to high costs of 153–4
individual (i-RCTs) 146
minimising selection biases in 146
nine-step approach to design of 144, *145*
optimum size of 149
quality of 145
risks of bias in 145
small sample sizes in 148–9
rapid evidence reviews (RERs) 209–13, **210**, 214
applying of to a meta-evaluation for an early years learning programme 211–12
definition and defining scope of **210**, **215**
in evaluation, three-phase approach to **210**
pros and cons of **213**
three-phase approach to
Phase 1: definition 209, **210**
Phase 2: sourcing and reduction 209, **210**
Phase 3: synthesis and reporting 209, **210**
rationale, differences of view of underpinning 57
RCTs *see* randomised control trials
RDD *see* regression discontinuity design
reach **301–2**
real time approach 64, 103, 104
realist synthesis 213–14, 217–18
four-step approach to **215**
Stage 1: Define the scope of the review **215**
Stage 2: Search for and appraise evidence **215**
Stage 3: Extract and synthesise findings **215**
Stage 4: Draw conclusions and make recommendations **215**
Realistic Evaluation (Pawson and Tilley) 181, 190
receipt and distribution of indicative content for evaluation reporting plan **267**

recommendations **215**, **276**, 295–7, **296**
recruitment of sufficient number of units 143–4
red/amber/green reports *see* RAG reports
regression discontinuity 169–71
regression discontinuity design (RDD) 170, 171
regulatory or standard-setting bodies as potential stakeholders **230**
reliability 285
reports and reporting 44, 77–8, **210**, 265–87, **267**, **277–8**, 308n1(ch14)
RERs *see* rapid evidence reviews
research questions (RQs) 51, 58, 60–1, 64, 207, **208**, 210, 214, 216, 239–40, 241, 274
researchers and research centres/teams 39, 43, 52–3, 56, 62, 65, 97, 133, 170, **230**, 274, 276, 280–1
resource management and constraints 76, 111–12, 123, 138, 241
responsiveness to (evolving) situation **111**
review
defining of the **208**
mandated evidence-based **292**
review mode 258–9
right of reply **74**
rigour 179, 206, 208, 212, 297–8
risk foresight and management 152, 254–5
risk registers 254–5, 262
risks 60, 67–8, 82, **117**, 126, 139, 149–50, 155, 189, 231–2, 246, **256**, **285**
RQs *see* research questions

S

samples and sample strategy 68, 147–9, 172, 177
scoping (purpose) 12–13, 32–4, 35, 44, 47, 229
and formative analyses 23
Scriven, Professor Michael 3, 8
search and selection **208**
search focus, setting of **208**
segmented group workshops, scoping through **41**
selection bias 150, 179

semi-variable costs **129**
sense-checking 63, 92
sensitivity analysis 126–7, 136, 298
sequencing 253–4
set theoretic methods 189 *see also* process tracing; qualitative comparative analysis
seven step process 191 *see also* contribution analysis
'SMART' (specific-measurable-achievable-realistic-timebound) objectives for purposeful evaluation, setting 53, **54**, 58
smoking gun 198
smoothed projection of effect 175, 176
social media **302**
social (science) research 65, 66, 76, 151, 155, 158, 172, 177, 181–2
social return on investment (SROI) 136–7
social values 125–6
source description 210
sourcing and reduction in RER **210**
specific-measurable-achievable-realistic-timebound objectives for purposeful evaluation, setting *see* 'SMART' objectives for purposeful evaluation, setting
spillover **178**
SROI *see* social return on investment
stakeholder credibility and confidence 120, 125, 197, 224
stakeholder differences on process priorities and use 119
stakeholder discussions and collaboration 64, 126, 229, 231, 233
stakeholder engagement 12–13, **38–9**, **41–2**, 43, 44, **74**, 75, 196, 204, 214, 217–18, 226–34, **234**, 243
stakeholder legacy 244
stakeholder panels 196
stakeholders 37–44, **38–9**, 47, 226, 228–34, **230**, 240, 250
standards, relevant external referred **117**
statistical power 147–8, 165
status (at delivery) of indicative content for evaluation reporting plan **267**
steering (or working) groups **257**
step costs **129**

step-wedge designs 147 *see also* cross-over designs
straw in the wind 198
substantiation 283–6, **285**, 287
substitution **178**
summary **275**
summative evaluation report, indicative structure and content for a **275–6**
summative (final) reporting 44, **45**, 46, 103, 104, 109, 272–4, 276
sunk costs **129**
supplementary delivery requirements, anticipating 281–3
support factors to evidence 108–9
synthesis **208**, **210**, 216
synthesis approaches 217–18
synthesis assessment 216
synthetic comparators 171–2
synthetic control designs 171–4, 179
systematic reviews 207–8, **208**, 209, 212, 213, **213**, 214, 250

T

tasks and task groups, required 251, **252**, 253, 254
TBE *see* theory-based *under* evaluation
Teaching and Learning Research Programme (TLRP) 50
technical options and requirements 138, 244
test and learn approach 234, 242, 266, 286, 293
theory of change (ToC) 21, 34, 36, 43, 49, 50, 59, 60, 114–15, 116, **117**, 119, 137, 182, *187*, 188–9, 190, 191, *192*, 192–3, **193**, 194, 196, 199, 201, **202**, 203–4, 275, 305n2(ch2), 308n8
theories of change (ToCs) 36, 37, 64
theory platforms and 20–1
theory platforms, harnessing 186–9, 203
thinking theory 182
threats to validity and unintended consequences 176–8
Tilley, Nick 181, 190
time constraints 216–17
time management 35, 99, 130, 167, 169, 221, 224, 231–2, 243, 261–2, 271

timeframes 33, 41, 105, 144, 157, 214, 234, 241, 243
timing (receipt and review) of indicative content for evaluation reporting plan **267**
tips, purposeful 46–7, 63–4, 80, **81**, 82, 98–9, 119–20, 137–9, 157–8, 178–80, 203–4, 216–18, 243–4, 261–2, 286–7
TLRP *see* Teaching and Learning Research Programme
ToCs *see* theories of change
trade-offs 154
traffic light reports **270**, 271
trajectory analysis 174, 175–6
transfer evidence 109
transitional outcomes effects **185**
transparency (of process) 34, 73
transport, safe 71
trial
  management and integrity 154
  summative 146–7
trial precision 155
trial size 147–9
truth table 201
type, choice of 91–3
type-approach-method sequence 86–7, 99

U

UK Evaluation Society 249
UN agencies *see* United Nations agencies
uncertainties 186
unconscious bias 150
unintended consequences 12, 156, 157, 177–8, **178**, 179, **230**, 237, 242–3
unit-cost methods 132
unit-cost ratios 131, 132
United Nations (UN) agencies 21
use and utility, Improving 288–91
user expectations 203
user/stakeholder 'peer' network events and websites **301**
user platform, widening the 30–1
user-evaluator relationships 293–5
users xiv, 6, 19, 30–1, 34, 38, **38–9**, 47, 49, 57–8, 59, 72, 75, 96, 98, 112–13, 121, 122, 132, 136, 140, 142, 154, 162, **166**, 174, 176, 184, **193**, **202**, 203,
207, 212, **213**, 214, **215**, 217, 241, 243, 268, 269, 270, 272, **275**, **277**, **278**, 281, 282, 283, 284, 287, 290, 291, 294, 297–8, 300, **301**, 302, **302**, 303
see also end users
utility 85, 123, 152, 154, 174
  gaps 241
  maximisation 123
value-based approach 19

V

validity 212
  external 142, **285**, 285–6
  internal 141–2, 146, **285**, 285–6
validity threats 153–7, 158
valuation 125, 126
valuation errors 125–6
value 90, 122, 123, 125, 138
  for money 90, 93, 122–3
variable costs **129**
variables, independent 242
VfM *see* for money *under* value
visualisation **302**
volatility in context or actions over course of intervention, likely **185**
voluntary engagement and informed consent 68–9, 229
voluntary opt-out comparators 165

W

wage (New York City, 1992), enhanced minimum 167–8
wants to needs, progression from 48–51
weight average effect 216
Weiss, Carol 8, 65, 291
whole team anticipation of ethical risks and prioritisation of early response 82
work packages **252**
working or task groups, scoping through **41**
workplans
  scheduling 250–4, 262
  stages of **252**

X

X **302**

Y

yardsticks 104, **105**, **117**

www.ingramcontent.com/pod-product-compliance
Lightning Source LLC
Chambersburg PA
CBHW051525020426
42333CB00016B/1783